June 14–16, 2017
Hilversum, The Netherlands

**Association for
Computing Machinery**

Advancing Computing as a Science & Profession

TVX'17

Proceedings of the 2017 ACM International Conference on
Interactive Experiences for TV and Online Video

Sponsored by:
ACM SIGCHI

Supported by:
ACM SIGWEB & ACM SIGMM

Supported by:
Beeld en Geluid, Nokia, Delft University of Technology, TNO, and Centrum Wiskunde & Informatica

Association for Computing Machinery

Advancing Computing as a Science & Profession

The Association for Computing Machinery
2 Penn Plaza, Suite 701
New York, New York 10121-0701

Copyright © 2017 by the Association for Computing Machinery, Inc. (ACM). Permission to make digital or hard copies of portions of this work for personal or classroom use is granted without fee provided that copies are not made or distributed for profit or commercial advantage and that copies bear this notice and the full citation on the first page. Copyright for components of this work owned by others than ACM must be honored. Abstracting with credit is permitted. To copy otherwise, to republish, to post on servers or to redistribute to lists, requires prior specific permission and/or a fee. Request permission to republish from: permissions@acm.org or Fax +1 (212) 869-0481.

For other copying of articles that carry a code at the bottom of the first or last page, copying is permitted provided that the per-copy fee indicated in the code is paid through www.copyright.com.

Notice to Past Authors of ACM-Published Articles

ACM intends to create a complete electronic archive of all articles and/or other material previously published by ACM. If you have written a work that has been previously published by ACM in any journal or conference proceedings prior to 1978, or any SIG Newsletter at any time, and you do NOT want this work to appear in the ACM Digital Library, please inform permissions@acm.org, stating the title of the work, the author(s), and where and when published.

ISBN: 978-1-4503-4529-3 (Digital)

ISBN: 978-1-4503-5595-7 (Print)

Additional copies may be ordered prepaid from:

ACM Order Department
PO Box 30777
New York, NY 10087-0777, USA

Phone: 1-800-342-6626 (USA and Canada)
+1-212-626-0500 (Global)
Fax: +1-212-944-1318
E-mail: acmhelp@acm.org
Hours of Operation: 8:30 am – 4:30 pm ET

Printed in the USA

Welcome from the General Chairs

It is our great pleasure to welcome you to Hilversum for the fourth edition of the *ACM International Conference on Interactive Experiences for Television and Online Video – ACM TVX2017*. The idea of hosting ACM TVX in the Netherlands came quite spontaneously through the interaction of three top Dutch research institutes: Delft University of Technology, TNO and CWI. Their combined, extensive track record in the design of television and online video experiences, and their strong joint interest in user-centered multimedia optimization, made the opportunity of organizing ACM TVX2017 exciting. We hope that, while at TVX2017, you will feel welcomed in this atmosphere that characterized the whole conference organization.

The conference takes place at the Netherlands Institute for Sound and Vision (NISV), which forms the heart of the Hilversum Media Park. The Media Park is the bustling hub of the Netherlands' media industry, where you will find traditional media broadcasters working alongside innovative media agencies. No fewer than 6.000 media professionals, specialists, creatives, presenters, technicians, enthusiasts and visionaries work here. The NISV building, a well-known architectural landmark in the Netherlands, hosts the greatest collection of Dutch audio-visual material heritage in the country. Over 750,000 hours of television, radio, music and film dating back to 1898 make this collection one of the largest in Europe, and the perfect place to host TVX2017.

TVX2017 follows the success of three previous editions of TVX conferences (held in Chicago, Brussels and Newcastle on Tyne), and builds upon the legacy of the EuroiTV conference series, organized between 2003 and 2013 all across Europe. The TVX community has always been highly multidisciplinary, welcoming experts from human-computer interaction, multimedia engineering and design to media studies, media psychology and sociology. In 2017 ACM TVX maintains this tradition, enforcing its quality standards by using double blind peer review for the full papers and notes in the main track. The conference also includes a wide range of formats for presentation and discussion of research, including Demos, Work-in-Progress and industry papers. To foster the participation of the newer generation of researchers, TVX also offers a Doctoral Consortium, while new ideas are stimulated through a set of five exciting workshops.

This conference would not be possible without the practical and financial support of many supporters. First of all, we would like to thank you for registering and attending the conference, as you are an important part of our community and your participation makes these events possible. We would also like to thank all the members of the organizing committee, who have worked very hard during more than a year to prepare the conference. Finally, we want to thank our sponsor, **ACM SIGCHI**, and our generous supporters, **The Netherlands Institute for Sound and Vision** and **Nokia**, who provided the welcomed logistic aid for making this conference an enjoyable experience.

We wish you have a great conference and hope that you will enjoy your stay in Hilversum!

Judith Redi
ACM TVX 2017 General Chair
Delft University of Technology

Omar Niamut
ACM TVX 2017 General Chair
TNO

Dick Bulterman
ACM TVX 2017 General Chair
CWI and Vrije Universiteit Amsterdam

Welcome from the Program Chairs

We are very pleased to present an exciting program for ACM TVX 2017, which has been put together based on submissions from scholars around the globe.

As the leading international conference for the presentation and discussion of research into interactive experiences for online video and TV, the conference brings together international researchers and practitioners from a wide range of disciplines, ranging from human-computer interaction, multimedia engineering and design to media studies, media psychology and sociology, to present and discuss the latest insights in the field. The ACM TVX 2017' conference theme is "Alternate Realities". Research on this topic will be presented together with topics such as Virtual Reality, new interaction technologies & techniques, user consumption patterns, the role of the audience and second screen interactions.

The call for papers attracted submissions from Asia, Europe and North and South America. 41 full and short papers were submitted and subjected to a rigorous double-blind review process. Each paper was assigned to an associate chair (AC) who recruited at least three reviewers for each paper and wrote a meta-review summarizing the main points of each review. The review process included at rebuttal period, giving authors the chance to respond to the reviewers' comments. During the TPC meeting on March 17, 2017 in Delft, the Netherlands, each paper was discussed in-depth and the final decision on the accepted papers was made, resulting in a high-quality program of 13 accepted full and short papers, accounting for an acceptance rate of 31%. Full papers, short papers, the abstracts of the four workshops co-located with TVX and of the TVX-in-Asia forum are part of the main proceedings and will be included in the ACM Digital Library.

In addition to these submissions, there were several other tracks that attracted a large number contributions, resulting into 10 Work-in-Progress papers, 9 Doctoral Consortium papers, 2 TVX in Industry presentations and 10 demos, which are all made available in the adjunct proceedings.

The ACM TVX 2017 conference also features two interesting keynote presentations related to the main topic of 'Alternate Realities'. We would definitely recommend attendees to attend these insightful keynote talks, a first one by Wijnand IJsselsteijn, Professor in Cognition and Affect in Human-Technology Interaction at Eindhoven University of Technology and a second one by Arthur van Hoff, Founder and CTO of Jaunt, leader in Cinematic VR experiences.

Putting together the program of ACM TVX 2017 was a team effort. We would therefore like to thank the authors for their submissions, the ACs who managed the whole review process for each individual paper and the reviewers who provided invaluable feedback for each of the papers. It is thanks to this joint effort that we are able to present you an interesting program.

We hope that the program we compiled for you provides you with some valuable food for thought and inspiration and that you can share ideas with other researchers and practitioners from all over the world at TVX 2017.

Wendy Van den Broeck
ACM TVX 2017 Technical Program Chair
Imec-smit, Vrije Universiteit Brussel, Belgium

Michael J. Darnell
ACM TVX 2017 Technical Program Chair
Samsung, USA

Roger Zimmermann
ACM TVX 2017 Technical Program Chair
National University of Singapore, Singapore

Table of Contents

Secondary Content and Companion Screens

Session Chair: Johan Oomen *(Netherlands Institute for Sound and Vision)*

Closing Keynote Address

Session Chair: Omar Aziz Niamut *(TNO)*

Workshop Summaries

ACM TVX 2017 Conference Organization

General Chairs: Judith Redi *(Delft University of Technology, The Netherlands)*
Omar Niamut *(TNO, The Netherlands)*
Dick Bulterman *(CWI and Vrije Universiteit Amsterdam, The Netherlands)*

Technical Program Chairs: Wendy van den Broeck *(imec-SMIT, Vrije Universiteit Brussel, Belgium)*
Michael J. Darnell *(Samsung, USA)*
Roger Zimmermann *(NUS, Singapore)*

Work in Progress Chairs: Mu Mu *(University of Northampton, UK)*
Elena Fedorovskaya *(Rochester Institute of Technology, USA)*

Workshop Chairs: Katrien de Moor *(NTNU, Norway)*
Rene Kaiser *(Know-Center Research Center, Austria)*
Hokyoung Blake Ryu *(Hanyang University, Republic of Korea)*

**Doctoral Consortium
Chairs:** Satu Jumisko Pyykko *(Tampere University of Technology, Finland)*
Ben Shirley *(University of Salford, UK)*

TVX in Industry Chairs: Johan Oomen *(NISV, The Netherlands)*
Ali C. Begen *(Networked Media and Ozyegin University, Turkey)*
Igor Curcio *(Nokia, Finland)*

Demo Chairs: Lucia D'Acunto *(TNO, The Netherlands)*
Andy Brown *(BBC R&D, UK)*

**Inclusion and
Accessibility Chairs:** Teresa Chambel *(University of Lisbon, Portugal)*
Hartmut Koenitz *(HKU University of the Arts Utrecht, The Netherlands)*

Local Production Chairs: Britta Meixner *(CWI, The Netherlands)*
Kelly Mostert *(Beeld en Geluid, The Netherlands)*
Latha Spelt *(Beeld en Geluid, The Netherlands)*
Mois Schuttert *(Beeld en Geluid, The Netherlands)*

Web Chair: Ernestasia Siahaan *(Delft University of Technology, The Netherlands)*

Steering Committee: Santosh Basapur *(Institute of Design, IIT, USA)*
Frank Bentley *(Yahoo/MIT, USA)*
Pablo Cesar *(CWI, The Netherlands)*
Teresa Chambel *(University of Lisbon, Portugal)*
Konstantinos Chorianopoulos *(Ionian University, Greece)*
David Geerts *(Mintlab (KU Leuven/IMEC), Belgium)*
Artur Lugmayr *(Tampere University of Technology, Finland)*
Marianna Obrist *(Sussex University, UK)*
David A. Shamma *(Yahoo! Research, USA)*

Program Committee: Alan Said *(University of Skövde, Sweden)*
Britta Meixner *(CWI, The Netherlands)*
Jacob Groshek *(Boston University, USA)*
Kyoungwon Seo *(Hanyang University, Republic of Korea)*
Lucia D'Acunto *(TNO, The Netherlands)*
Maarten Wijnants *(IMEC, Hasselt University, Belgium)*
Niall Murray *(Athlone IT, Ireland)*
Nuno Correia *(FCT NOVA, Portugal)*
Oliver Korn *(Offenburg University, Germany)*
Patrick Le Callet *(Université de Nantes, France)*
Rene Kaiser *(Know-Center Research Center, Austria)*
Rodrigo Laiola Guimarães *(IBM Research, Brazil)*
Sebastian Arndt *(NTNU, Norway)*
Shuichi Aoki *(NHK, Japan)*
Sid Ahmed Fezza *(National Institute of Telecommunications & ICT, Algeria)*
Timothy Neate *(Swansea University, UK)*
Toinon Vigier *(Université de Nantes, France)*
Tom Bartindale *(Newcastle University, UK)*

Sponsor:

In cooperation with:

Supporters:

Institutional Supporters:

'Here's Looking At You, Kid'
Interactive Entertainment In The Age of Machine-Readable Humans

Wijnand IJsselsteijn
Eindhoven University of
Technology
Eindhoven, The Netherlands
w.a.ijsselsteijn@tue.nl

ABSTRACT

Today, while you're watching television, your television is watching you too. With the introduction of cameras, microphones, and other sensors integrated with our networked, smart TV sets and mobile devices, opportunities arise that go well beyond videocommunication, gesture-based interaction, or consumer segmentation. Machines are learning to recognise human identity, contexts, activities, and emotions, and your TV is no exception.

Armed with such knowledge, new horizons for personalised, interactive and immersive entertainment as well as marketing emerge. At the same time, some such proposals may be at variance with human values many of us hold dear, including privacy, trust, and control. In addition, with increasingly powerful personal profiling and machine understanding of humans, the potential psychological consequences of breaches in cybersecurity (e.g., hacking, phishing) increase in similar measure.

In this keynote talk, I will highlight some of the progress in machine understanding of human behavior and emotions, its potential in interactive and personalised entertainment, as well as some legitimate concerns in terms of human values and human psychology as we enter the Age of Machine-Readable Humans.

ACM Classification Keywords
H.5.2. User Interfaces; J.4. Social and Behavioural Sciences: Psychology

Author Keywords
Affective computing; Machine-readable humans; Personal profiling; Interactive television; Value-sensitive design

Permission to make digital or hard copies of part or all of this work for personal or classroom use is granted without fee provided that copies are not made or distributed for profit or commercial advantage and that copies bear this notice and the full citation on the first page. Copyrights for third-party components of this work must be honored. For all other uses, contact the owner/author(s). Copyright is held by the author/owner(s).
TVX 2017, June 14–16, 2017, Hilversum, The Netherlands.
ACM ISBN 978-1-4503-4529-3/17/06.
http://dx.doi.org/10.1145/3077548.3077562

BIOGRAPHY

Prof.dr. Wijnand IJsselsteijn has a background in artificial intelligence (AI) and cognitive neuropsychology. He obtained his PhD in 2004 on the topic of telepresence. Since 2012, he is full professor of Cognition and Affect in Human-Technology Interaction at Eindhoven University of Technology (TU/e). He has an active research program on the impact of media technology on human psychology, and the use of psychology to improve technology design. His current projects deal with the ways in which media technology can transform our sense of self and others, can affect decision making, influence prosocial and healthy behaviours, and promote stress reduction and wellbeing. He has a keen interest in the relation between data science, AI and psychology, and works on technological innovations (e.g., sensor-enabled mobile technologies, virtual environments) that make possible novel forms of human behaviour tracking, combining methodological rigor with ecological validity.

He is a member of the Jheronimus Academy of Data Science in Den Bosch (http://www.jads.nl), and is scientific director of the interdisciplinary Center for Humans and Technology at TU/e (http://www.tue.nl/CenterHT), which explicitly focuses on people- and value-centred perspectives of technology understanding and design. He has published over 200 peer-reviewed academic papers in journals and conferences, and has (co-)edited 10 volumes. His most recent co-edited book "*Immersed in Media: Telepresence Theory, Measurement, and Technology*" appeared in 2015, at Springer.

Media Multitasking at Home: A Video Observation Study of Concurrent TV and Mobile Device Usage

Jacob M. Rigby[1], Duncan P. Brumby[1], Sandy J.J. Gould[2], Anna L. Cox[1]

[1]UCL Interaction Centre, University College London, London, WC1E 6EA, UK

[2]School of Computer Science, University of Birmingham, Birmingham, B15 2TT, UK

[1]{j.rigby.14, d.brumby, anna.cox}@ucl.ac.uk, [2]s.gould@cs.bham.ac.uk

ABSTRACT

Increasingly people interact with their mobile devices while watching television. We evolve an understanding of this kind of everyday media multitasking behaviour through an analysis of video data. In our study, four households were recorded watching television over three evenings. We analysed 55 hours of footage in which participants were watching the TV. We found that mobile device habits were highly variable between participants during this time, ranging from 0% to 23% of the time that the TV was on. To help us understand this variability, participants completed the Media Multitasking Index (MMI) questionnaire. Results showed that participants with a higher MMI score used their mobile device more while watching TV at home. We also saw evidence that the TV was being used as a hub in the home: multiple people were often present when the time the TV was on, providing a background for other household activities. We argue that video analysis can give valuable insights into media multitasking in the home.

ACM Classification Keywords

H.5.m. Information Interfaces and Presentation (e.g. HCI): Miscellaneous

Author Keywords

Media multitasking; mobile; television; in the wild; video observation; dual screen; multitasking; task switching

INTRODUCTION

In recent years, using mobile devices while watching television has become a common activity [11, 30, 2]. This concurrent use of multiple media is known as media multitasking. In the UK, communications regulator Ofcom found that 53% of UK adults reported that they regularly media multitasked in 2013 [25], and a 2014 report showed that 99% of adults media multitask at some point during the week, for an average of 2 hours and 3 minutes every day [26]. Multitasking in our living rooms may not have safety implications as in aviation [9, 20] or driving [6], or be directly detrimental to productivity as in workplace

Permission to make digital or hard copies of part or all of this work for personal or classroom use is granted without fee provided that copies are not made or distributed for profit or commercial advantage and that copies bear this notice and the full citation on the first page. Copyrights for third-party components of this work must be honored. For all other uses, contact the owner/author(s).

TVX '17 June 14-16, 2017, Hilversum, Netherlands

© 2017 Copyright held by the owner/author(s).

ACM ISBN 978-1-4503-4529-3/17/06.

DOI: http://dx.doi.org/10.1145/3077548.3077560

environments [22], but nonetheless this changing behaviour is of interest to a number of groups. TV networks wish to retain their audiences by increasing engagement. Content producers want to create better TV experiences for viewers. Advertisers will want to know whether viewers are switching to their mobile devices during breaks as a way to avoid adverts.

Studies conducted to better understand the prevalence of media multitasking behaviour have typically relied on self reporting from participants (e.g. [11, 29, 36, 37]). However, it is possible that people are poor at estimating just how much time they are spending on digital devices and so misrepresent the extent to which they media multitask. In response to this, a small number of observational studies have also been conducted, for instance using direct observation [38] or sensor-based telemetry [13]. While these methods are more accurate than self-report data, fine-grained video data has the potential to offer a more detailed and nuanced impression of behaviour in situated contexts (e.g. [3, 28]).

In this paper, we used video observation to establish a detailed and accurate understanding of mobile device usage and TV consumption in the home. To do this, we recorded the behaviour of four households over a 72 hour period. Before describing the results of this video observation study, we review related prior research on media multitasking.

RELATED WORK

A number of previous studies have investigated media multitasking behaviours and habits, often using self reporting methods such as surveys [11, 27, 29], diary studies [11, 29, 36, 37], and interviews [36]. Such methods facilitate the collection of large amounts of data, giving a general view of many peoples' media multitasking behaviours and habits. However, self-reported data can be inaccurate and lack granularity. This has led to a need for observational studies to be performed to obtain an accurate view of everyday media multitasking.

In order to better understand when people used their devices while watching TV and exactly what they were doing, Voorveld and Viswanathan [38] conducted an analysis of observational data obtained by directly observing participants from the USA. They found that media multitasking was most prevalent when watching sport and channel surfing, during morning and afternoon, and when individuals were watching television alone. Observations were made every 10 seconds to give a fine-grained view, but were not video recorded and so could not be played back for further post-hoc analysis. Activities performed on mobile devices were also not recorded in detail.

Another situated study was performed by Holz et al. [13]. They used a device logging system installed on participants' phones and tablets. Various information was logged, including apps launched and websites visited. This was cross-referenced with the TV programme being watched at the time, which was established using audio fingerprinting. It was found that although the majority of device usage was unrelated to the programme being watched, device usage did differ based on the type of show being watched. Furthermore, device usage seemed to correspond to the events in the show. For example, Holz et al. found that when people were watching crime dramas they tended to use their devices less often towards the end of the programme, presumably because the plot becomes more engaging as it reaches the finale. While this study also gave a very fine-grained view of device usage, it was not video recorded and so the physical behaviour of participants could not be studied to verify what they were doing. For example, mobile device usage was inferred based on application logs. However, without additional observational video data it is difficult to establish whether the participant was actively interacting with the device or whether it had been put aside.

Rooksby et al. [31] used an approach in which device logs were complemented by video observations to identify periods of media multitasking. In this study, parallel TV and device usage was inferred through a device logging system. These logged events were then augmented with an analysis of video observation data. This work was further expanded on [32], but the results focus more on the social implications of how media multitasking affects home life, presented as a small number of vignettes. Furthermore, the participants had to manually turn on the cameras every time they wished to record data, meaning naturalistic data may have been omitted and the fact they were being recorded would have been fresh in their minds.

While the research by Holz et al. [13] and Rooksby et al. [31] is valuable in establishing media multitasking habits in the home, it leaves open an important question of what drives these behaviours. Is it the case that media multitasking behaviour reflects situational factors, such as becoming bored with the television programme or wanting to look up some relevant information, or is it that some people are more inclined to media multitask than others?

Ophir et al. [27] argue that a person's propensity to media multitask is not driven by situational levels of engagement but more reflects a stable individual trait — some people just prefer to media multitask while others do not. To support this claim, Ophir et al. developed the Media Multitasking Index (MMI), a measure used to establish individual media multitasking preferences. Research using the MMI has investigated cognitive differences between media multitaskers [1, 18, 19]. However, little research has been done to investigate this specifically in the context of concurrent TV and phone usage in the home. In other words, are those people that self-report a high MMI actually more inclined to use a device while watching television?

Household	Duration
A	19:07:52
B	07:23:05
C	17:48:07
D	10:04:49

Table 1: Total duration TV was turned on, by household.

The study presented here further investigated individuals' media multitasking behaviour through means of video observation over three evenings. Two surveillance cameras were used. One recorded participants' seating areas and televisions to allow for a greater understanding of physical behaviour and other non-phone and tablet tasks that may occur, and another recorded the television to allow us to see when the TV was turned on and what was being watched. The participants also completed an MMI questionnaire to measure general media multitasking preferences.

METHOD

Participants
Five households were recruited through opportunity sampling. Each household was required to have a dedicated TV set. At least one person in each household was required to watch TV regularly (at least 1 hour evening), who was also required to have a smartphone as their primary device. Households were paid £75 (~$94 USD) for three evenings of continuous participation.

Household A consisted of a male and female couple, aged 67 and 56 respectively, living in a house in Worcestershire, England. Their TV was located in their living room.

Household B consisted of three cohabiting professional females aged 26, 27, and 29, living in a shared flat in Oxford, England. Their TV was located in their living room area, which adjoined the kitchen and dining area.

Household C consisted of a male and female couple, aged 58 and 59 respectively, living in a house in Worcestershire, England. Their TV was located in their living room area, which adjoined the kitchen and dining area.

Household D consisted of two parents (39 and 45 years old) and their three children (17, 12, and 9 years old) living in a house in Oxford, England. Their TV was situated in their living room.

The final household, **household E**, consisted of two parents in their thirties and their three young children (all under 8 years old) living in a house in Worcestershire, England. Their TV was situated in their living room. Due to technical issues, large portions of the data collected from this household was unusable. For this reason, household E was excluded from this study. The mean age of the remaining participants was 37 ($SD = 19.88$).

Materials
For each household participating, a small mains-powered surveillance camera was used to record a view of the TV for the purposes of programme detection, and another identical camera was angled towards the seating area to record

Part-icipant	Age	Time present when TV on (% of TV on time)	Device use while present (% of time present)	Mean time per use	Number of uses	Uses per hour of time present	MMI
A1	67	17:27:05 (91.22%)	00:51:12 (4.89%)	00:06:24	8	.46	2.27
A2	56	17:30:05 (91.48%)	02:24:02 (13.72%)	00:13:06	11	.63	2.82
B1	27	04:41:28 (63.53%)	00:40:46 (14.48%)	00:02:24	17	3.62	2.7
B2	26	04:04:10 (55.11%)	00:40:24 (16.55%)	00:01:27	28	6.88	4.02
B3	29	02:02:41 (27.69%)	00:05:47 (4.72%)	00:00:58	6	2.93	2.16
C1	58	08:04:50 (44.39%)	00:00:00 (0%)	00:00:00	0	0	0
C2	59	11:39:30 (65.49%)	02:39:45 (22.84%)	00:15:58	10	.86	2.63
D1	39	03:14:43 (32.19%)	00:25:52 (13.29%)	00:03:42	7	2.16	2.68
D2	45	01:30:09 (14.90%)	00:05:52 (6.51%)	00:01:57	3	2	1.04
D3	17	03:59:27 (39.59%)	00:00:00 (0%)	00:00:00	0	0	1.18
D4	10	01:22:03 (13.56%)	00:00:00 (0%)	00:00:00	0	0	1.37
D5	12	04:09:30 (41.25%)	00:22:32 (9.03%)	00:11:16	2	.48	6.45*

Table 2: **Results for all participants, grouped by household (all times HH:MM:SS).** *Note: value marked * denotes anomalous value removed from analysis.*

the participants themselves. Video footage was recorded onto micro SD cards. Participants were expected to use their own dedicated televisions for viewing; this study did not record viewing on other devices.

The study utilised a pre-session questionnaire to collect demographic and technology usage data, and the Media Multitasking Index questionnaire [27] to indicate individual media multitasking preferences in general.

Ethical considerations

The presence of surveillance equipment in people's homes presented some ethical and privacy issues. While ethical clearance was given to recruit households with participants under the age of 18 with parental consent, it was possible that visitors under the age of 18 could become part of the study. It was also possible that adults could unknowingly participate. For these reasons, each household was required to display a poster informing visitors of the study taking place in a prominent position near the property entrance.

Procedure

The study took place in participants' homes, wherever their TV was situated. Once participants were recruited, a suitable time was arranged with them for a researcher to visit their property and install surveillance cameras. Clocks across all devices were also synchronised. During this session, the participants were shown the information sheet and given the opportunity to ask questions, then asked to sign a consent form. Finally, they were asked to fill in the questionnaire about demographics and technology usage. Once everything was set up, three evenings' worth of data were logged. These were consecutive evenings where possible, though as some participants said they would not be in the house during that time, evenings were not necessarily consecutive. A time was also agreed for the researcher to collect equipment and pay the participants.

RESULTS

TV watching and device usage

In total, 24 hours' worth of footage for each camera was collected per household, resulting in a total of 192 hours

of footage (96 hours the seating cameras and a further 96 hours for the TV camera). The cameras automatically split the footage into consecutive 30 minute sections. As this study is only concerned with behaviour during TV time, the sections showing the TV were first reviewed in order to discard sections where the TV was turned off. The corresponding footage of the seating areas were also discarded for these times. Once all of the sections with TV activity were identified, the corresponding clips were combined into a one file per evening to keep file sizes manageable - one file for the camera looking at the TV and one for the seating. Both video feeds for each evening were then synchronized and coded using Chronoviz[1]. During the coding process, the video was first annotated to show when the TV was on, then all further codes were performed focusing on these periods. During these subsections, the video was annotated to show when each participant was present and when they were using any mobile devices. Further to this, any other notable or interesting events were also annotated, such as use of on-demand services.

The total amount of time participants' TVs were turned on across all households was 54:23:53. This equates to about 57% of the total video recordings. As can be seen in Table 1, there was considerable variability in the total amount of time that the TV was on in each household (*range*: 07:23:05 - 19:07:52).

Results for individual participants can be seen in Table 2. It can be seen that for individual participants, mean total time present when the TV was on was 07:45:15 ($SD = 07:15:56$), mean total device usage when present was 00:46:36 ($SD = 00:48:38$), and mean number of uses was 7.33 ($SD = 8.19$). It can also be seen in Table 2 that there were large individual differences in media multitasking habits between participants. Some participants did not use their devices at all (C1, D3 and D4) while others used their devices for nearly a quarter of the time they were watching (C2). Furthermore, some participants favoured shorter, more frequent uses while others exhibited fewer but longer uses.

---

[1]http://www.chronoviz.com/ [Last access 27th October 2016]

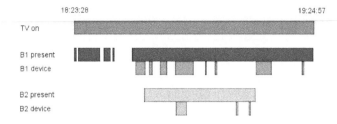

Figure 1: Frequent but short device uses from household B.

Figure 2: Long but infrequent device uses from household C.

To illustrate some of the differences in media multitasking strategies that were observed, we focus in on two participants with the highest percentage of TV time spent using their devices — these were participants C2 and B2. Participant B2 used their device 28 times for an average of 1 minute and 27 seconds, at a rate of .115 uses per minute, whereas C2 only used their device 10 times, but for an average 11 minutes and 16 seconds at a rate of .014 uses per minute. This can be seen in Figure 1 and Figure 2 respectively, which shows a snapshot of behaviour over a ~1 hour period. However, these individuals did not necessarily sustain the same usage pattern uniformly over the course of their viewing.

Device usage and MMI score
We next consider the relationship between MMI score and total device usage (as a percentage of time participants are present while the TV is on), and between MMI score and device uses per hour. One participant was removed from these analyses due to misunderstanding the MMI questionnaire, leading to an artificially high value. Across the remaining sample of 11 participants, mean MMI score was 2.08 ($SD =$ 1.1). Figures 4 and 3 are scatterplots showing the relationship between MMI and time using device and device uses per hour. As can be seen in these figures, participants who had a higher MMI score tended to use their devices for longer periods in total when in front of the TV ($r^2 = .60$), and use their devices more frequently ($r^2 = .48$). Statistical analyses support these observations, showing that MMI score was a significant predictor of time spent using devices in front of the TV, $F(1,9) = 13.66, p = .005$, and number of devices uses per hour $F(1,9) = 8.36, p = .018$. In other words, MMI scores were predictive of people's actual observed media multitasking behaviour at home.

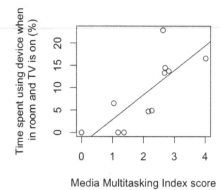

Figure 3: Scatterplot of device usage time against MMI.

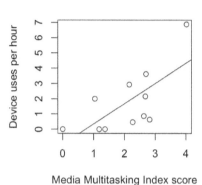

Figure 4: Scatterplot of device uses per hour against MMI.

The TV as a meeting point
Previous literature has shown how the living room and television are used as a meeting place where family and friends gather to be with one another, both to watch programmes together and also to do other tasks while not actively watching [15, 17, 8]. Figure 5 shows some examples of participants using the TV as a background to other activities performed together. Times when there were more than one person present while the TV was on accounted for 28:59:13 (53% of total TV time) across households.

Three of the households were recorded completing some kind of work in front of the TV. Participant A2 was recording completing some accounting work (see Figure 6a), B1 and B3, both teachers, were recorded marking work (see Figure 6b), and the children from household D were recorded doing homework (see Figure 6c).

DISCUSSION
The results of this study revealed large individual differences in concurrent TV watching and device use habits between participants. Some participants were frequent device users, while others used no devices whatsoever. Looking at the demographic make-up information of the households, the household made of females in their late 20s (household B) recorded the largest proportion of concurrent mobile device usage while

(a) Wrapping a present.

(b) Sleeping.

(c) Knitting.

(d) Reading together.

Figure 5: Participants performing tasks in front of the TV with others present.

(a) Participant A2 doing paperwork, while A1 watches TV.

(b) Participant B1, a teacher, marks work in front of the TV, while B2 uses her phone.

(c) Child from household D doing homework.

Figure 6: Participants working in front of the TV.

watching TV. This may be in line with expectations that millennials use more technology than older people [7]. To further understand this, we examined their domestic circumstances, and found that two of the participants had partners that lived in different cities, whereas all of the other households consisted of couples or children. It is possible that this increased usage could be through messaging their partners. This is supported by the high number of uses recorded, which supports the type of phone checking pattern resulting from asynchronous communication.

The MMI questionnaire asks participants to assess their general multitasking preferences across a range of media. Our results show that MMI score was a good predictor of actual media multitasking behaviour. It is interesting to note that the MMI scores of participants in our study were considerably lower than that reported in previous studies that used the MMI — mean MMI score for our participants was 2.08, compared to 4.38 in [27], 3.82 in [21] and 4.07 in [1]. This difference in MMI scores between studies is most likely due to our sample of older participants, compared to the participants in previous studies, which were mainly college students in their early 20s. Both media multitasking and general multitasking has been found to be less common among older generations [7, 10], which would explain this discrepancy. In general, our results suggest that the rate of media multitasking in the home might vary considerably between households.

Different patterns of device usage were observed, ranging from fewer uses lasting for long periods, to many short uses. This raises interesting questions as to how media multitasking is defined. We observed multitasking behaviour at different points on the multitasking continuum [35]. Frequent, shorter uses could be considered instances of concurrent multitasking, were two tasks are being performed simultaneously (e.g. talking and driving). On the other hand, longer uses with fewer switches could be considered instances of sequential multitasking, where only one task at a time is being actively performed before switching to the other task. This means that when the user is purely concentrating on their device, the TV is likely blurring into the background and they stop following what is happening on the TV. Indeed, in our data there were many occurrences of the TV on in the background while the participants were engaged in other activities (e.g. those shown in Figure 5d and Figure 6b). Such nuances may be difficult to convey when using self-reported methods or log analysis to establish how prevalent media multitasking really is, which may call into question the veracity of such methods — simply asking participants if they use their phones and tablets while watching TV may not give a full picture of their behaviour.

The impact of the types of media multitasking we observed should also be considered. It is widely accepted that humans have limited cognitive resources, and so to perform two tasks concurrently they must be interleaved [23, 5, 34]. This results in switch costs, which can impede performance [24]. It may be that negative effects also transfer to the TV domain, for instance in terms of reduced engagement [12]. With regard to processing media messages, we can look to the Limited Capacity Model of Motivated Mediated Message Processing (LC4MP) which attempts to explain such cognitive limitations specifically in relation to mediated communication, such as TV watching [16]. Furthermore, it has also been shown that media multitasking specifically can also have detrimental effects, for instance when attempting to work in front of the TV [4, 19], and there is evidence to suggest that those who media multitask the most are often the worst at it [27].

Our data showed that of the entire time the television was on across households, more than one person was present for at least half of the time. In line with prior research, this shows that the television was very much a meeting point for the households in this study [15, 17, 8]. Watching TV was frequently a social activity, and in addition to coming together to watch programmes together, the participants would leave the TV on while doing other tasks seemingly just to be together. This suggests that although the television landscape has changed and fragmented, people still value the social aspect of sitting together whether or not they are watching TV together. This is supported by the findings of Kubey [14], who found that family viewing is associated with a more challenging, cheerful, and sociable experience than viewing alone. Furthermore, social interaction has also been found to be a motivation for television viewing [33].

LIMITATIONS AND FUTURE DIRECTIONS
This study has described an analysis of video data that gives an interesting snapshot of daily mobile device use in front of the TV. This has allowed these media multitasking moments to be isolated and analysed to give a better understanding of how often and how long they occur in the home. Due to the high level of individual differences observed across participants, and the small sample size, it could be argued that it is difficult to draw strong generalisable conclusions.

However, the results do provide good evidence of a strong link between self-reported MMI and observed device usage.

A number of difficulties were had with the technology. Setting up the cameras was not a trivial task, and at times they malfunctioned resulting in data loss. Furthermore, image quality was lower than desired, which made analysing small movements and glances difficult or impossible. The cameras are intended for basic home surveillance and so were not entirely fit for our purposes, but we were limited by the need to have mains-powered, "set-and-forget" equipment, and by cost.

While the video data can provide a rich perspective into events, it can take significant amounts of time to process and analyse. A number of passes were required to prepare, collate, and synchronise the video files, including a lengthy re-encoding process. The actual video analysis and annotation also required a number of passes in order to make sure each type of relevant behaviour and each participant was accounted for. Nevertheless, our efforts have resulted in a detailed dataset which would be difficult to obtain using alternative methods.

Future work could aim to provide a deeper understanding of these media multitasking moments. It might also be useful to recruit a larger sample to allow for more generalisable patterns of behaviour to be established. However, the resources needed to run such a study, for even small numbers, makes this prohibitive. Furthermore, this study has only focused on viewing in the living room. It would also be beneficial to see how this fits in with content consumption outside of the living room, such as on mobile devices via on-demand services.

CONCLUSION
In this study, we observed four households watching TV for three evenings, with cameras observing both the participants and the television. During the 96 hours of observation across each household, participants' televisions were turned on for 54.4 hours (57% of the time), with a mean of 13.6 hours. Our results suggest that viewing and device usage habits for individual participants were highly variable. Some participants watched a lot of TV while others watched less. Some participants frequently used their mobile device while other did not use devices at all. MMI was found to be a good predictor of observed media multitasking, taking into account both total device usage and the number of uses, suggesting that people who media multitask with their phone and TV probably do so with other media too. We also observed differing patterns of device use in front of the television, which could be classified at different points on the multitasking continuum.

Our observations confirmed a common theme in prior studies that the TV has a social function in the household. We observed that for 53% of the total time the TV was turned on, more than one person was present. The TV acted as a household hub, with participants gathering around it even when focusing on other tasks, such as work, using mobile devices, and reading. This suggests that although it is changing, the TV remains a focal point for family life in the home.

ACKNOWLEDGEMENTS
This research was supported by EPSRC grant EP/G037159/1.

REFERENCES

1. Reem Alzahabi and Mark W Becker. 2013. The association between media multitasking, task-switching, and dual-task performance. *Journal of Experimental Psychology: Human Perception and Performance* 39, 5 (2013), 1485. DOI:http://dx.doi.org/10.1037/a0031208

2. S Adam Brasel and James Gips. 2011. Media multitasking behavior: Concurrent television and computer usage. *Cyberpsychology, Behavior, and Social Networking* 14, 9 (2011), 527–534. DOI: http://dx.doi.org/10.1089/cyber.2010.0350

3. Barry Brown, Moira McGregor, and Eric Laurier. 2013. iPhone in vivo: video analysis of mobile device use. In *Proceedings of the SIGCHI conference on Human Factors in computing systems*. ACM, 1031–1040. DOI: http://dx.doi.org/10.1145/2470654.2466132

4. Duncan P. Brumby, Helena Du Toit, Harry J. Griffin, Ana Tajadura-Jiménez, and Anna L. Cox. 2014. Working with the Television on: An Investigation into Media Multitasking. In *Proceedings of the Extended Abstracts of the 32Nd Annual ACM Conference on Human Factors in Computing Systems (CHI EA '14)*. ACM, New York, NY, USA, 1807–1812. DOI: http://dx.doi.org/10.1145/2559206.2581210

5. Paul W Burgess, Emma Veitch, Angela de Lacy Costello, and Tim Shallice. 2000. The cognitive and neuroanatomical correlates of multitasking. *Neuropsychologia* 38, 6 (2000), 848 – 863. DOI: http://dx.doi.org/10.1016/S0028-3932(99)00134-7

6. Jeff K. Caird, Chelsea R. Willness, Piers Steel, and Chip Scialfa. 2008. A meta-analysis of the effects of cell phones on driver performance. *Accident Analysis & Prevention* 40, 4 (2008), 1282 – 1293. DOI: http://dx.doi.org/10.1016/j.aap.2008.01.009

7. L Mark Carrier, Nancy A Cheever, Larry D Rosen, Sandra Benitez, and Jennifer Chang. 2009. Multitasking across generations: Multitasking choices and difficulty ratings in three generations of Americans. *Computers in Human Behavior* 25, 2 (2009), 483–489. DOI: http://dx.doi.org/10.1016/j.chb.2008.10.012

8. Evelien D'heer, Cédric Courtois, and Steve Paulussen. 2012. Everyday Life in (Front of) the Screen: The Consumption of Multiple Screen Technologies in the Living Room Context. In *Proceedings of the 10th European Conference on Interactive Tv and Video (EuroiTV '12)*. ACM, New York, NY, USA, 195–198. DOI:http://dx.doi.org/10.1145/2325616.2325654

9. R Key Dismukes, Loukia D Loukopoulos, and Kimberly K Jobe. 2001. The challenges of managing concurrent and deferred tasks. In *Proceedings of the Eleventh International Symposium on Aviation Psychology. Columbus, OH: The Ohio State University*. Citeseer.

10. Brittany R-L Duff, Gunwoo Yoon, Zongyuan Wang, and George Anghelcev. 2014. Doing it all: An exploratory study of predictors of media multitasking. *Journal of Interactive Advertising* 14, 1 (2014), 11–23. DOI: http://dx.doi.org/10.1080/15252019.2014.884480

11. Ulla G Foehr. 2006. Media Multitasking among American Youth: Prevalence, Predictors and Pairings. *Henry J. Kaiser Family Foundation* (2006).

12. Michael E. Holmes, Sheree Josephson, and Ryan E. Carney. 2012. Visual Attention to Television Programs with a Second-screen Application. In *Proceedings of the Symposium on Eye Tracking Research and Applications (ETRA '12)*. ACM, New York, NY, USA, 397–400. DOI: http://dx.doi.org/10.1145/2168556.2168646

13. Christian Holz, Frank Bentley, Karen Church, and Mitesh Patel. 2015. "I'm Just on My Phone and They're Watching TV": Quantifying Mobile Device Use While Watching Television. In *Proceedings of the ACM International Conference on Interactive Experiences for TV and Online Video (TVX '15)*. ACM, New York, NY, USA, 93–102. DOI: http://dx.doi.org/10.1145/2745197.2745210

14. Robert Kubey. 1990. Television and the quality of family life. *Communication Quarterly* 38, 4 (1990), 312–324. DOI:http://dx.doi.org/10.1080/01463379009369769

15. Robert W Kubey. 1986. Television use in everyday life: Coping with unstructured time. *Journal of communication* 36, 3 (1986), 108–123. DOI: http://dx.doi.org/10.1111/j.1460-2466.1986.tb01441.x

16. A Lang. 2000. The limited capacity model of mediated message processing. *Journal of Communication* 50, 1 (2000), 46–70. DOI: http://dx.doi.org/10.1111/j.1460-2466.2000.tb02833.x

17. Robert J Logan, Sheila Augaitis, Robert H Miller, and Keith Wehmeyer. 1995. Living room culture - an anthropological study of television usage behaviors. In *Proceedings of the Human Factors and Ergonomics Society Annual Meeting*, Vol. 39. SAGE Publications Sage CA: Los Angeles, CA, 326–330. DOI: http://dx.doi.org/10.1177/154193129503900507

18. Kep Kee Loh and Ryota Kanai. 2014. Higher media multi-tasking activity is associated with smaller gray-matter density in the anterior cingulate cortex. *Plos one* 9, 9 (2014), e106698. DOI: http://dx.doi.org/10.1371/journal.pone.0106698

19. Danielle M. Lottridge, Christine Rosakranse, Catherine S. Oh, Sean J. Westwood, Katherine A. Baldoni, Abrey S. Mann, and Clifford I. Nass. 2015. The Effects of Chronic Multitasking on Analytical Writing. In *Proceedings of the 33rd Annual ACM Conference on Human Factors in Computing Systems (CHI '15)*. ACM, New York, NY, USA, 2967–2970. DOI: http://dx.doi.org/10.1145/2702123.2702367

20. Loukia D Loukopoulos, R Key Dismukes, and Immanuel Barshi. 2003. Concurrent task demands in the cockpit: Challenges and vulnerabilities in routine flight operations. In *Proceedings of the 12th international symposium on aviation psychology*. Wright State University Press Dayton, OH, 737–742.

21. Kelvin FH Lui and Alan C-N Wong. 2012. Does media multitasking always hurt? A positive correlation between multitasking and multisensory integration. *Psychonomic bulletin & review* 19, 4 (2012), 647–653. DOI: http://dx.doi.org/10.3758/s13423-012-0245-7

22. Gloria Mark, Shamsi T. Iqbal, Mary Czerwinski, Paul Johns, and Akane Sano. 2016. Neurotics Can't Focus: An in Situ Study of Online Multitasking in the Workplace. In *Proceedings of the 2016 CHI Conference on Human Factors in Computing Systems (CHI '16)*. ACM, New York, NY, USA, 1739–1744. DOI: http://dx.doi.org/10.1145/2858036.2858202

23. David E Meyer and David E Kieras. 1997. A computational theory of executive cognitive processes and multiple-task performance: Part I. Basic mechanisms. *Psychological review* 104, 1 (1997), 3. DOI: http://dx.doi.org/10.1037/0033-295x.104.1.3

24. Stephen Monsell. 2003. Task switching. *Trends in cognitive sciences* 7, 3 (2003), 134–140. DOI: http://dx.doi.org/10.1016/s1364-6613(03)00028-7

25. Ofcom. 2013. The Communications Market Report 2013. (2013). http://stakeholders.ofcom.org.uk/binaries/research/cmr/cmr13/2013_UK_CMR.pdf

26. Ofcom. 2014. The Communications Market Report 2014. (2014). http://stakeholders.ofcom.org.uk/binaries/research/cmr/cmr14/2014_UK_CMR.pdf

27. Eyal Ophir, Clifford Nass, and Anthony D. Wagner. 2009. Cognitive control in media multitaskers. *Proceedings of the National Academy of Sciences* 106, 37 (2009), 15583–15587. DOI: http://dx.doi.org/10.1073/pnas.0903620106

28. Stefania Pizza, Barry Brown, Donald McMillan, and Airi Lampinen. 2016. Smartwatch in vivo. In *Proceedings of the 2016 CHI Conference on Human Factors in Computing Systems*. ACM, 5456–5469. DOI: http://dx.doi.org/10.1145/2858036.2858522

29. Victoria J Rideout, Ulla G Foehr, and Donald F Roberts. 2010. Generation M ^{2}: Media in the Lives of 8-to 18-Year-Olds. *Henry J. Kaiser Family Foundation* (2010).

30. Donald F Roberts and Ulla G Foehr. 2008. Trends in media use. *The future of children* 18, 1 (2008), 11–37. DOI:http://dx.doi.org/10.1353/foc.0.0000

31. John Rooksby, Mattias Rost, Alistair Morrison, Marek Bell, and Matthew Chalmers. 2014. Practices of Parallel Media: Using Mobile Devices When Watching Television. *Designing with Users for Domestic Environments: Methods, Challenges and Lessons Learned. Workshop at CSCW '14* (2014).

32. John Rooksby, Timothy E Smith, Alistair Morrison, Mattias Rost, and Matthew Chalmers. 2015. Configuring Attention in the Multiscreen Living Room. In *ECSCW 2015: Proceedings of the 14th European Conference on Computer Supported Cooperative Work, 19-23 September 2015, Oslo, Norway*. Springer, 243–261. DOI: http://dx.doi.org/10.1007/978-3-319-20499-4_13

33. Alan M. Rubin. 1981. An Examination of Television Viewing Motivations. *Communication Research* 8, 2 (1981), 141–165. DOI: http://dx.doi.org/10.1177/009365028100800201

34. Dario D Salvucci and Niels A Taatgen. 2008. Threaded cognition: an integrated theory of concurrent multitasking. *Psychological review* 115, 1 (2008), 101. DOI:http://dx.doi.org/10.1037/0033-295x.115.1.101

35. Dario D. Salvucci, Niels A. Taatgen, and Jelmer P. Borst. 2009. Toward a Unified Theory of the Multitasking Continuum: From Concurrent Performance to Task Switching, Interruption, and Resumption. In *Proceedings of the SIGCHI Conference on Human Factors in Computing Systems (CHI '09)*. ACM, New York, NY, USA, 1819–1828. DOI: http://dx.doi.org/10.1145/1518701.1518981

36. Jeroen Vanattenhoven and David Geerts. 2012. Second-screen use in the home: An ethnographic study. In *Proceedings 3rd International Workshop on Future Television, EuroITV*. 12.

37. Hilde A. M. Voorveld and Margot van der Goot. 2013. Age Differences in Media Multitasking: A Diary Study. *Journal of Broadcasting & Electronic Media* 57, 3 (2013), 392–408. DOI: http://dx.doi.org/10.1080/08838151.2013.816709

38. Hilde A. M. Voorveld and Vijay Viswanathan. 2014. An Observational Study on How Situational Factors Influence Media Multitasking With TV: The Role of Genres, Dayparts, and Social Viewing. *Media Psychology* 0, 0 (2014), 1–28. DOI: http://dx.doi.org/10.1080/15213269.2013.872038

How People Multitask While Watching TV

Auriana Shokrpour
Samsung Research America
655 Clyde Ave. Mountain
View, CA 94043
a.shokrpour@samsung.com

Michael J. Darnell
Samsung Research America
655 Clyde Ave. Mountain
View, CA 94043
mike.darnell@samsung.com

ABSTRACT

We often think of TV watching as the activity where people are fully engaged and immersed in the TV program. However, research has shown that there is a continuum of levels of attention while watching TV. We set out to understand multitasking behaviors as well as users' motivation and intention behind simultaneous tasks performed in front of the television. We conducted an in-home qualitative research methods study inside ten households across the San Francisco Bay Area and used a quantitative method for analysis of the large amount of behavioral data we gathered. We recorded participants' television watching behaviors using cameras that were placed in their homes and used retrospective interviews to gather purpose behind events that were observed in the video recordings. We defined eye gaze elsewhere than on the TV as accounting for a multitasking event. It was found that multitasking occurred almost 40% of the time when people were seated in front of the television. Most multitasking occurred during TV programs — not during the interval between TV programs. Of the time people spent multitasking, 36% was spent on a device, mostly a smartphone. However, only 10% of device-related multitasking was related to the content being played on the TV. With our study, we contribute to the greater body of foundational knowledge around common multitasking behaviors that are conducted in front of the television.

Author Keywords

Television; multitasking; behaviors; smartphone; social watching; media-multitasking, attention; distraction; ethnography; TV.

ACM Classification Keywords

H.5.m. Information interfaces and presentation (e.g., HCI): Miscellaneous.

Permission to make digital or hard copies of all or part of this work for personal or classroom use is granted without fee provided that copies are not made or distributed for profit or commercial advantage and that copies bear this notice and the full citation on the first page. Copyrights for components of this work owned by others than ACM must be honored. Abstracting with credit is permitted. To copy otherwise, or republish, to post on servers or to redistribute to lists, requires prior specific permission and/or fee. Request permissions from Permissions@acm.org.

TVX '17, June 14-16, 2017, Hilversum, Netherlands
© 2017 Association for Commuting Machinery.
ACM ISBN 978-1-4503-4529-3/17/06...$15.00
http://dx.doi.org/10.1145/3077548.3077558

INTRODUCTION

We often think of TV watching as the activity where people are fully engaged and immersed in the TV program. However, previous research by Lee and Lee (1995) shows that there may be 4 levels of engagement with TV watching: (1) TV watching is sole activity, (2) TV watching is one of two activities (user is still in front of set), (3) TV watching is peripheral activity (user is not in front of the set most of the time) and (4) TV is background noise [5]. Ostrem (personal communication, 2013) asked survey respondents across the United States to best describe their last TV watching experience in relation to the 4 levels of engagement, and found that 24% only watched TV and did nothing else, 54% did something else but primarily attended to the TV, 17% did something else primarily but also watched TV and lastly, 7% did another task with TV on in the background.

According to Deloitte's latest Digital Democracy Survey, 90% of consumers are typically multitasking while watching TV [3]. While research around multitasking during TV watching time has focused on the frequency of media multitasking, or multiple devices being used, whether they are used during ads or during the show and whether they interrupt or enhance the TV watching experience, there is relatively little research around which tasks people are actually doing during their television-watching time at a more general, behavioral level, device-related or not.

Many questions remain around what is occurring in peoples' television watching-space while the television is on. For example, are people attending to extraneous tasks while somewhat engaged with television content being played? And when do these simultaneous tasks occur in relation to the timing of television content? For example, while concurrent tasks are being performed during television-watching time, is the television content in a transition state such in closing credits of a show, or in a browsing state such as on a guide or menu, during ads or during the show itself? Do these extraneous tasks involve secondary devices to the television and remote, and if so, which extraneous devices are commonly used during TV watching time? And are the tasks conducted on the devices related or unrelated to the content being viewed on the television?

Traditionally, research around multitasking are lab or survey-based [1, 3, 4, 6, 7, 8]. While the survey methodology approach gathers a large amount of insight, survey results depend on people's beliefs and knowledge regarding their own and other people's behavior and may bear little resemblance to their actual behavior. Similarly, data from instrumenting TVs and other devices reveal great detail about function use on the devices but relatively little about the users' task or goals. Lab studies can reveal how people use TVs in new controlled situations, but reveal little about how people actually use their TV at home. In contrast, In-Home research allows one to observe people naturally while watching television and potentially engage in extraneous tasks.

Observing people in their natural environments as they watch television is important because it increases our body of knowledge for common tasks that occur while watching TV without the restrictions posed by survey, television usage data and lab studies. Given predictions around the future of television moving towards an ambient, more responsive device, it is a critical time for understanding which tasks occur simultaneously during television-watching time and the extent to which those tasks are related to the TV content. Gathering insight on people watching television in their homes helps television companies and content providers invent the future of television.

While previous research answers questions around multitasking using survey and laboratory methodologies, there is relatively little research that has explored what people are doing while watching television in their natural home environment. The goal of this study was to explore the questions asked above. In order to do so, this research study employs an ethnographic approach, where ten households were observed through video recordings over the course of two weeks in order to capture natural human behaviors in relation to television watching.

RELATED WORK
A substantial amount of survey data exists from the growing interest of media multitasking conducted by several different organizations. The most recent annual Multitasking and Social Media TV Survey by TiVo found that 53% of viewers are multitasking every time or almost every time they watch TV [8]. Of these respondents 36% self reported that they use a smartphone device while multitasking. When multitasking, it was found that only 6% of the 806 respondents across the U.S. reported that tasks were related to content being viewed on the TV.

Deloitte conducted a large self-report study asking people what tasks they typically do while watching TV [3]. They found that only 10% of respondents reported that they typically just watch TV. Of the 90% who reported that they typically multitask while watching television, the top five task activities were all device-related, listed in successive order as such: surf web, read email, text message, use social media, browse products online. It was also found that 22%

of overall multitasking activities are directly related to the programs that they are watching.

The PEW Research Center coined the term "connected viewer" for the 74% of smartphone owners who reported to have used their smartphone in one way or another while watching television within 30 days prior to taking the online survey [7]. Smartphone owners used their phones to multitask while TV watching and reported doing so in a variety of ways, including as a distraction tool during ads (58%), to validate information absorbed in television content (37%), to visit a website mentioned on TV (35%) or to view user-generated material about television content (20%). The three latter findings indicate a stronger relationship between multitasking on the smartphone and TV content, which contradicts findings reported from the TiVo survey, where only 6% of respondents reported TV content-related device usage [7, 8].

Brasel and Gips (2011) conducted a one-on-one laboratory experiment and post-hoc survey that investigated multitasking by how frequently people switch between gazing at the television and gazing at a secondary device screen [1]. A naturalistic media environment in a lab was simulated using a laptop computer and television; stimuli were based on findings from the Neilsen Research Group that 57 percent of people who reported to watch TV with others (two or more in room) surfed the Internet at the same time [6]. Brasel and Gips found that on average participants spent 69 percent of the time with their eye gaze on the laptop, and 31 percent of the time with their eye gaze on the television [1]. Moreover, they found that participants viewed more than double the amount of websites (12) than channels (5) during their session. The amount of attentional switching, measured by their eye gaze, averaged 120 switches in under 30 minutes. Interestingly, Brasel and Gips found that participants underestimated the frequency of switching by 88% in the post-hoc self-report survey, giving weight to the importance of behavioral observations for understanding multitasking over self-report surveys.

Holz, Bentley, Church, and Patel (2015) explored multitasking on smartphones and tablets in relation to the timing of television content (ads or show) using a mixed qualitative and quantitative approach. An app logger was installed in 7 households, tracking app and webpage launches during television watching [4]. A sound-printing tool was used to help identify whether an ad or show was being played on the TV during the timing of when the secondary device was used. Holz et al. found that the volume of device multitasking was relatively similar regardless of whether an ad or show was playing on the TV, with rates differing by only 5% (35.5% during show and 30.2% during ad) [4]. However, only 3.6% of the 415 hours of TV logged consisted of ads (15 hours total), posing a foggy area as to whether it can be concluded that little difference in multitasking occurred between ads and shows.

The method employed by Holz et al. exerted a level of control in observing only specified devices that people used to multitask while watching TV. This method gets closer to the ethnographic approach used in this study to investigate people multitasking while watching TV at home, which was replicated after a naturalistic research study conducted by Darnell (2007) [2]. Darnell recounts an in-home research method used for gathering natural Digital TV and DVR interactions in the home environment. In this study, he placed cameras in the homes of ten participants and after all video footage was taken, people were interviewed as they watched video footage of their TV watching as to gather insight around their goals and behaviors. This current study replicates this method of naturalistic observation with retrospective interviews.

METHOD

This study used naturalistic observation methodology, where video cameras were placed in ten homes across the San Francisco Bay Area in order to capture how people watch television in their own home over the course of two-weeks. After the video recordings were completed, retrospective interviews were conducted with each of the participants in order to gain rich qualitative insight on their intentions for various events that were conducted while interacting with the television.

Participants

A representative sample of smart TV owners were recruited who fit the criteria for varying levels of live TV, streaming, and DVR usage across either dish and cable subscriptions. Experienced television watchers were selected and reported to regularly watch 21 hours or more of television per week. Ten people participated, 8 males and 2 females, all between the ages of 27 and 61 and all lived in multi-person households.

Participant	Gen	Age	Num in House	System
1	M	61	2	Dish, DVR
2	M	45	4	Cable TV, DVR
3	F	29	3	Cable TV, DVR
4	M	39	2	Cable TV
5	M	27	2	Cable TV
6	M	30	2	Direct TV, DVR
7	M	37	3	Cable TV, DVR
8	F	28	3	Cable TV, DVR
9	M	47	4	Cable TV
10	M	61	2	Cable TV, DVR

Table 1. Participants' Characteristics.

Figure 1. Output video stream with two inputs showing from left: (1) video camera view of TV from opposite side of room; (2) video camera view of living room from TV area.

Equipment

A multi-channel mini DVR device was used in order to support capturing multiple video angles and audio at the same time. Two video cameras were placed in the viewing area for the primary television in each of the ten homes. One of the video cameras was placed near the television in order to capture the room and the participant as they watched TV, while the other video camera was placed behind the participant viewing area facing the TV, in order to capture the TV screen. The two video cameras and their outputs fed into the multi-input video processer device and scaled the video feeds equally and arranged them into a single output stream (see Figure 1). The output video and audio stream were recorded onto memory cards for later review.

Procedure

The study began in January 2016 and was conducted in three 2-hour long home visits, an initial visit at the beginning of the two-week period, a visit at the end of the first week, and a final visit at the end of the second week, concluding the in-home visits:

1) The first visit of our two-week session consisted of short semi-structured interviews where the participants' TV watching area was documented using a photo camera. Participants briefly demonstrated their TV watching behaviors using their remotes.

During the initial interview, two video cameras were set up in the participants' home, one to record the participants' TV screen itself and the other to record the participants as they watched TV in their own environment (see Figure 1).

At the end of the initial interviews, each participant determined the days and times for which the multi-input video processing device would store recordings from the camera inputs over the course of their normal television watching times for the week. A total of 6 hours of video recording sessions were scheduled for the first week and were stored on the memory card in the video processing device. Over the course of the first week, participants were told to watch television as usual and that the red light indicator on the multi-input video processing device confirmed that recording times were as scheduled. This resulted in more confidence for the participants to feel comfortable in knowing they were not continuously being recorded over the course of the two-week period that the video cameras were installed in their homes.

2) The second visit consisted of reviewing the video recordings that were stored on the memory device using a retrospective review technique. Due to a time limitation of 2-hour long visit per participant, the recordings that were most proximal to our second home visit were prioritized for review first. The intent behind this was that recall of reasoning behind events would be more clear to participants if the video being reviewed were more recent in time. Another requirement was that the primary participant was present during the video recording. Participants watched recordings and provided commentary when notable events occurred. If there were multiple people in the room during the recorded videos, the primary participant provided detailed commentary for behaviors of secondary viewer during commentary interviews. In cases where the secondary participant was present during commentary interviews, the secondary participant provided commentary on events as well. Comments were noted in an excel spreadsheet as well as the time for which the event occurred.

At the end of this visit, participants scheduled six more hours of television watching time to be stored on the memory card in the video processing device. A total of twelve hours of video recordings was collected over the course of the two-weeks.

3) The final in-home interview consisted of retrospective review of the second set of video recordings, with all of the same criteria upheld as during the retrospective review session in visit 2. At the end of this visit, all video cameras and recording equipment were collected from the homes, which concluded the two-week long logging period with participants.

First we determined which recordings qualified for analysis. We established the least number of usable recorded session hours to analyze based on the following criteria: recordings where participants were out of the room were not included; recordings where the TV was turned off were not included. We analyzed recording sessions of people watching alone as well as people watching with others. For video recordings with multiple viewers, cases where secondary viewer was not present during commentary interviews, or primary participant had not commented on secondary viewer, were not included for analysis. Entire recording session blocks were used for analysis, unless the recording did not adhere to the requirements that the primary participant was present and the TV was turned on during the scheduled recording time. An equal amount of video recordings per participant were analyzed in order to make sure each household contributed the same amount of data to the study.

Second, we analyzed the video recordings through an organized data tracking technique using an excel spreadsheet with time-stamped commentary from the retrospective interviews. Metrics for behavioral trends were defined based on observations of events in the usable videos. Every 5min during the TV-watching sessions, it was noted where the participant's eyes were looking. Eye gaze was used as the metric for multitask events in this study based on the methodology from the Brasil and Gips study, where eye gaze was used to determine multitask events in the lab between a laptop and television [1].

Results

One hundred and twenty hours of television watching recordings were collected across all ten participant households, resulting in a large amount of data whereby a quantitative method for analysis was used. Sixty-five of the one hundred twenty hours were reviewed and used as data for the study. The sixty-five hours of reviewed TV watching video (10 participants X 6.5 hours) was analyzed for multitasking in the following way. Every 5 minutes in the video it was determined where the principal participant was looking (e.g., at the TV, at a person, at their smartphone). This was used to estimate the proportion of time spent in various multitasking activities. As such there were 738 data points in total, 621 of which were usable; 103 data points were declared unusable because the primary person stepped out of the camera view, and 14 data points were declared inconclusive because eye gaze was unclear due to blurriness of the camera or an object temporarily covering a participant's face (117 unusable data points total). The purpose behind the 5 minute samples was largely a practical consideration given the large amount of data to analyze. We compared the representativeness of frequency of multitask events between samples analyzed at 1 minute intervals versus samples analyzed at 5 minute intervals for three participants (3 of 10) who were particularly active during their session recordings. The reason why we chose these 3 participants is because a wide range of multitask events took place at high frequencies during each of their sessions, resulting in greater understanding for impact on normalizing the data between analyzing samples at 1 min intervals versus 5 min intervals. While the frequency counts of tasks observed at the 5 minute mark are fewer than the frequency counts of tasks observed at the minute mark, our comparisons led us to conclude that the samples analyzed at 5 minute intervals of the recordings were a sufficient representation for frequency of the type of multitask events that occurred during sessions (see Fig. 2). From this, we found that while "watching TV", people spent about 40% of the time NOT looking at the TV.

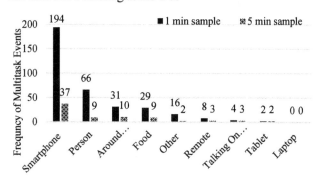

Figure 2. The sum of multitasking events taken at 1min samples and 5 min samples for P2, P3 and P8.

14

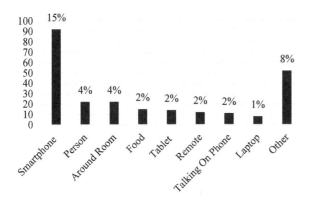

Figure 3. The overall frequency of multitasking events.

The most commonly observed position for eye gaze was on a smartphone, which was observed in 9 participants and accounted for 15% of 5-minute events in the overall TV-watching time (see Figure 3 and Figure 4). While looking around the room (n = 10), engaging with another person (n = 9), eating food or drinking (n = 8) and looking at the remote (n = 9) were tasks that many participants conducted while watching TV, these tasks accounted for an especially small amount of overall TV watching time at 3%, 3%, 2% and 2%, respectively.

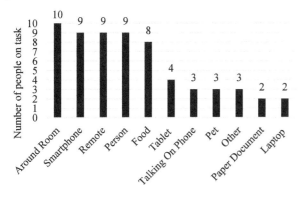

Figure 4. Multitasking behaviors observed in the most participants.

Engaging with another person All ten participants lived in multi-person households (see Table 1). More than half of the time, people watched television in company, with 40% of that statistic consisting of 2 people watching TV together at the same time. During the times when people watched together, the other person was either engaged most of the time or on a device multitasking. Instances where the primary viewer looked at another person were mostly because they were conversing about what was happening in their TV program or movie. In some instances, the primary viewer paused the TV show in order to talk about the content being played on TV.

Timing of multitasking activities in relation to TV content Multitasking events occurred during shows, during ads, during paused content, while browsing in the smarthub, while browsing in saved DVR recordings, during the automatic start of a series in Netflix, or while browsing the Live guide.

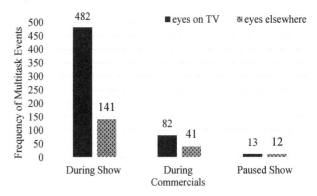

Figure 5. Timing of multitasking activities in relation to what was happening on the TV.

Multitasks were most dense when content was paused on the television, accounting for 92% of all tasks. Multitasks accounted for 50% of all tasks during ads, and 29% of tasks during a programs (see Figure 5).

Multitasking during a program Multitasking events mostly occurred during a program (see Figure 5).

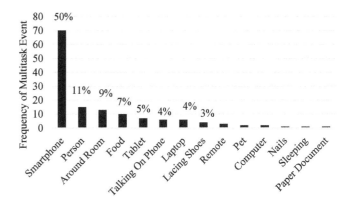

Figure 6. The overall frequency of multitasking events during show.

Of the 5 min samples taken from the 65 hours of video footage, multitasking events during programs most frequently involved a smartphone, which occurred 50% of the time (see Figure 6). Events where the participant was looking at another person during a show or movie occurred 11% of the time. Nine percent of the time that multitasking was observed during programs, people were gazing around the room at something off camera, while 7% of the time, people were looking at their food or drink.

Eight of the 10 participants were observed on their phone during programs. Of the 10 multi-person households, 8 of the participants were directly observed engaging with the other person(s) during a program. Seven of the ten participants were observed looking at things around the room that were off camera, and 6 people were observed looking at their food or drink during programs.

Other multitasking activities that occurred during programs included browsing the smarthub (this is the main menu of apps on a Samsung Smart TV) for something to stream, browsing saved DVR recordings, browsing the live guide and when Netflix was automatically launching the next show in a streamed series.

Multitasking during ads Simultaneous tasks commonly observed during ads accounted for 20% of the overall multitasking time (see Figure 5).

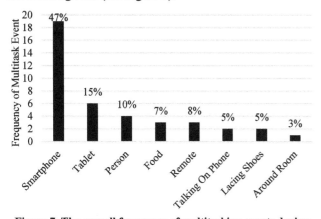

Figure 7. The overall frequency of multitasking events during ads.

Multitasking events during ads most frequently involved a smartphone, which occurred 47% of the time and observed in 7 out of 10 participants (see Figure 7). Events where participants were looking at their tablet occurred 15% of the time, although only 2 participants were observed in this task during ads. Events where the participant was looking at another person during ads occurred 10% of the time and was observed in 3 participants. Other events that occurred during ads include looking at the remote 8% of the time (n = 2), food 5% of the time (n = 3), talking on the phone 5% of the time (n = 2), lacing shoes 5% of the time (n = 1), and looking at various things around the room 2% of the time (n = 1). Tasks that occurred during the program that did not occur during ads include those conducted on a laptop device, computer, or paper documents.

Multitasking during paused content Six percent of all multitasking events consisted of the participant pausing the television program in order to conduct the task, which was an observed behavior in half of the participants (see Figure 5).

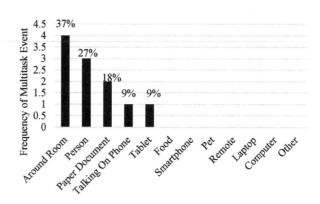

Figure 8. The overall frequency of multitasking events during paused content on TV.

Of the 5 min samples taken from the 65 hours of video footage, multitasking events during paused content (n = 5) most frequently involved the participant gazing at items around the room which was observed in 3 participants, accounting for 37% of the time (see Figure 8). Interestingly, 27% of the time that the content was paused, the participant was looking at another person (n = 2).

Figure 9. Left: TV program paused; (2) camera view participant looking at wife and chatting about *Downtown Abbey*.

Retrospective interviews revealed that participants were discussing program-related events in the show while the content was paused and they were looking at another person while doing so. P10 recalled that he had paused the show *Downtown Abbey* in order to ask his wife for clarification on a character's role (see Figure 9).

Looking at a paper document occurred 18% of the time that the program was paused in order to multitask and was observed in one participant. Overall, two people jotted notes down while watching TV, one during DVR recording on a news segment on the stock crash, and the other during live TV in order to keep track of baseball statistics for specific players. In this case, the participant who had paused the show in order to take notes was watching a recorded news segment on stocks. While the content on TV was paused, 8% of the time it was because someone was on the phone (n = 1) or on their tablet (n = 1).

Device-related multitasking activities while TV watching Thirty-four percent of multitasking activities while watching TV involved a device. The three devices that were discovered to have been used for multitasking include a smartphone, laptop and tablet.

Relatedness of device usage Comments from participants provided in retrospective review revealed that while multitasking on a device, 10% of the time, it's related to content being watched on TV. Of the events where a device was used (112), all of the activities that were reported as related to television content (11) were conducted on a smartphone, while tasks conducted on a laptop or tablet were reported as unrelated to television content. Of all smartphone-related multitasking (92), 11 events were reported as related to the content on the television, resulting in about 12% of relatedness between smartphone multitasking and TV content. The relatedness was found to be around information-seeking about the content in the programs that were simultaneously being watched. All of the cases where this took place were on programs that played on live TV.

P2 discussed his habits for keeping up with fantasy baseball by watching baseball talk shows and games on live TV while simultaneously looking up supplementary player statistics on his smartphone: "*I'm always on my phone…searching online, using apps, whatever…but right now I put a lot of money in fantasy baseball…so while I'm watching a game or 'Hot Stove' or something, I'll search on my phone which players they're talking about to find out more information about them. I won a lot of money one year because I constantly stay up-to-date this way.*"

P3 commented on her habits for looking up foods she sees on cooking shows using yelp on her smartphone: "*I'm going to Southern California in a few weeks and I wanted to go to Gordon Ramsay's restaurant down there, so I looked it up and saw that it is closed…I love Hell's kitchen. Sometimes I'll look up things they're making on the show…Oh! One time they made Dim Sum and so then we were craving Dim Sum…so I used yelp to find nearby restaurants that were open. We ended up having to drive really far because nothing was open around us. It was late.*"

P4 spoke on his instance of using the PBS smartphone application while watching a program on PBS live. "*My wife and I loved the program about raccoons. It was so interesting…so I pulled my phone out and opened the PBS app to see what the scheduled for programs will be for the week. We liked this one so much we wanted to find others that were similar so that we could watch those too. Live TV has so much content on it…so this is what I like to do to find something that's actually interesting to me. It's usually hard to find good stuff because there's so much on my TV.*"

While these participants commentated on experiences where they searched additional information that was related to television content using their smartphone, others had a more interactive experience between both their TV and smartphone device. P5 commented on his instance of sharing information from the program *Jeopardy* on TV using his Facebook smartphone application: "*I thought the contestant was really cute, so I held my phone up to the screen to take a photo of the guy on my TV and uploaded it to Facebook. A few of my friends were also watching, so they*

had commented on it, and a whole discussion started… it was pretty funny."

Although all TV-related activities occurred on smartphones, most smartphone-related activities were unrelated to television content. Some unrelated activities on the smartphone included checking social media, email and text messages. One participant who used his tablet frequently commented that he used it to watch basketball games while ads played during the program he was watching on live TV. A few unrelated activities on the laptop included one participant searching Universities for his niece and another participant filing taxes while watching TV.

LIMITATIONS
While ethnographic research provides rich and detailed insights on how people multitask while watching TV, it is limited by a small sample size. The ten households we visited provided clear trends in multitasking amongst each other, however, ten households is not representative of the entire TV watching population. Moving forward, larger-scale studies can help validate the trends observed in this study.

Given the intrusive nature of placing cameras in homes, we specified certain days and times that each participant typically watched television and stored recordings for only those times. This method allowed participants to feel confident that they were not consistently being recorded over the course of the 2 weeks that the cameras were placed in their homes. The limitation is that during these session recording times, we had to be sure the television was on and the participant was present in order to gather meaningful data. The participants were instructed to mostly be watching TV during their specified recording schedule. Participants had an awareness that cameras were there to record them watching television, and could have altered their behaviors based on this factor.

The video recordings we collected were very comprehensive and required hours of video analysis. That said, another limitation of this study is the consistency in which coding behavioral data occurs. With the 65 hours of video recordings, it is inevitable that some in-between cases existed where a behavior seemed to fit in two alternate categories. In such cases, a decision had to be made on how the behavior was coded for analysis, often times upholding inter-rater reliability of two researchers' opinions. In cases where the camera was covered, or the picture was blurred to the point where eye gaze was unclear, the data point was tossed, resulting in 621 usable data points, as 117 were declared inconclusive due to the person being away from the camera or their eye gaze being unclear.

DISCUSSION AND IMPLICATIONS
In this current research study, we provide rich and detailed qualitative analysis on how people multitask in front of the TV. Recording participant behaviors in their homes and reviewing the videos with participants afterwards allowed us to understand reasoning behind multitasking events that

occurred while watching TV. Having two cameras, one that recorded participants as they watched television and one that recorded the television itself allowed us to precisely map actions to the timing of content being played on the TV, such as during a program, during ads, or during paused content. This analysis allowed us to understand multitasking while watching TV, and we will now discuss the data we synthesized in greater detail.

Based on eye gaze and the commentary provided by participants during retrospective interviews, television watching indeed fell within a continuum of varying levels of attendance. In our study, multitasking events mostly occurred during shows themselves. The ability to multitask while watching television was particularly notable through the process of reviewing video recordings with participants, who often expressed that they were surprised to see themselves on screen looking like they were completely ignoring the TV, yet they were able to recall the information quite well. Similar types of multitasking activities that occurred during a show also occurred during ads.

Most of the activities during programs and ads seemed to have a similar theme of either filling time or browsing other content with the smartphone being the most notable focal point. Smartphone usage was mostly unrelated to the content on the TV. However, the times where mobile usage was related, it was to seek out information that was initiated from content on the television, versus transferring content from one screen to another. During a program, for example, participants more frequently used their mobile devices to find related information based on something in the show that triggered a related question. Only one case was observed where the participant held the mobile device up to the TV hardware to take a picture and transfer information.

In contrast, people seemed to pause content in order to attend to something around the room (off camera), or to talk with another person. Retrospective interviews revealed that the conversations that occurred during paused content typically involved questions or conversations about the plot or characters of a program being watched on TV. Interestingly, people also looked at others during a show for social conversation. Although this occurred far less frequently during a show than when a person dedicated time to the conversation through pausing a show, it leads to the question of how engaged a person must be in order to pause content to converse versus casually conversing while the content plays. A possible explanation for pausing content to engage in conversation is that the person is fully immersed in the program on the television, giving merit to interrupting the experience in order to converse about it. While the smartphone was the front-runner for carrying out multitasking events during programs and ads, it was completely absent in tasks that people conducted during paused TV content. A possible explanation for no smartphone usage during paused content is that engaging in personal smartphone device is a more individualistic experience and since over half of the time in this study people

watched TV with at least one other person, it makes sense that a participant would not have paused content in order to attend to their personal matters on their smartphone while making others viewing with them wait to watch.

The fact that most device usage was unrelated begs the question of whether there is enough TV-related multitasking going on to justify special features on the TV that rely heavily on smartphone applications to better facilitate the TV experience. It is apparent that the relatedness frequency of smartphone usage while watching TV is quite low. Based on the frequency estimates in this study, in a typical 30 hour week of TV watching, the average person might seldom think to multi-task on the smartphone in a way related to the TV programming.

On the other hand, it is also apparent from our study that the smartphone is a reachable tool that is commonly used in front of the TV, and at times, use was initiated from content on the TV evoking information-seeking behaviors on the smartphone. In these cases, the TV content triggered smartphone usage. However, we have yet to see content from the smartphone influence the TV experience in regards to content surfaced on the TV UI. Incoming calls to a landline phone surfaces the number and name of the caller on the TV UI. However, this concept has yet to be transferred to the smartphone. Could there be an area of opportunity in allowing our television display content based on activities that occur on the smartphone?

Our study opens up further questions for follow up studies. In particular, applying this research study method across different cultures would increase our understanding of what people are doing in front of the TV at a larger scale than the San Francisco Bay Area. Also, using an eye tracking method along with retrospective interviews would provide a more accurate snapshot as to where peoples' eye gaze is while watching television.

SUMMARY

This paper describes a study that investigates multitasking while watching TV. In this study, one hundred and twenty hours of television watching recordings were collected across all ten participant households, sixty-five of which were analyzed and used as data for the study. Of the 738 data points, we found that while "watching TV", people spent about 40% of the time looking at things other than the TV. We used a qualitative retrospective interview technique to gather insight behind the events where simultaneous tasks occurred in front of the television. We have shown how multitasking occurs while watching TV, what tasks are commonly performed while watching TV, and the timing in the television content for which the simultaneous tasks occur (i.e., during programs, during ads, during paused content).

ACKNOWLEDGMENTS

We would like to thank Samsung Research America for supporting this research. We also thank our participants for allowing us into their homes to make this research possible.

REFERENCES

1. Brasel, S. A., & Gips, J. (2011). Media multitasking behavior: Concurrent television and computer usage. *Cyberpsychology, Behavior, and Social Networking, 14*(9), 527–534. https://doi.org/10.1089/cyber.2010.0350

2. Darnell, M.J., How do people really interact with TV? Naturalistic observations of digital TV and digital video recorder users. *ACM Computer Entertainment 5*(2). http://doi.acm.org/10.1145/1279540.1279550

3. Deloitte LLP. (2016). *Digital democracy survey*. Retrieved from https://www2.deloitte.com/us/en/pages/technology-media-and-telecommunications/articles/digital-democracy-survey-generational-media-consumption-trends.html

4. Holz, C., Bentley, F., Church, K., Patel, M., "I'm just on my phone and they're watching TV": Quantifying mobile device use while watching television. *Proc. TVX '15*. http://dx.doi.org/10.1145/2745197.2745210

5. Lee, B. and Lee, R.S. 1995. How and why people watch TV: Implications for the future of interactive television. J. *Advertising Research 35*(6), 9-18.

6. Neilsen. (2009). *Three screen report*. Retrieved from http://www.nielsen.com/us/en/insights/reports/2010/three-screen-report-q4-2009.html

7. PEW Research Center. (July 2012). *The rise of the "connected viewer"*. Retrieved from http://pewinternet.org/Reports/2012/Connected-viewers.aspx

8. TiVo. (November 2015). *Distracted, but still watching: TiVo survey finds 99 percent of viewers are multitasking while watching TV*. Retrieved from http://ir.tivo.com/Cache/1001214132.PDF?O=PDF&T=&Y=&D=&FID=1001214132&iid=4206196

Countering Contextual Bias in TV Watching Behavior: Introducing Social Trend as External Contextual Factor in TV Recommenders

Felix Lorenz[1], Jing Yuan[2], Andreas Lommatzsch[2], Mu Mu[3],
Nicholas Race[4], Frank Hopfgartner[5], Sahin Albayrak[2]
[1]Technische Universität Berlin, Berlin, Germany, f.lorenz@campus.tu-berlin.de
[2]TU Berlin – DAI-Lab, Berlin, Germany, {firstname.lastname}@dai-labor.de
[3]The University of Northampton, Northampton, United Kingdom, Mu.Mu@northampton.ac.uk
[4]School of Computing & Communications, Lancaster University, Lancaster, UK, n.race@lancaster.ac.uk
[5]University of Glasgow, Glasgow, UK, frank.hopfgartner@glasgow.ac.uk

ABSTRACT

Context-awareness has become a critical factor in improving the predictions of user interest in modern online TV recommendation systems. In addition to individual user preferences, existing context-aware approaches such as tensor factorization incorporate system-level contextual bias to increase predicting accuracy. We analyzed a user interaction dataset from a WebTV platform, and identified that such contextual bias creates a skewed selection of recommended programs which ultimately locks users in a filter bubble. To address this issue, we introduce the Twitter social stream as a source of external context to extend the choice with items related to social media events. We apply two trend indicators, Trend Momentum and SigniScore, to the Twitter histories of relevant programs. The evaluation reveals that Trend Momentum outperforms SigniScore and signalizes 96% of all peaks ahead of time regarding the selected candidate program titles.

ACM Classification Keywords

H.5.1 Information Interfaces and Presentation (e.g., HCI): Multimedia Information Systems; H.3.3 Information Storage and Retrieval: information filtering, relevance feedback; H.2.8 Database Applications: Data mining

Author Keywords

privacy reserving recommender; video on demand; user experience; context-aware applications; trend detection

INTRODUCTION

With the rapid growth of Internet connectivity, movies and videos are increasingly available online. Whilst streaming services continuously expand their market share, channel-based linear TV also remains very popular [17]. IP Television (IPTV)

Permission to make digital or hard copies of all or part of this work for personal or classroom use is granted without fee provided that copies are not made or distributed for profit or commercial advantage and that copies bear this notice and the full citation on the first page. Copyrights for components of this work owned by others than the author(s) must be honored. Abstracting with credit is permitted. To copy otherwise, or republish, to post on servers or to redistribute to lists, requires prior specific permission and/or a fee. Request permissions from permissions@acm.org.

TVX '17, June 14-16, 2017, Hilversum, Netherlands

© 2017 Copyright held by the owner/author(s). Publication rights licensed to ACM.
ISBN 978-1-4503-4529-3/17/06...$15.00

DOI: http://dx.doi.org/10.1145/3077548.3077552

providers therefore typically offer their customers access to both Live and VoD content. Recommenders in such TV systems play a key role in unburdening users from the choice of whether to watch linear TV channels or browsing through a confusingly vast catalog of recorded TV programs [28]. TV program recommenders have their own unique characteristics when compared with other recommending scenarios. Usually, TV broadcasters try to incorporate their assumptions about viewers preferences and habits in their schedule to achieve high viewing figures. For example, news and weather reports are mostly arranged in the morning while dramas and sports-related content is generally scheduled in the evening or during the weekend. Thus when we analyze users' viewing behavior in a linear TV scenario, the patterns we observe reflect the arrangement of TV schedules to some degree. This characteristic often limits the benefit of a traditional Context-aware Recommender (CAR) for TV content since the observed user preferences are highly biased by the broadcasted TV programs.

A CAR usually defines a system's internally traceable auxiliary information (e.g. "time of day", "day of week", "location") as contextual factors [9]. Using logged clickstream data with detailed playback statistics, we analyze users' viewing habits in the "Vision" system, a production-level live and on-demand streaming service used by a large Living Lab user community at Lancaster University, UK. We find a significant portion of the users' consumption habits with respect to both live linear and on-demand TV content to be attributed to *contextual bias*. It is not surprising that recommendation algorithms that reliably predict items according to this *filter bubble* bias show high performance in laboratory tests. However, the resulting recommendations can be monotonous and repetitive to the end users. In order to escape from this self-fulfilling prophecy, additional external information is required. In this paper, we propose using TV domain relevant late-breaking events detected from social media as an external contextual factor to provide more diverse and precise recommendations.

Incorporating social media and crowd-sourced supplemental attributes has become an increasingly popular approach in recent recommender designs [41, 16, 27]. However, most social aware recommenders consider such factors only from the perspective of analyzing large-scale social graphs constructed from user-item relations. Though methods known from time series analysis such as "anomaly detection" and "trending topics analysis" are widely used for use cases like earthquake detection [35], breaking news event detection [29], and reputation monitoring [39], they haven't been attemped in social source analysis in recommender area to our best knowledge. There is a distinct lack of research investigating the utility of hot events or trends in social media as a recommendation factor. Our work make up for this vacancy by introducing trend analysis of domain related social media streams as an external contextual factor in a TV recommendation scenario. At the same time, since no internal information is needed prior to producing recommendations, the *cold start* problem with new users is addresses by our approach.

The introduction of social media trends as an external contextual factor for TV recommenders involves a number of challenges. For example, there is no concise statistical model of a trend, though some work summarizes frequently used features [33] and creates taxonomy of different trend types [4]. In addition, the relationship between the events in the social domain (e.g. Twitter stream) and the Online TV domain (e.g. users' content browsing and playback activities) is not well understood. To address these challenges, the present paper makes two main contributions: 1) we provide quantifications for the measurements of trend in both TV user watching data streams and Twitter social media text streams; and 2) we show that the trends detected in the Twitter social stream highly cover peaks observed in the user data (but not necessarily vice versa), proving it's not contrary to user behavior and applicable in a TV platform. Specifically, we use two indicators known from stock market analysis – Trend Momentum [29] and SigniScore [37] to capture the hotness of specific TV programs in the "Vision" user data via their related Twitter timelines, which we obtained by crawling the results from a keyword based Twitter search. Through investigation of the two parallel datasets, we identify the best hyper parameters for both trend measures through a grid search. The quantified evaluation of Omission rate (OR) and time difference between the trend indication and consumption peaks demonstrates that: 1) Trend Momentum (TM) can better predict points of high user demand in IPTV services; 2) OR can serve as a criterion for filtering out the programs which do not lend themselves well to the proposed approach.

The remainder of the paper is structured as follows. Sect. 2 summarizes related work on recommenders in TV services and social trend analysis. Contextual bias within online TV dataset is analyzed in Sect. 3, while the definition of external context is introduced in Sect. 4. Our approach towards TV domain trend analysis in Twitter streams combined with user activity data is presented in Sect. 5. Finally, Sect. 6 evaluates the trend measures and a conclusion and an outlook on future work is given in Sect. 7.

RELATED WORK
In this section, we review the literature with respect to three aspects: Recommender systems for IPTV services, the use of contextual factors in recommenders, and trend analysis in social networks.

Recommender System in IPTV Services
Recommender systems have been broadly applied by IPTV providers to increase users' Quality of Experience (QoE) when they watch TV programs over the internet [5]. The classical recommendation strategy Collaborative Filtering (CF) essentially clusters users based on their choice of content in the past [40] and infers potentially interesting items using similarity between clusters [21]. Unfortunately neither item-based CF nor user-based CF addresses the *cold start* problem, which arises when a new user or item is added to the system without any prior information on usage. A similar issue surfaces for outlier content (i.e. *gray sheep* problem) and is highly undesirable in the TV domain [15]. Solutions include using demographic user information obtained from user profiles or a linked social media account to generate group-based recommendations for new users [7]. However, profile information creates new concerns about user privacy, many systems thus deploy hybrid algorithms that use Content-based Filtering (CB) to compensate CF drawbacks.

In the TV domain, Electronic Program Guide (EPG) data serves as a standardized source for CB models. The similarity between programs is often calculated through semantic analysis of their EPG descriptions [32, 6, 11]. Extensions via online databases like Internet Movie Database (IMDb) and DBpedia[1] [19] can help to enhance the descriptiveness of representations. Given the availability of meta-data, a wide range of well-known techniques from the field of information retrieval and extraction are then employed to compute similarity scores in textual feature space [2]. Nevertheless, CB recommenders tend to over-specialize and constrain their recommendations to a *filter bubble* of similar items [6]. As a result, recommenders often fail to adapt to new trends and changes in user preferences.

Contextual Factors in Recommenders
Abreu et al. conducted a survey of TV viewer behaviors, according to which more than half of the relevant determinants for program selection depend on the situational context of the user [1]. Furthermore, 60% of respondents state that the presence of company and the available time are important contextual factors to select a program. Context-aware recommender algorithms, e.g. based on tensor factorization [24, 23] incorporate time [26, 45, 9] or location [14, 28] as additional parameters to encode contextual information. In addition, some advocate to model the local social environment [43, 30] and propose strategies to improve recommendations in households with multiple users sharing a single device [38].

Although existing context-aware approaches take influential factors into consideration to improve diversity of recommendations, contextual bias still exhibits significant influence even in state of the art model encodings [34]. The problem is mainly attributed to the restriction of the training set to system-level internal user behavior data. In the TV domain such contextual bias from user behavior is more prevalent, because programs

---

[1] http://wiki.dbpedia.org last accessed Oct. 23, 2016

are intentionally arranged by TV stations to match temporal preferences and target audiences. To address this issue, we extend the notion of context to domain relevant trends detected in online social media streams like Twitter, such that the selection presented to a user is not restricted to content that is biased towards the usual choices at the specific moment in time.

Social Trend Analysis

Defining "hot" events as trends in the external context of social media creates the need for techniques such as trend detection and prediction, which have been successfully applied to social streams to identify trending topics [18, 31], political opinions [42, 39], and news stories [46, 20]. Directly modeling the time series with keyword co-occurrence [36] is a typical approach to detect and observe trending conditions. Others apply clustering methods [3] and incorporate user authority information to improve detection rate [10]. Qualitative examinations by Asur et al. [4] reveal typical emergence and decay patterns of twitter trends that can be exploited at model creation time, e.g. when selecting sensible ranges for hyper parameter search. Since 2015, Twitter provides an API endpoint for locally sensitive trending topics[2] [22]. To quantitatively define the trend indication, Lu and Yang introduce TM, a smoothed version of Moving Average Convergence-Divergence (MACD) and use a threshold crossing point as trend indication signal [29]. Meanwhile, Schubert et al. [37] propose a *z-score* based on Exponentially Weighted Moving Average (EWMA) and Exponentially Weighted Moving Average Variance (EWMAVar) as a quantitative measure of trendiness. However, to our knowledge, there is currently no research adopting mentioned methods for the purpose of TV program recommendation.

CONTEXTUAL BIAS

In this section, we introduce the concept of *contextual bias* to the evaluation of recommender systems. We intuitively explain its influence on user behavior using a concrete scenario, namely the IPTV service "Vision", operated by Lancaster University.

The computation of recommendations is usually seen as a data mining or machine learning task. Thus a specific evaluation protocol and adequate metrics (like *precision* and *recall*) are used to determine how well the predicted results fit with the ground truth of static datasets (c.f. [12, 25]). Normally, the more accurate the algorithm predicts missing values, the better it is considered to be. Recommender algorithms taking into account contextual factors in their models often outperform "normal" approaches. This has been observed in some recent studies where time is used to track the evolution of user preferences [44] and to identify periodicity in user behavior [8]. However, once bias exists in the dataset, its fingerprint is visible in the statistical patterns allowing a targeted improvement of recommendation quality. To the present date there has not been extensive research on the impact of this bias information. We analyze the phenomenon that users become increasingly trapped in a limited selection of items and receive very few new recommendations due to *contextual bias*.

[2]https://dev.twitter.com/rest/reference/get/trends/place Oct. 26, 2016

In IPTV services, TV programs are often scheduled for a long duration of one to several hours. Therefore, temporal bias of users' choices is more prevalent than in other services such as YouTube. We use users' behaviors as captured by "Vision" to quantitatively analyze *contextual bias* in detail. In "Vision", TV programs are broadcasted as live TV and also recorded by a cloud-based service for on-demand retrieval beyond their original broadcast time. Users can decide themselves how and when they retrieve arbitrary content. The dataset from "Vision" contains fine details of user interactions with the service including clickstream data and playback statistics (e.g., play, pause, resume, etc). The dataset also encapsulates EPG data of 106,710 programs videos from a set of 12,809 unique titles over 23 genres and 62 channels. Over a period of 26 months, 2241 users made 204,920 requests to the site that are labeled "live" (142,011) or "vod" (62,909) depending on how the request was served. The cumulative playback duration over all requests was about 90,000 hours, about a third of which were streamed via Video-On-Demand (VOD). The majority of the programs are provided with genre specification via EPG and a third party TV catalog service. Exploration of this dataset reveals typical "time of day" *contextual bias* in the selection of channels, genres and programs in both Live and VOD mode.

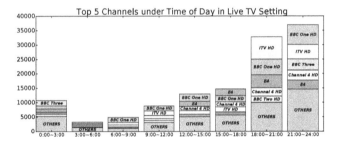

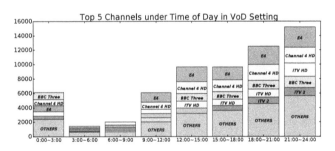

Figure 1: Frequency distribution on channels per "time of the day" for VOD and live.

For visualization, we split a day by grouping every three hours as a time segment, such that 8 time segments span a whole day. Figure 1 shows the ranked frequency statistics of channels (channels ranked after 5 are colored gray) in different time segments. From such ranked channels under both live (upper sub-figure) and VOD (bottom sub-figure) environment, we can see that within each time segment, the top 5 out of 62 distinct channels always hold more than half of the watching consumption. Though the channels consumed in a live environment are more diverse than under VOD, five most dominant channels in each categorical time bin are already sufficient to make a satisfactory suggestion for over half of the users of Live TV. Regarding the VOD environment, the pattern is more obvious that the rank of the top 5 channels is consistently *E4*, *Channel 4 HD*, *BBC Three*, *ITV HD*, and *ITV2* over all time segments. The observation is a typical example where relying on the statistical property of temporal bias can serve as a "good" recommendation strategy for both linear Live TV and a VOD yet at the expense of sacrificing diversity.

In Figure 2 we present a bar chart for the viewing frequency statistics on genres with respect to "time of day" in both Live and VOD consumption mode. Similar to our observations regarding the channel popularity distribution, the top 5 genres (*Sitcom*, *Drama*, *Entertainment*, *Soap*, *Comedy*) rank stably under VOD in each time segment, while such a distribution is slightly more diverse in the Live setting.

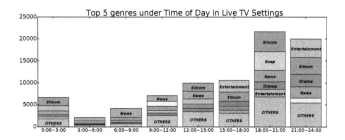

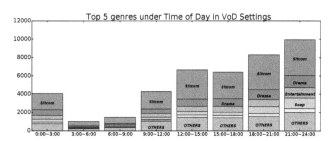

Figure 2: Frequency distribution on genres per "time of the day" for VOD and live.

In Figure 3, the frequency of viewing of the top 30 most retrieved programs is plotted (black dots) for each time segment in both Live and VOD settings. The most viewed program title and its proportion in this time category is also filled in a box in the place near its own solid circle. In addition, the percentage of the top 30 programs in each time segment is also written as text in middle area of every sub-figure. The frequency distribution of programs in each time segment depicts power law distribution. Out of 12,809 unique program titles, the proportion occupied by the top 30 programs in each temporal category ranges from 30% (21:00 - 24:00 in live settings) to 56.6% (3:00 - 6:00 in live settings), with an outlier of 70.18% (6:00 - 9:00 in live settings). It appears that a very small proportion (0.23%) of the programs attract around 30% to 50% of user playback requests within every temporal category. This proves that *contextual bias* exists not only in high-level user selections (such as channels and genres) but also at the individual program-level.

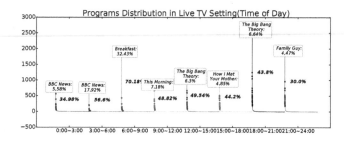

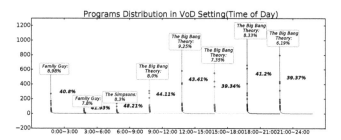

Figure 3: Frequency distribution on programs per "time of the day" for VOD and live.

Figure 4 in the next page displays frequency statistics concerning the time lag between airing and subsequent VOD request for four popular programs over the whole time-span in the dataset. We observe distinctive user behaviors on two types of programs. First, programs like *Gogglebox* and *Match of the Day* receive periodic attractions over a long period of time after their initial broadcast. This reflects the stable "time of day" regularity, which we identified in Figure 3. For this type of program, it makes sense to break its temporal bias and also recommend content at special moments determined by external factors. Conversely, some programs such as *This Morning* and *Coronation Street* can be grouped as the second type, which receive most of their on-demand playback requests within the first few hours after broadcast. Their popularity then suddenly drops to a minimal level, and no obvious periodic pattern can be caught. For these programs, only relying on system internal record information limits the possibility of their appearance in the recommendation list, thus introducing an external source thereby creates new opportunities for them to come back to users' sight.

Our exploration of the user interaction data indicates some strong contextual bias, which suppresses the diversity of recommendations in IPTV services. We thus introduce TV domain related trends in social media as an external contextual factor to help the users escape from the unfavorable filter bubble.

EXTERNAL CONTEXT

To address the problem of contextual bias, we opt to include Twitter as external context source for TV domain recommendation. Though Twitter is one of the most popular social media platforms for second screen usage, its user base is eventually heterogeneous and its applicability to the TV domain needs to be evaluated. We obtained our data by crawling only tweets related to relevant program names. To narrow the investiga-

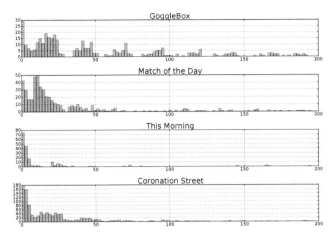

Figure 4: Delayed hours of watching from the first time aired for selected programs under VOD setting.

tion range, we select 12 titles from the 30 most requested TV programs on the "Vision" platform and perform a Twitter keyword search[3] to crawl Twitter histories. In total, the crawler gathered 4.7 million tweets for the 12 TV programs across a 26 month period parallel to user request dataset. Detailed statistics about the crawled tweets and user requests are provided in Sect. 6.

We group tweets according to the associated program title into one hour time bins. The histogram of tweets frequency in each time bin is first drawn to tell whether Twitter data really contains trend information regarding TV programs. Figure 5 depicts the frequency distribution of two typical kind of programs: *EastEnders* and *Gogglebox*. Programs like *EastEnders* show a generally stable frequency throughout the observed period, with rare bursts in the trending moments further called *peaks*, i.e. timeslots with a significantly higher number of tweets, that occur at uncertain points in time. In this case, the trend information is particularly valuable, because it reflects the uncertain external trending moment rather than other fixed bias regularity. On the other hand, *Gogglebox* represents another kind of trend phenomenon. The *peaks* of these TV programs in tweets even shows periodic regularities, which often correlate with their airing time.

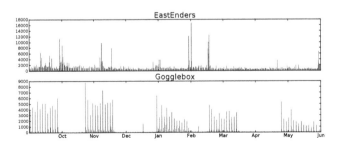

Figure 5: Tweet frequency distribution of two selected programs.

---

[3]https://twitter.com/i/search/

Knowing that *trends* exist in the external source, we investigate how trend information correlates with users' behavior in choosing programs to watch. In Figure 6, frequencies of user requests for the program *Coronation Street* are plotted in red, while the tweet frequency of the same program is plotted in green. This data from a short period (1 week) of time series demonstrates how both tweeting and playback request activities correspond to the same social events. A *peak* in tweet frequency often follows a *peak* in playback requests, while the rising flank of the tweet *peak* can actually happen ahead of the *peak* in requests. Crossing points of Trend Momentum and SigniScore w.r.t. the highest peak of program viewing frequency have been marked in green and blue scatters respectively, which show the forecasting effect of trend indicators in Twitter regarding frequency peaks in TV user requests data. Our ultimate aim is to use this earlier detection effect of Twitter *trends* on user request *peaks* to improve recommendations. To this end, the concept of both *trends* and *peaks* must be quantified.

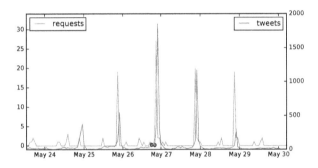

Figure 6: Parallel comparison of data distributions between tweets and user requests for program *Coronation Street*. The two dots mark the threshold crossings of both trend indicators closest to the center peak.

TREND MEASUREMENTS

To model the dynamics in popularity of a specific program in both internal user request data and external tweet data, we unify two concepts. First, a *peak* represents a point with significantly higher number of tweets/requests compared to the average number over the full period of discrete time-bins. Second, a *trend* is described by the rising phase of a *peak* and often appears shortly before the corresponding *peak*. That is to say *trends*, the early indications of upcoming *peaks*, are more valuable because they can help foretell an increase in popularity of a program in the near future, such that users receive recommendations for the program prior to its extensive discussion in social media. At the end of our literature review, we identified two promising trend measurements that can be used in our scenario.

$$MA(n,k) = \frac{\sum_{i=n-k+1}^{n} x(i)}{k} \quad (1)$$

$$MACD(n) = MA(n, k_{\text{fast}}) - MA(n, k_{\text{slow}}) \quad (2)$$

$$TM(n) = MA(n, k_{\text{fast}}) - MA(n, k_{\text{slow}})^{\alpha} \quad (3)$$

$$Momentum(n) = MA(TM(n), k_{\text{smooth}}) \quad (4)$$

The first one is the TM score listed in Eq. 3 proposed by Lu and Yang [29]. It is a smoothed version of MACD stock trend indicator and has been deployed to detect trending news in the Twitter stream. The definition stems from the concept of Moving Average (MA) (as Eq. 1 shows), which captures at the n_{th} time bin, the average frequency of k previous time bins. Considering that this average is not enough to represent a rising or decreasing trend, MACD (as shown in Eq. 2) utilizes the difference between the MA in k_{fast} (shorter) time windows and the MA in k_{slow} (longer) time windows to determine whether there is a trend appearing. In addition, with the discount parameter α assigned as exponential term to longer period MA in MACD, TM is defined as Eq. 3, and the sign change of its value from negative to positive or reversely indicates the appearance of a rising or declining trend. Furthermore, to avoid a volatile condition, MA is applied again with a third, even shorter time window k_{smooth} to further smooth the trend indicator as presented in Eq. 4. Throughout the remainder of this paper, we will simply use the name TM to refer to the final *Momentum* value (Eq. 4). By using this measure of momentum, a trend is said to be emerging when there is a turning point from negative to positive. Apart from the typical values recommended by the textbook, the four hyperparameters (k_{fast}, k_{slow}, k_{smooth} and α) can be tuned to improve accuracy of predicting *peaks*.

$$\Delta \leftarrow x - EWMA \qquad (5)$$

$$EWMA \leftarrow EWMA + \alpha \cdot \Delta \qquad (6)$$

$$EWMVar \leftarrow (1 - \alpha) \cdot (EWMVar + \alpha \cdot \Delta^2) \qquad (7)$$

$$\alpha = 1 - \exp\left(\frac{\log(0.5)}{t_{half}}\right) \qquad (8)$$

$$\text{SigniScore}(x, \beta) = \frac{x - \max(EWMA, \beta)}{\sqrt{EWMVar + \beta}} \qquad (9)$$

Another trend indicator as defined in Eq. 9 is called *SigniScore* and was introduced by Schubert et al. [37]. It is also a member of the MA family. With x being the frequency of occurrence within a time bin, the definition of Δ in Eq. 5 represents the deviation of this time bin from the EWMA calculated over preceding bins. After the current time bin has been observed, Δ is added to the EWMA in Eq. 6, where α is used as a weighting factor, similar to a learning rate. Corresponding to the accumulated mean, i.e. EWMA along the frequency stream, the formula for the accumulated variance is given in Eq. 7. As shown in Eq. 8, α can be derived from the half-life time t_{half} according to domain expert's knowledge. In our case, the critical parameter t_{half} is used as one of the hyperparameters to be optimized. On top of EWMA and EWMAVar, *SigniScore* is defined in Eq. 9 in the form of a *z-score*. Here β is the bias term that avoids division by 0 and at the same time filters noise. It constitutes the second hyperparameter which will be searched for in the case of *SigniScore*. Telling the (normalized) significance of a trend rather than solely relying on the sign change is an advantage of this measurement. It makes the comparison between different trending moments possible.

EVALUATION

Having introduced the two trend measures in the previous section, we proceed to apply them to the Twitter stream dataset over a timespan parallel to the user request data. Given the fact that "Vision" is a UK TV platform, for the 12 targeted TV titles, we choose 10 UK productions and 2 US productions. In addition, some program titles mostly consist of stop-word-like terms, e.g. *This Morning* and *My Wife and Kids*. For these program titles, the obtained tweets contain much more noise than others, and we include them to estimate the extend to which unrelated tweets influence the peak alignment. In Table 1, for both user request data and the crawled Twitter data, the number of data points, average number of points per non-empty bin μ, standard deviation σ, number of peaks occurring over the whole evaluation period #*peaks* and number of times where two concecutive peaks appear within 12 hours δ_{12} are displayed. We evaluate the precision of using *trends* in Twitter stream to predict *peaks* in user request data by two scores: OR and earliness of signal Δt.

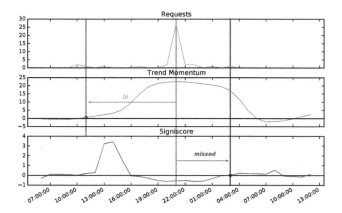

Figure 7: Visual comparison of a successful trend indication (TM) versus a *miss* (*SigniScore*).

The evaluation of our approach employs the concept of *peaks* in demand as time slots where the number of tweets/requests exceeds two standard deviations over the mean per (non-empty) time bin in the respective data stream. Following this definition, as Table 1 shows, the user dataset contains a total of 464 *peaks* for the targeted 12 TV programs, while in the comparably bigger Twitter dataset exist 3,455 such *peaks*. Even though there are relatively few peaks in the user request dataset, δ_{12} (the number of times where two consecutive peaks appear within a range of 12 hours) excludes the risk that they all belong to a few major *peak windows*. In accordance with the literature, we define the point when a trend measure crosses a threshold as the signal for the potential arrival of a *peak*. If the closest threshold crossing point occurs after the corresponding peak, we count the trend prediction as *missed* or as an *omission*. Otherwise, the crossing point can be seen as a successful indication of the incoming *peak*. A special example can be found in Fig. 7, where Trend Momentum successfully predicts the peak while Signiscore misses the chance because of the late capturing of this peak. For every successful trend indication, we compute the time delay between the threshold crossing and the highest *peak* point as Δt, which shows how

	User request data					Twitter data			
	N	μ	σ	#peaks	δ_{12}	N	μ	σ	#peaks
Made in Chelsea	1235	2.0	3.5	20	0	649523	36.2	312.4	111
EastEnders	1195	1.8	1.4	38	1	1276494	65.8	337.0	310
Hollyoaks	2070	1.7	1.1	91	13	1010904	52.7	223.8	375
Gogglebox	911	1.4	1.1	28	0	502954	31.5	257.0	128
Match of the Day	1122	1.7	1.7	23	2	189331	10.7	42.4	275
Emmerdale	1601	1.9	1.5	67	1	457419	24.5	149.7	175
Coronation Street	2624	2.0	2.1	43	7	295738	15.6	61.3	221
Britain's Got Talent	683	2.6	3.6	13	3	126100	7.1	34.8	102
Frasier	1413	1.4	0.7	72	23	116387	6.0	4.3	531
North West Tonight	1338	2.0	1.6	20	0	76512	1.8	1.3	430
This Morning	1046	1.5	0.8	21	0	17415	1.7	1.4	223
My Wife and Kids	756	1.8	1.1	28	6	10115	4.3	4.6	574

Table 1: Comparative statistics per evaluated program for the two datasets in use. N is the number of data points. For bin size of 1 hour, μ is the average number of points per non-empty bin and σ the respective standard deviation. Peaks are bins with more than $\mu + 2\sigma$ datapoints. δ_{12} counts the number of times where two consecutive peaks appear within a range of 12 hours.

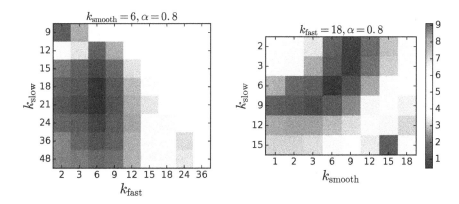

Figure 8: Omission rate under combinations of k_{fast}, k_{slow}, and k_{smooth}. Heat map shows the omission rate (in %)

early Twitter stream *trend* can predict user choice *peaks* (just as Δt shown in Fig. 7). The threshold can later be used to trade off between precision and recall but during the evaluation we use a fixed threshold $\theta = 0$ for finding crossings. In addition to the two trend measurements, we add a baseline trend indication in the evaluation. The baseline indication directly use the *peaks* in tweets frequency as trend indication signal, where the crossing threshold is a two standard deviations increase over the mean. The calculation of the baseline is straightforward and no parameters need to be tuned.

The performance of a trend indicator in a particular domain depends on the values assigned to its hyperparameters. We deploy grid search to find the best parameter settings for our target application. The ranges of the grids are derived from examination of contextual bias in Sect. 3. The performance criterion to be minimized is the average number of missed peaks (OR), over the 8 target programs. Since all preliminary trials reported the best value of α to be 0.8 in TM, we keep it constant throughout optimization. Then we conduct a 3-dimensional grid search with ranges $k_{slow} \in [2,\ldots,48], k_{fast} \in [2,\ldots,36], k_{smooth} \in [1,\ldots,18]$ and skip trials where $k_{fast} > k_{slow}$. For the 2-d heatmaps as display in Fig. 8 we fix k_{smooth} at 6 and k_{fast} at 18 respectively as they achieved lowest omission

rate throughout the full search. The parameters settings falling in the dark blue area turned out to be better in reducing the omission rate. The results indicate that the best parameter settings for TM are $[k_{slow} = 18, k_{fast} = 6, k_{smooth} = 6, \alpha = 0.8]$.

For *SigniScore*, as described in Sect. 5, the bias term β and half-life setting t_{half} are the parameters to be tuned. Since there are only two parameters to be searched, one grid is directly applied in the range as depicted in Figure 9. The results show that $[\beta = 9, t_{half} = 9]$ is the optimal parameter combination for the problem at hand.

The best hyper parameters determined by the grid search are used to examine the per-program performance. In addition to the OR, for each program, we compute the average on Δt, i.e. time difference between threshold crossing and *peak*, to denote how early the trend indicator takes effect. Aside from that, the deviation σ on Δt is also provided. Contrary to the usual case where trend detection is favored to be as early as possible, in our setup, lower delays represents higher correlation between trend signal in tweets and *peaks* in user data. Thus we consider a small Δt (and small $\sigma(\Delta t)$) to be better.

Among the 12 programs under consideration, the evaluation result for 8 of them turned out to be better (Table 2). The

	Trend Momentum			SigniScore			Baseline		
	OR	Δt	σ	OR	Δt	σ	OR	Δt	σ
Made in Chelsea (20)	**5.0%**	**11.0**	1.5	**5.0%**	14.3	4.8	15.0%	3.9	1.6
EastEnders (38)	**2.6%**	**8.7**	2.1	7.9%	10.7	9.5	26.3%	11.3	15.1
Hollyoaks (91)	**3.3%**	8.0	2.6	20.9%	**6.6**	3.2	31.9%	17.6	23.4
Gogglebox (28)	**3.6%**	7.6	1.8	7.1%	**7.0**	2.0	35.7%	69.1	15.9
Match of the Day (23)	**0.0%**	**4.4**	2.3	39.1%	20.0	14.6	39.13%	33.9	14.2
Emmerdale (67)	**1.5%**	8.2	2.2	9.0%	**6.6**	2.8	49.3%	112.5	122.5
Coronation Street (43)	**2.3%**	9.8	2.5	25.6%	**6.2**	4.0	51.2%	31.5	25.9
Britain's Got Talent (13)	30.77%	**9.4**	2.0	**7.69%**	10.7	9.5	100.0%	-	-

Table 2: Evaluation of trend indicators and baseline. The number of peaks per program is displayed in braces.

	Trend Momentum			SigniScore			Baseline		
	OR	Δt	σ	OR	Δt	σ	OR	Δt	σ
My Wife and Kids (28)	21.4%	7.8	6.9	25.0%	12.5	10.4	25.0%	106.8	220.6
Frasier (72)	47.2%	13.3	12.4	40.3%	1.6	1.8	45.8%	19.4	20.9
This Morning (21)	95.2%	17.0	0.0	61.9%	153.1	80.5	57.1%	11.6	8.5
North West Tonight (20)	70.0%	10.0	2.7	50.0%	476.5	335.8	60.0%	87.4	75.7

Table 3: Evaluation of trend indicators and baseline over the excluded programs. The number of peaks per program is displayed in braces.

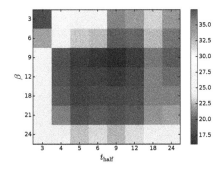

Figure 9: Omission rate for various combinations of t_{half} and β. Heat map shows the omission rate (in %)

comparison reveals that TM outperforms *SigniScore* and *baseline* for most of the target programs in terms of OR, Δt and σ(Δt). The threshold crossing has a relatively consistent Δt before *peaks* of about 8 hours. This early increase in communication is observed for all soaps and reality shows (like *EastEnders* and *Gogglebox*) in the dataset. To a lesser extent, sports programs such as *Match of the Day* very well reflect a general characteristic of Twitter second screen usage. The reality TV show *Britain's Got Talent* constitutes the only case where *SigniScore* achieves lower OR, but its data is particularly sparse with only 13 peaks in total. Another special case is marked by *Made in Chelsea*, for which *baseline* already shows reasonable performance (the value of Δt is 3.9), while both trend measurements cross the threshold much earlier.

The varied evaluation results over different programs suggest that the applicability of the trend indicator is program dependent. For the other 4 programs out of 12 candidates, the performance as displayed in Table 3 sets a negative example of the trend indicators adaptability. Considering programs like *This Morning* and *North West Tonight*, their terms collocations

are not unique, thus the tweet crawler tends to retrieve a significant number of unrelated tweets. This might be one important explanation for the poor performance of trend indicators. Similarly expected are the failures over the US programs like *My Wife and Kids*, for which the matching between Twitter trends and program interest in Vision, a system based in the UK, is skewed due to different time zones. In summary, we benefit from our evaluation in terms of both performance comparison and adaptable program grouping.

CONCLUSIONS AND FUTURE WORK

This paper introduces a novel approach to enhancing TV program recommendation based on external social context. We analyzed user interaction with a hybrid VOD/linear TV platform and identified a prevalent *contextual bias*. TV consumers' choices tend to fall in a strong temporal regularity, in which a few dominant programs or channels account for the majority in consumption. To overcome the issue of *contextual bias* and improve the diversity in recommendation, we harvest Twitter conversations as a source of social context. Using trend scores to detect early signs of increasing interest in program-related Twitter streams we explain *peaks* in the user request data. After hyperparameter optimization, we find that the MACD-based Trend Momentum indicator can very well achieve that goal, successfully forecasting about 96% of all peaks in TV programs' consumption dataset.

Our method comes with numerous advantages over previous approaches to context-sensitive recommendation. First and foremost, it alleviates the issue of *contextual bias* by extending the notion of context to a societal level, thus increasing the diversity of recommendations. Secondly, exploiting social context helps address *cold start* problem, because a significant portion of programs is new in TV recommendation scenario. Since Twitter is an external source, its utilization deprecates the need for any user- or program-related data prior to model deployment. A further strength of our method is that it particularly lends itself to the detection of individually popular episodes of repetitive programs without the scaling issues that come with CB alternatives. Finally, recommendation based on Twitter trends obtains the potential to create a feedback loop when it leads to more participants joining social conversation and reinforcing the trend. Appropriate access points can help the user directly engage the relevant discussion thereby facilitating VOD collaborative watching and the increasingly popular second screen usage.

Recommendation based on Twitter trends is not a silver bullet. Its applicability depends on the means by which program related conversations are collected. Filtering for programs with distinctive names is trivial as demonstrated by our analysis. In other cases, if we intend to discern TV program through the whole context in a Tweet, the approach proposed by Cremonesi et al. in [13] can be a good work to refer to. In addition, Tweets about programs with an international audience may show reduced correlation to *peaks* in consumption on platforms with a specific national target audience. Geolocation information as an additional filter can be used to reduce noise and augment tweets relevance in the future [41]. Admittedly, the analysis in the current paper can only illustrate the applicability of social trend in TV recommendation tasks. Yet to which degree it can enhance the user experience or how much they can overcome the contextual bias, is to be determined through future work.

ACKNOWLEDGEMENTS
This work was supported in part by the German Federal Ministry of Education and Research (BMBF) under the grant number 01IS16046. It was also partially supported by the European Commission through the Horizon 2020 programme under grant agreement No. 687921, project MPAT (Multi-Platform Application Toolkit). The second author of the paper has been supported by China Scholarship Council (CSC). We are also grateful to Jamie Jellicoe for assistance with data extraction from the "Vision" platform.

REFERENCES
1. J. Abreu, P. Almeida, B. Teles, and M. Reis. Viewer behaviors and practices in the (new) television environment. In *Procs. of the 11th european conf. on Interactive TV and video*, pages 5–12. ACM, 2013.

2. G. Adomavicius and A. Tuzhilin. Toward the next generation of recommender systems: A survey of the state-of-the-art and possible extensions. *Knowledge and Data Engineering, IEEE Transactions on*, 17(6):734–749, 2005.

3. C. C. Aggarwal and K. Subbian. Event detection in social streams. In *SDM*, volume 12, pages 624–635. SIAM, 2012.

4. S. Asur, B. A. Huberman, G. Szabo, and C. Wang. Trends in social media: Persistence and decay. *Available at SSRN 1755748*, 2011.

5. R. Bambini, P. Cremonesi, and R. Turrin. A recommender system for an iptv service provider: a real large-scale production environment. In F. Ricci, L. Rokach, B. Shapira, and P. B. Kantor, editors, *Recommender Systems Handbook*, pages 299–331. Springer US, 2011.

6. A. B. Barragáns-Martínez, E. Costa-Montenegro, J. C. Burguillo, M. Rey-López, F. A. Mikic-Fonte, and A. Peleteiro. A hybrid content-based and item-based collaborative filtering approach to recommend tv programs enhanced with singular value decomposition. *Information Sciences*, 180(22):4290–4311, 2010.

7. P. Bellekens, G.-J. Houben, L. Aroyo, K. Schaap, and A. Kaptein. User model elicitation and enrichment for context-sensitive personalization in a multiplatform tv environment. In *Proceedings of the seventh european conference on European interactive television conference*, pages 119–128. ACM, 2009.

8. P. G. Campos, A. Bellogín, F. Díez, and J. E. Chavarriaga. Simple time-biased knn-based recommendations. In *Proceedings of the Workshop on Context-Aware Movie Recommendation*, pages 20–23. ACM, 2010.

9. P. G. Campos, F. Díez, and I. Cantador. Time-aware recommender systems: a comprehensive survey and analysis of existing evaluation protocols. *User Modeling and User-Adapted Interaction*, 24(1-2):67–119, 2014.

10. M. Cataldi, L. Di Caro, and C. Schifanella. Emerging topic detection on twitter based on temporal and social terms evaluation. In *Proceedings of the Tenth International Workshop on Multimedia Data Mining*, page 4. ACM, 2010.

11. N. Chang, M. Irvan, and T. Terano. A tv program recommender framework. *Procedia Computer Science*, 22:561–570, 2013.

12. P. Cremonesi, Y. Koren, and R. Turrin. Performance of recommender algorithms on top-n recommendation tasks. In *Proceedings of the fourth ACM conference on Recommender systems*, pages 39–46. ACM, 2010.

13. P. Cremonesi, R. Pagano, S. Pasquali, and R. Turrin. Tv program detection in tweets. In *Proceedings of the 11th european conference on Interactive TV and video*, pages 45–54. ACM, 2013.

14. F. S. da Silva, L. G. P. Alves, and G. Bressan. Personaltvware: A proposal of architecture to support the context-aware personalized recommendation of tv programs. In *European Interactive TV Conference (EuroITV 2009), Leuven, Belgium*, 2009.

15. D. Das and H. ter Horst. Recommender systems for tv. In *Recommender Systems, Papers from the 1998 Workshop, Technical Report WS-98-08*, pages 35–36, 1998.

16. Y. Dong, J. Tang, S. Wu, J. Tian, N. V. Chawla, J. Rao, and H. Cao. Link prediction and recommendation across heterogeneous social networks. In *Proceedings - IEEE Intl. Conf. on Data Mining, ICDM*, pages 181–190, 2012.

17. Ericsson ConsumerLab. Tv and media 2015. Technical report, Ericsson ConsumerLab, 2015.

18. Y. Fang, H. Zhang, Y. Ye, and X. Li. Detecting hot topics from twitter: A multiview approach. *Journal of Information Science*, page 0165551514541614, 2014.

19. Y. B. Fernández, J. J. P. Arias, M. L. Nores, A. G. Solla, and M. R. Cabrer. Avatar: an improved solution for personalized tv based on semantic inference. *Consumer Electronics, IEEE Transactions on*, 52(1):223–231, 2006.

20. J. Freitas and H. Ji. Identifying news from tweets. *NLP+CSS 2016*, page 11, 2016.

21. D. Goldberg, D. Nichols, B. M. Oki, and D. Terry. Using collaborative filtering to weave an information tapestry. *Communications of the ACM*, 35(12):61–70, 1992.

22. S. Hendrickson, J. Kolb, B. Lehman, and J. Montague. Trend detection in social data. Technical report, Twitter, 2015.

23. B. Hidasi and D. Tikk. General factorization framework for context-aware recommendations. *Data Mining and Knowledge Discovery*, 30(2):342–371, 2016.

24. A. Karatzoglou, X. Amatriain, L. Baltrunas, and N. Oliver. Multiverse recommendation: n-dimensional tensor factorization for context-aware collaborative filtering. In *Proceedings of the fourth ACM conference on Recommender systems*, pages 79–86. ACM, 2010.

25. Y. Koren. Collaborative filtering with temporal dynamics. *Communications of the ACM*, 53(4):89–97, 2010.

26. M. Krstic and M. Bjelica. Context-aware personalized program guide based on neural network. *IEEE Trans. on Consumer Electronics*, 58(4):1301–1306, 2012.

27. J. Kunegis, G. Gröner, and T. Gottron. Online dating recommender systems: the split-complex number approach. In *ACM RecSys workshop on Recommender systems and the social web*, pages 37–44, 2012.

28. W.-P. Lee, C. Kaoli, and J.-Y. Huang. A smart tv system with body-gesture control, tag-based rating and context-aware recommendation. *Knowledge-Based Systems*, 56:167–178, 2014.

29. R. Lu and Q. Yang. Trend analysis of news topics on twitter. *International Journal of Machine Learning and Computing*, 2(3):327, 2012.

30. A. Q. Macedo, L. B. Marinho, and R. L. Santos. Context-aware event recommendation in event-based social networks. In *Procs. of the 9th ACM Conf. on Recommender Systems*, pages 123–130. ACM, 2015.

31. A. Madani, O. Boussaid, and D. E. Zegour. Real-time trending topics detection and description from twitter content. *Social Network Analysis and Mining*, 5(1):59, 2015.

32. A. B. B. Martínez, J. J. P. Arias, A. F. Vilas, J. G. Duque, and M. L. Nores. What's on tv tonight? an efficient and effective personalized recommender system of tv programs. *IEEE Transactions on Consumer Electronics*, 55(1):286–294, 2009.

33. M. Naaman, H. Becker, and L. Gravano. Hip and trendy: Characterizing emerging trends on twitter. *Journal of the American Society for Information Science and Technology*, 62(5):902–918, 2011.

34. U. Panniello, A. Tuzhilin, and M. Gorgoglione. Comparing context-aware recommender systems in terms of accuracy and diversity. *User Modeling and User-Adapted Interaction*, 24(1-2):35–65, 2014.

35. T. Sakaki, M. Okazaki, and Y. Matsuo. Earthquake shakes twitter users: real-time event detection by social sensors. In *Proceedings of the 19th international conference on World wide web*, pages 851–860. ACM, 2010.

36. H. Sayyadi, M. Hurst, and A. Maykov. Event detection and tracking in social streams. In *Icwsm*, 2009.

37. E. Schubert, M. Weiler, and H.-P. Kriegel. Signitrend: scalable detection of emerging topics in textual streams by hashed significance thresholds. In *Proc.s of the 20th ACM SIGKDD Intl. Conf. on Knowledge Discovery and Data Mining*, pages 871–880. ACM, 2014.

38. C. Shin and W. Woo. Socially aware tv program recommender for multiple viewers. *IEEE Transactions on Consumer Electronics*, 55(2):927–932, 2009.

39. D. Spina. *Entity-based filtering and topic detection For online reputation monitoring in Twitter*. PhD thesis, Universidad Nacional de Educación a Distancia, 2014.

40. D. Véras, T. Prota, A. Bispo, R. Prudêncio, and C. Ferraz. A literature review of recommender systems in the television domain. *Expert Systems with Applications*, 42(22):9046–9076, 2015.

41. S. Wakamiya, R. Lee, and K. Sumiya. Towards better tv viewing rates: exploiting crowd's media life logs over twitter for tv rating. In *Proceedings of the 5th International Conference on Ubiquitous Information Management and Communication*, page 39. ACM, 2011.

42. J. Weng and B.-S. Lee. Event detection in twitter. *ICWSM*, 11:401–408, 2011.

43. C.-C. Wu and M.-J. Shih. A context-aware recommender system based on social media. In *International Conference on Computer Science, Data Mining & Mechanical Engineering*, 2015.

44. L. Xiang, Q. Yuan, S. Zhao, L. Chen, X. Zhang, Q. Yang, and J. Sun. Temporal recommendation on graphs via long-and short-term preference fusion. In *Procs. of the 16th ACM SIGKDD Intl. Conf. on Knowledge Discovery and Data Mining*, pages 723–732. ACM, 2010.

45. H. Yin, B. Cui, L. Chen, Z. Hu, and Z. Huang. A temporal context-aware model for user behavior modeling in social media systems. In *Proceedings of the 2014 ACM SIGMOD international conference on Management of data*, pages 1543–1554. ACM, 2014.

46. A. Zubiaga, D. Spina, R. Martinez, and V. Fresno. Real-time classification of twitter trends. *Journal of the Association for Information Science and Technology*, 66(3):462–473, 2015.

How Millennials and Teens Consume Mobile Video

Jennifer McNally
Verizon
San Jose, CA
jennifer.mcnally@verizon.com

Beth Harrington
Verizon
Waltham, MA
beth.harrington@verizon.com

ABSTRACT

A majority of teens now have mobile phones and there is an increase in younger users watching video through paid subscriptions. Technology and services available for mobile video have also changed since previous studies were conducted. We set out to describe the current scenarios in which Millennials and teens view mobile video, their motivations, and how they access video. Twenty-four participants completed diary entries over a five-day period. Nine of these participants also took part in individual interviews that followed. Our findings describe the scenarios and motivations in detail and highlight two main findings. 1) Several mood and emotional states, beyond boredom and killing time, lead to viewing mobile video. 2) When accessing video, choices are made based on mood, desired level of engagement, stimulation, and length. This study provides information that can be used to inform mobile video experiences and proposes opportunities for future research.

Author Keywords

Human factors; diary studies; mobile video; smartphones; tablets; Millennials; teenagers; user experience and interaction design.

ACM Classification Keywords

H.5.m. Information interfaces and presentation (e.g., HCI): Miscellaneous.

INTRODUCTION

Viewing video on a mobile device has been possible since 2002, according to the National Consumer Research Centre in Finland [12]. Since then we've seen the introduction of smartphones and tablets and evolution of technological capabilities and services available for video on mobile devices. It is now possible to download and stream short clips, TV shows, movies, and live events using a variety of free and paid apps and websites. Video specific services like YouTube, Netflix, and Hulu make it easy to do this as

Permission to make digital or hard copies of all or part of this work for personal or classroom use is granted without fee provided that copies are not made or distributed for profit or commercial advantage and that copies bear this notice and the full citation on the first page. Copyrights for components of this work owned by others than ACM must be honored. Abstracting with credit is permitted. To copy otherwise, or republish, to post on servers or to redistribute to lists, requires prior specific permission and/or a fee. Request permissions from Permissions@acm.org.

TVX '17, June 14-16, 2017, Hilversum, Netherlands
© 2017 Association for Computing Machinery.
ACM ISBN 978-1-4503-4529-3/17/06...$15.00
http://dx.doi.org/10.1145/3077548.3077555

do social networking and media sites where video has been heavily integrated. It is even possible to access what was once only available through a cable box and television.

Previous research has contributed to understanding of how mobile and online video is consumed. Mobile and online video consumption takes place both inside and outside of the home [2,3,7,8], can be an individual and a shared experience [2,9,10], is often mixed with other activities [3]. Mood and emotional states also play a role, particularly boredom and passing time [2,3]. To the best of our knowledge, however, there has not been a recent comprehensive study on mobile video consumption inclusive of the varied types of mobile video available today on smartphones and tablets. There also has not been focus placed on mobile video consumption of Millennial and teenage users.

In their book Millennials Rising: The next great generation, Howe and Strauss define Millennials as the generation beginning with those born in 1982 [5]. They argue this generation is unique because, compared to other population segments, it is large, affluent, highly educated, and ethnically diverse.

In addition to being a unique and diverse segment, Millennials also represent a large and growing group of mobile video consumers. The Nielsen Company found Millennials, aged 18-34 at the time of this study, to be the largest segment of smartphone owners as well as one of the largest population segments [8]. And according to the Pew Research Center, use of mobile devices to watch movies or TV through paid subscriptions has increased among the younger portion of this group (ages 18-29) [1].

There is evidence that teenagers are also an important group of smartphone users to consider. In a recent study on teens, social media, and technology, Pew Research Center reported a majority of teens (ages 13-17) have smartphones [6]. While this study did not report specifically on video use, findings included frequent use of social media sites and apps which all now have video. Videos play automatically in many of these products as users scroll in the feed.

Because it is important to conduct an up-to-date study to understand mobile video consumption of Millennials and teenagers, the primary goal of our study was to identify and describe scenarios in which Millennials and teens watch mobile video. Focus was placed on identifying behaviors, motivations, and how videos are accessed in these scenarios.

To do this, we designed a study combining two research methods. We used the diary method to collect natural behavior data and the interview method to probe deeper into diary findings while observing behavior. Participants completed a digital diary entry using their mobile device right after they watched mobile video. After the five-day diary portion of the study, we invited a subset of participants to take part in individual in-person interviews.

This work provides up-to-date observations and findings about mobile video consumption behaviors of Millennials and Teenagers. Findings support previous research that mobile video is consumed inside the home as well as on the go, is sometimes a shared experience, is often mixed with other activities, and mood and emotional states play a role. This study contributes to mobile video research by describing scenarios of mobile video use, motivation, and how videos are accessed with current devices and technology. We also describe types of decisions users make when accessing video.

RELATED WORK

Several studies have provided valuable insight into mobile video consumption behaviors prior to the development of devices and technology we have today. Researchers at The National Consumer Research Centre in Finland conducted one of the earliest studies [12]. They sought to identify what mobile video experiences would be meaningful, focusing on what they referred to as "physical and social contexts". Participants were provided a Nokia 7650 with video software and access to a predetermined set of videos. After watching video and providing feedback over a one-week period, two kinds of situations for mobile video emerged, avoiding boredom and sharing in experiences with others.

It was revealed in a 2009 study that inside the home was a frequent location where mobile Internet and video is accessed [7]. In this study, Nylander, et al. discovered mobile internet was accessed most frequently at home, followed by outdoors, in transit, indoors at such places as stores, cafes, at work or a friend's house. And in over half of the cases in this diary study, participants (aged 20-55years old) used mobile devices even though they had access to a computer.

These findings supported those of O'Hara et al. in 2007 that mobile video was often consumed at home by participants in the UK and US aged 14-47 [9]. Findings challenged assumptions that mobile video is primarily short and on the go or to pass time. In this study using the diary method and in-depth-interviews, researchers discovered mobile videos varied in length and were sometimes consumed individually for reasons like managing solitude and disengaging from others. However, they also found mobile video to sometimes be consumed more socially.

In another study published the same year, Cui et al. revealed similar findings based on interviews with users of

a paid, live mobile TV service in Seoul [2]. Researchers identified at home, commuting, breaks, and secret use as contexts of use. They defined secret use as situations when watching TV was not socially acceptable, like in the classroom and library. They also identified boredom and staying up to date with popular events as drivers for mobile TV consumption. And similar to other studies, they found some viewing to be a shared experience.

Oksman et al. reported contrasting findings in their field study of a mobile TV service in Finland [10]. Participants in this 2007 study, ages 23-56, primarily consumed video individually. However, the content in this study was limited to News content. This suggests content type could influence consumption behaviors.

Although not specific to mobile devices, Cunningham and Nichols investigated how users find video online [3]. In their 2008 study, researchers interviewed and observed University students in New Zealand as they searched for videos on sites like YouTube, Google Video, and Yahoo Video. They identified "video surfing" as an activity mixed with other everyday activities such as studying, waiting for dinner, or using IM to chat with friends. They also found mood and emotional state were drivers of video searches. However, specific moods and emotional states were not mentioned beyond boredom and distraction. It's also important to note that this study did not focus specifically on mobile video.

In a more recent study on mobile device use while watching TV, Holz et al. found participants often did so to physically be together with family members [4]. They also found none of the mobile use to be directly related to what was on the TV. However, this study didn't focus specifically on video. Reported behaviors were open to any type of app or website.

Because previous research has identified moods and emotional states as playing a role in mobile video consumption, it is important to reference Dolf Zillman's work on mood management and content choices [14]. According to this theory, content can alter mood states and content choice is often made to regulate mood states. However, choices are not necessarily made with focused deliberation or thought.

Strizhakova and Krcmar conducted a study utilizing Mood Management Theory to investigate the relationship between moods and content choices when renting video [13]. Surprising to researchers were choices of those with more negative mood states. Nervous participants tended to choose more horror movies as opposed to fewer. Sad participants chose more dramas and crime dramas but tended to avoid dramatic comedies. The authors concluded that content choices are not always made to promote a more positive mood, rather a desirable mood. Choices to promote a desirable mood, they propose, are made considering arousal level and environment in addition to mood state.

Overall, the literature shows there are various scenarios for mobile video consumption, which are influenced by boredom and distraction as primary moods and emotional states. However much time has passed since publication of previous work on mobile video consumption and new opportunities have presented themselves for research. There

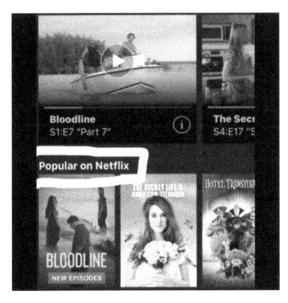

Figure 1. Sample of a submitted diary entry as it appears when accessed for review at https://dscout.com.

are younger mobile device users, updated technology, and new video products and services. Questions that have not recently been addressed include, what are current scenarios in which mobile video is viewed by Millennials and teenagers? What are motivations in these scenarios? How are videos found in these scenarios? And what is important to users when accessing videos in these scenarios?

METHODS

We used two research methods to answer these questions. The diary method was chosen as a way to collect data reflecting everyday behavior in a natural environment. We chose to schedule in-depth interviews following the diary portion to ask diary follow-up questions, probe deeper, and observe participant interaction with their mobile video products.

Participants

A recruiting agency was used to recruit participants across the United States who watch mobile video. We also recruited participants from an internal panel to include users of go90, which is a Verizon video product. It was required that all participants watch mobile video, on a smartphone or tablet, at least twice a day. We also aimed to obtain a mix of individuals based on sex, age, smartphone OS, and use of paid and free video services. While we aimed to recruit participants across the United States, we also requested some to be located in the San Francisco Bay Area who would be willing to participate in in-person interviews.

Twenty-four individuals participated in the diary portion of the study, nine of which also participated in the in-depth interviews that followed. Thirty participants were initially recruited. Six dropped out or didn't complete enough diary entries to fulfill the participation requirement of submitting at least two entries per day over a period of five days.

Although we aimed to obtain an even mix, our set of participants contained more females (n=16) than males (n=8). Ages ranged from 13-34 and represented three groups: teenagers ages 13-17 (n=6), young adults ages 18-25 (n=10), and adults ages 26-34 (n=8). Fourteen used smartphones with iOS and ten used Android smartphones. Some also used tablets. Fifteen participants lived outside the San Francisco Bay Area, while nine lived in the Bay Area. Finally, eleven participants used mobile video paid services in addition to free video services.

Procedure

Diary study
Participants were instructed to complete a diary entry after watching mobile video on a mobile phone or tablet using dscout, a digital diary tool available as a mobile app (https://dscout.com). They were not asked to watch any specific type of video other than what they normally watch. A minimum of two entries per day was required over a period of five days, which began on a Wednesday and ended on a Sunday because we wanted to capture data representing weekday and weekend behaviors. Diaries

included ten questions about the video watched, or the last one watched if it was a longer session. Questions prompted participants to describe the video, how they found it, where they were, what they were doing, whom they were with, what caught their interest, difficulties, and what they did after. Participants were also asked to attach a screenshot of the discovery point for the video watched. A sample of a completed diary entry is shown in Figure 1.

In-depth interview
Participants located in the San Francisco Bay area were invited to participate in individual interviews the week following the diary portion of the study. Sessions were scheduled for 60 minutes and took place in the research lab at our office in San Jose, CA. Participants provided consent and were aware the session would be recorded for note taking purposes. Sessions began with an introduction and background discussion, followed by an activity where participants thought about a typical weekday and weekend day. They then drew a timeline of activities for each on a magnetic whiteboard and placed magnets representing the device the use to watch video on their timeline. We allowed participants to indicate any type of video and any type of device. In other words, maps could include watching cable service on a TV, a website on a laptop, and an app on a Tablet. Participants described their timeline and demonstrated how they access videos for each moment in a typical day when they watch video. Finally, if questions remained, follow-up questions were asked about the activity and diary entries. An example of a participant timeline can be seen in Figure 2.

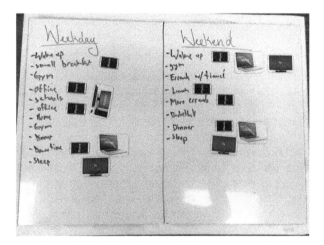

Figure 2. Participant map of video use on a typical weekday and weekend.

RESULTS
Participants in this study reported watching various types of mobile videos, including music videos, fails, pranks, sports highlights, documentaries, news, live, video games, movie trailers, and TV shows. Videos were accessed using a variety of services, such as Buzzfeed, HBO, Google search, Facebook, Netflix, and Snapchat. We describe the motivations and scenarios below and in Table 1.

Motivations
Qualitative data from diary entries and interview data revealed multiple motivations for watching mobile video. As found in previous studies, many of these can be described as a mood or emotional state. Participants indicated they watched mobile video to:

- Fill time, kill time, pass time, boredom
- Procrastinate
- Relax, relieve stress
- Wind down, rest mind
- Become alert
- Keep up to date
- Seek information, inspiration
- Respond to an alert, notification (ex: email, message, push notification)
- Background noise, distraction
- Lonely, seeking company
- Share information, emotional experiences with others
- Anticipate an upcoming event
- Prolong, revisit an experience or event

Scenarios
Several scenarios emerged in which participants described watching mobile video. Consistent with previous research, mobile video was consumed both inside and outside of the home. Although some tablet use was reported, the Smartphone was described as more convenient because it is always with participants and easy to take out and put away.

First thing in the morning
Waking up in the morning, participants browsed apps they regularly use to catch up on what happened while they were sleeping. Reasons for mobile video at this time included to keep updated, to procrastinate getting out of bed, and to help become alert. Participant 8 described watching a video to catch up: *"I was scrolling through Instagram and one of the bakery accounts I follow posted a behind-the-scenes video. I like to check out all the things I missed on Instagram while I was sleeping each morning."*

Some participants described more than one motivation leading to watching mobile video in this scenario. Participant 16 explained becoming alert while delaying getting out of bed: *"It's a way to get my mind active in the morning slowly that offers entertainment without having to get up."*

Browsing was commonly described as how videos were accessed. The goal was not always to watch anything specific or even to watch video. Participant 16 went on to describe how a video was accessed while browsing for updates: *"I just browsed my feed because it was easy to access and I didn't know what I wanted to watch."*

Videos in this scenario were often described as short, although more than one may have been viewed. Participants knew they would eventually have to get up to start their day. The morning scenario is not the time to invest in a video that cannot be finished.

Scenario	Motivations
First thing in the morning	Keep updated, procrastinate, become alert
Just before going to sleep	Wind down, relax, pass time, check for updates
While watching TV	Keep updated, boredom, pass time, seek information, prolong experience
During independent activities	Background noise, distraction, company
Socializing	Share emotion, share information
Together but alone	Relax, keep updated, bored, fill time
Taking a break	Boredom, interruption, rest mind, relieve stress, fill time, keep updated
Waiting	Pass time
Downtime	Relax, relieve stress, boredom
In Transit	Pass time, anticipation

Table 1. Scenarios and motivations, including mood and emotional states.

Just before going to sleep
Participants watched videos to help them relax, pass time, and as part of a final check for updates at the close of the day. This was often after they had watched shows or a movie on any device as part of their downtime in the evening. Just before going to sleep, some watched short videos and some watched a longer TV show or movie. However, the TV show or movie was usually one that the participant did not mind missing if he or she fell asleep. These were typically shows or movies they had seen before or did not care much about. Participant 19 described video in this scenario as a way to wind down: *"I find it good to watch videos so I can wind down before I go to bed."* Similarly, participant 7 described watching to kill time and to relax to a sleepier state: *"I had moved to my room, and was essentially killing time before I get ready for bed. I debated about reading but I felt like I couldn't focus due to*

how tired I am. It's easier to digest moving media. It helps me to be sleepy."

In this scenario, participants described searching or browsing for videos they knew would help them go to sleep rather than startle them. Participant 23 searched a specific source for the type of video he needed to wind down: *"I searched FailArmy in the search bar of YouTube. I was in bed because I couldn't get to sleep and those videos help me sleep."*

Participants also came across videos while doing a final check for updates on products they regularly visit such as Facebook, YouTube, and messaging apps. Participant 3 explains this and how she does not watch videos that will startle her: *"Before going to bed, I go on social media and answer texts. My brother sends me funny stuff as something we do, a ritual. Funny videos won't startle my brain and so when I go to sleep, I won't have scary dreams or feel stressed."*

While watching TV
Watching short videos on smartphones while also watching video on a TV or Laptop was commonly reported. In this scenario, finding the right video sometimes mattered more and sometimes it mattered less.

Finding a good video or the right video was less important when participants needed to relax and pass the time during boring parts on TV like commercials. In these moments participants accessed video while browsing apps they visit regularly, such as social media and YouTube, for updates and additional entertainment. Participant 12 described two mood states for a moment in this scenario, boredom and relaxation: *"I'm watching TV and browsing through my feed as I'm relaxing on my couch. I'm just bored and am always watching TV and on my phone at the same time when relaxing."* Participant 22 described mobile video in this scenario as killing time and of low importance: *"Video during commercials is not that important. It's just killing time."*

Finding the right video was important when participants wanted to get more information about something they just saw while watching TV. In these moments, participants typically searched. Participant 4 described, *"I had just finished watching a movie all about her...I was interested in seeing who the real Joy was and hearing her QVC infomercial."*

Finding the right video was also important when participants wanted to prolong the experience of what they had been enjoying on the bigger screen. Participant 20 explained wanting to maintain the enjoyment he felt after watching a TV episode. *"I went on YouTube to see some of his best moments and I was just cracking up. I couldn't get enough of it."*

During independent activities

Mobile video was used in this scenario for background noise while doing other activities, including cooking, chores, exercising, walking the dog, working, and getting ready. Participant 7 explained, *"I was doing other mindless things like tidying and it was just playing kind of in the background to entertain me."* The same participant described why she chose to use her mobile device. *"It was convenient. I had my phone with me and I can move my phone with me if I go from room to room."*

Participants also chose mobile video to provide them with company during solitary activities. Participant 18 explained, *"I'm just used to always having something going on when I'm not interacting socially. It makes me feel less by myself. It's like calling someone."*

Video can also provide distraction to make an activity more enjoyable. Participant 18 described why she chose to watch a sitcom while exercising. *"It is a funny and feel-good show. I like watching video while I work out because it distracts and entertains me."*

Participants deliberately chose longer videos so they wouldn't have to stop what they were doing to select another video. Specific videos were often accessed from a home section of the app that presented shows they have watched before. Participants also chose videos that didn't require visuals to see what was going on. These included shows participants were re-watching, shows they are very familiar with or have been watching a long time, and those they did not need or care to pay close attention to. Participant 19 explained, *"It's mostly shows I watch randomly...and I don't mind if I miss something."*

Socializing

Videos were accessed and played to show other people while socializing. Participants described wanting to share an emotion (ex: laughter and anger), information, or clarify a point. They reported looking for videos they had seen before that were related to the conversation. Participant 1 described searching for a video to share in an emotion: *"My roommate and I were watching an interview on (a political candidate) and I wanted to show her that funny video because he makes us so angry."* Participant 8 explained wanting to clarify a point: *"I was at a party with family and friends and we were all discussing the topic of human puppies. I watched it with other people to show them what I was talking about and to better explain my story."*

Participants reported looking for specific videos and topics by searching for profiles and pages in social apps. Participant 16 remembered where she could find a video like the ones others were sharing: *"Everyone was showing cute videos and it was my turn. I checked out my animal friend's page and found a cute puppy video."* Similarly, Participant 3 explained why she used search for a video she had seen before: *"I searched it because I had already seen*

it before and wanted to show someone. I was with a friend of mine watching stuff on Instagram, like funny videos."*

Together but alone

In these moments, participants watched video on their own as a way to spend time with others even though they were not partaking in the same activity. Video was not specific to any type or length or accessed in a specific way. Some participants watched longer shows and programs while others watched shorter clips. Participant 2 reported, *"Hanging out with my parents while they were getting some paperwork done"*. Similarly, participant 18 described, *"I'm binge watching the show. It is easy and comfortable to hold my phone while lying down. I was sitting with my boyfriend who is sick so I didn't want to disturb him."*

Some participants watched on their smartphone while those they wanted to spend time with also watched video, but on a different device. Participant 20 explained how he and his fiancé watch video in the same room and on separate devices: *"I might watch more basketball stuff and she'll watch reality shows on her phone...We're together, but on separate ends of the couch."* Participant 19 reported a similar moment: *"I was sitting on the couch using headphones while my mom watched TV in the evening."*

Taking a break

Participants consumed mobile video during short breaks from activities such as work, homework, personal projects, and chores. Participants took breaks on their own and welcomed interruptions either because of boredom or needing to rest their mind. They accessed videos through notifications, by browsing, looking for something specific, or watching a video they did not have time to watch earlier. Sometimes they went back to messages from others to access the videos they had not had time to watch. One participant described it as being similar to taking a smoke break.

Taking a break is a habit for Participant 9 who explained, *"It's almost a habit to get on Facebook and watch videos to take a break from other things."* Participant 20 described boredom, *"I was just bored and YouTube is usually spot on with stuff they think I like to see. I'm doing party favors for our wedding and took a break and watched videos. I just did it to pass the time before getting back to putting favors together."* Participant 13 described taking a welcomed break when distracted by a notification. *"My friend Devin posted it on Facebook and I had a notification. I was taking a break from writing my paper. I watched it because I needed a mental break from writing the paper and it was a meaningful video."* And participant 21 explained why a mobile device was more convenient than the laptop she had available: *"I was taking a break from cleaning my place. I wanted to chill for a minute and listen to some good tunes. It was easier to look it up on my phone than search it on the computer. My phone is right in my pocket whereas my laptop is still in my bag."*

Waiting

Previous studies have shown that video is watched while waiting to pass the time. Participants in this study revealed they often chose shorter videos because they didn't know how long they would be waiting. They didn't want to have to stop in the middle so they preferred to choose videos they would likely finish.

In this scenario, participants found videos in a variety of ways, including browsing and searching for videos they had previously seen. Participant 24 explained watching a suggested video on YouTube because, *"I was waiting in the living room for my mom to get ready so we could leave. I just needed a quick video that I could finish and not start something new and stop in the middle of it since I was only waiting a while."* Participant 1 explained using the search feature to find a previously viewed video, *"I had seen it before and wanted to watch it again. I was waiting for my roommate to finish her shower and wanted to kill some time by watching a video."*

Downtime

Downtime is when participants had a more time to themselves than other parts of their day. These moments included after school, after work, after dinner, and while eating a meal. They watched mobile video as a way to rest, relax, and relieve stress or boredom. Videos watched included both short clips and long episodes. Longer videos included episodes on Netflix and Hulu and were often accessed on the home page in an area dedicated to what they can continue watching.

In some cases, participants chose to watch mobile video even though they had access to a TV. Participant 10 explained, *"I was sitting on my couch eating lunch and I just decided to watch YouTube instead of TV. Watching video on my phone is easy and it's in my hands so it's right in front of me."*

As in other scenarios, participants described more than one mood or emotional state leading to mobile video consumption. Participant 11 was bored and wanted to relax: *"I was very bored and I had a long day so I wanted to be able to relax. So I just sat in bed and watched it on my phone."* Participant 23 also described boredom and seeking something funny: *"I was in my room after school. It was around 4:15 in the afternoon. I got bored after school and wanted to laugh at baseball bloopers."*

In transit

Participants watched mobile video to pass time while in cars and on public transit. Previous research has shown that mobile video is a form of entertainment while traveling on public transportation. In this study, participants also reported watching video as a passenger in a car. Teenagers included in this study may often be passengers in cars instead of drivers. Participant 17, in the 13-17 age group stated, *"I watched the Snapchat story because I was keeping myself busy in the car and I have an interest in politics."*

The emotional state of anticipating an event was also observed in this scenario. Participant 6 described watching in the car with friends on the way to an event: *"I'm heading to PVD fest soon and wanted to see what is going on! I'm a passenger in a car and we are in traffic so I am entertaining myself."*

ISSUES

Participants described issues with video playback and with search as areas they found most difficult or frustrating during a mobile video experience.

Issues watching video included responsiveness to selecting the play, delayed auto play while scrolling, poor video quality, slow loading both initially and when re-watching. With search, participants did not like having to sift through a lot of search results. They also sometimes needed to use exact search terms to get sufficient results.

DISCUSSION AND IMPLICATIONS

Some findings in this study are consistent with previous studies, indicating some behaviors have remained consistent over time. Consistent behaviors include consuming mobile video inside the home and elsewhere, socially and individually, mixed with other activities, and to deal with boredom or to pass time. However, this study also identifies scenarios and behaviors not previously discussed.

The scenarios identified here are important because they provide a current and comprehensive view of how mobile video fits into daily lives of Millennials and teenagers. Details about these scenarios provide insight into aspects of mobile video important to users so that experiences can be improved to better meet their needs. These details include mood and emotional states and the decisions users make when choosing video. We will discuss these details and identify opportunities for future research.

Mood and Emotional States

We identified multiple motivations for watching mobile video and observed that mood and emotional states vary. Some emotional states are less pleasurable, such as boredom and loneliness, while some are more positive, such as anticipating an event or prolonging/revisiting an experience. Designers and product teams could tap into these positive emotions in order to create positive associations with their product.

Findings from this study expand on previous research on mobile video as a shared experience. In this study, we found that the shared experience fulfilled a need to socialize and spend time with others. Some participants viewed mobile video with others to share in an emotion and to clarify a point in a discussion. Mobile devices have a reputation for contributing to reduced in-person communication, but our findings indicate that there are times when they are used to be closer to others, both physically and emotionally. Designers and product teams could explore ways to encourage users to share emotions with others as another way to create a positive association with their product.

However, considering Mood Management Theory and research, it should be noted that a positive mood state may not always be the end goal and video choices may not always be easy to predict based on mood states.

Choosing Video
Findings from this study seem to be supported by Mood Management work in that while moods and emotions play a role, video choice cannot always be predicted solely based on mood state. Decisions are not always made to alter a mood toward a more positive state and sometimes consider other factors of the environment such as level of arousal and environment. Most important to note, is that decisions may not necessarily made with a lot of deliberation.

In many of the scenarios, we observed participants making decisions about the type of video that would best suit their needs in that specific scenario. One decision was related to how stimulated they wanted to be. Participants' intentions were sometimes to be stimulated, as in the scenario of "waking up", and sometimes to wind down or become less alert, as in the scenario "just before bed". The same type of video may not work for both.

Participants also chose videos based on how engaged they planned to be with the video. They sometimes chose videos they wanted to pay close attention to, as in the downtime scenario, and sometimes chose video they cared less about and would not pay close attention to, as in the scenario referred to as during independent activities.

Another factor in choosing a video was length, described here as "longer" or "shorter" due to the qualitative nature of this study. There were reasons participants often chose shorter videos while waking up, taking a break, and waiting. It was either because they did not have much time or because they did not know how much time they would have. Longer videos were chosen in scenarios such as downtime and independent activities because participants either had more time or because they did not want to stop what they were doing when the video ended.

Understanding the choices users make when accessing video is important because these choices highlight different intentions in different scenarios and that video delivery and access needs to be flexible. This presents an opportunity for designers and product teams to explore ways to create systems that allow for flexibility that users need.

Future Research
This research provides information that can be used in design and to further understand mobile video consumption. Questions remain about the frequency and relationships between variables. Quantifying the frequency of scenarios relative to one another and with a larger sample could be useful to designers and product teams when making decisions about priorities and tradeoffs. Usage data could be leveraged to better quantify and understand video access for the scenarios we identified. While we were able to identify whether participants browsed or searched in each scenario, we were not able to capture real time behavior or all possible actions. There are a variety of ways to accomplish actions, which may also vary by product. Such findings could inform specific designs to better meet needs for specific scenarios.

CONCLUSIONS
We have described scenarios in which Millennials and teenagers consume mobile video. In this study, we used the diary and interview methods with participants across the United States. We identified a variety of mood and emotional states, indicating that mobile video is more than just dealing with boredom. Positive emotional states like anticipation can also lead to viewing mobile video. Finally, we identified types of decisions made when accessing videos, indicating a need to provide flexibility to accommodate for these choices. Choices go beyond mood state to include choosing video by level of stimulation, planned level of engagement, and length. Finally, we identified opportunities to further understand scenarios and inform the design of mobile video experiences.

REFERENCES
1. Monica Anderson, Pew Research Center. More Americans Using Smartphones for Getting Directions, Streaming TV. 2016. Retrieved January 9, 2017 from http://www.pewresearch.org/fact-tank/2016/01/29/us-smartphone-use/

2. Yanqing Cui, Jan Chipchase, and Younghee Jung. 2007. Personal TV: A qualitative study of mobile TV users. In *European Conference on Interactive Television*, 195-204.

3. Sally Jo Cunningham, and David M. Nichols. 2008. How people find videos. In *Proceedings of the ACM/IEEE-CS joint conference on Digital libraries*, 201-210.

4. Christian Holz, Frank Bentley, Karen Church, and Mitesh Patel. 2015. "I'm just on my phone and they're watching TV": Quantifying mobile device use while watching television. In *Proceedings of the ACM International Conference on Interactive Experiences for TV and Online Video*, 93-102.

5. Neil Howe and William Strauss. 2009. *Millennials Rising: The next great generation.* Vintage.

6. Amanda Lenhart, Pew Research Center. Teen, Social Media and Technology Overview 2015. 2015. Retrieved January 9, 2017 from http://www.pewinternet.org/2015/04/09/teens-social-media-technology-2015/

7. Stina Nylander, Terés Lundquiest, and Andreas Brännström. 2009. At home and with computer access: why and where people use cell phones to access the internet. In *Proceedings of the SIGCHI Conference on Human Factors in Computing Systems* (CHI '09). 1639-1642.

8. The Nielsen Company. Millennials Are Top Smartphone Users. 2016. Retrieved January 9, 2017 from http://www.nielsen.com/us/en/insights/news/2016/millennials-are-top-smartphone-users.html

9. Kenton O'Hara, April Slayden Mitchell, and Alex Vorbau. 2007. Consuming video on mobile devices. In *Proceedings of the CIGCHI conference on Human factors in computing systems* (CHI'07), 857-866.

10. Virpi Oksman, Elina Noppari, Antti Tammela, Maarit Mäkinen, and Ville Ollikainen. 2007. Mobile TV in everyday life contexts – Individual entertainment or shared experiences? In *Proceedings of the European Conference on Interactive Television*, 215-225.

11. Pew Research Center. U.S. Smartphone Use in 2015. 2015. Retrieved January 9, 2017 from http://www.pewinternet.org/2015/04/01/us-smartphone-use-in-2015/

12. Petteri Repo, Kaarina Hyvönen, Mika Pantzar, and Päivi Timonen. 2003. *Mobile Video.* National Consumer Research Centre.

13. Yuliya Strizhakova & Marina Krcmar. 2007. Mood management and video rental choices. *Media Psychology, 10(1)*, 91-112.

14. Dolf Zillmann. 1988. Mood management through communication choices. *American Behavioral Scientist, 31(3)*, 327-340.

The Social Construction of Targeted Television Advertising: The Importance of 'Social Arrangements' in the Development of Targeted Television Advertising in Flanders

Iris Jennes
Vrije Universiteit Brussel /
imec-SMIT
Brussels, Belgium
iris.jennes@vub.be

Wendy Van den Broeck
Vrije Universiteit Brussel /
imec-SMIT
Brussels, Belgium
wendy.van.den.broeck@vub.be

ABSTRACT

This paper focuses on the social construction of targeted TV advertising. In 2016, experiments with targeted TV commercials started in Flanders (Belgium). We apply a Social Construction of Technology (SCOT) approach to understand how targeted television advertising is being developed. We underline the importance of social arrangements in the development of this particular technology. Social arrangements can be defined as the relations between relevant social groups that work together to stabilize a technology. The development of targeted TV advertising can be seen as a moment of 'interpretive flexibility', implying that different relevant social groups can give a different meaning to targeted advertising as a technological artifact. To steer the development of the technology towards the most beneficial solution to their agenda, different social groups use different strategies. In our paper, we argue that in the case of targeted TV advertising, the audience should be approached as a relevant social group. Our empirical research thus incorporates both television industry and user perspectives on the development of targeted TV advertising in Flanders between 2012 and 2017. Based on expert interviews with industry representatives and focus group interviews with end-users, we provide an analysis of the different strategies, opportunities and challenges that different stakeholders (TV-industry, viewers and policy actors) are faced with. To conclude, we also formulate specific recommendations for a successful implementation of targeted TV advertising in Flanders.

Permission to make digital or hard copies of all or part of this work for personal or classroom use is granted without fee provided that copies are not made or distributed for profit or commercial advantage and that copies bear this notice and the full citation on the first page. Copyrights for components of this work owned by others than the author(s) must be honored. Abstracting with credit is permitted. To copy otherwise, or republish, to post on servers or to redistribute to lists, requires prior specific permission and/or a fee. Request permissions from Permissions@acm.org. Permissions@acm.org.

TVX '17, June 14-16, 2017, Hilversum, Netherlands
© 2017 Copyright is held by the owner/author(s). Publication rights licensed to ACM. ACM ISBN 978-1-4503-4529-3/17/06…$15.00
http://dx.doi.org/10.1145/3077548.3077553

Author Keywords
Targeted television advertising, commercial television, television audience, social arrangements, interpretive flexibility.

ACM Classification Keywords
Business modeling and marketing

INTRODUCTION

Digitization of television and convergence of digital technologies has challenged both commercial broadcasters and advertisers. Audience fragmentation across television channels and across devices has increased the competition for audience attention. Audience autonomy -viewers can watch what they want, when they want to, using the device of their choice- has challenged the traditional audience measurement systems, creating a mismatch between the estimated, measured and actual audience [25]. In contrast, digital devices also provide opportunities to reach audiences in a less traditional way. Interactivity and personalization offer interesting possibilities for both traditional commercial broadcasters as well as for online and over-the-top (OTT) players. For commercial television broadcasters, this signifies a shift from broadcasting towards narrowcasting in which they offer a more interactive and tailored service to specific user profiles [5, 8, 28]. The sustainability of traditional 30-second spot advertising on television is questioned as well, and the advertising industry expects it to be replaced by new advertising formats [19].

More concretely, targeted or personalized advertising would also come to the television screen [10]. Personalization is considered an opportunity for the commercial television industry as it promises to reduce waste and to increase the effectiveness of television advertising [21]. Today we see that the traditional 30-second spot still exists, but new advertising formats such as personalized or targeted advertising indeed emerge. The current format of targeted TV advertising is that of a personalized 30 second spot, but tailored to the profile of the viewer. As such, people will see different spots during the commercial breaks depending on their specific profile.

People without pets will not get pet-related commercials, while someone who is interested in sports, will get to see a gym-commercial.

While targeted TV advertising offers a clear opportunity for broadcasters and advertisers, it represents more than a mere technological innovation that needs to be adopted by the television industry. Personalization requires a shift in audience measurement from its current measurement system in the form of aggregated panel data to a combination of behavioral, personal and even third party data [21]. Thus, the development of targeted television advertising should not just be studied as a technological innovation that requires implementation, but as a social process in which different actors play a role in shaping targeted advertising. Therefore, we apply the framework of Social Construction Of Technology (SCOT) as developed by Pinch & Bijker. Central is "*the claim that technological artifacts are open to sociological analysis, not just in their usage but especially with respect to their design and technical 'content'*" [6]. SCOT puts forward the idea that our technologies reflect society and that they could be shaped differently [7]. In the theoretical framework, we discuss the SCOT-approach, the changing commercial television ecosystem, changing audience practices and changing relations between television industry and audience. Based on this framework, we argue that the television audience is an important and relevant social group that needs to be involved to fully understand how and by which means this technology might become stabilized.

Thus, the empirical research addresses two perspectives on targeted advertising: the commercial television industry as well as the television viewer. We provide insights into the concrete strategies, opportunities and challenges related to the development of targeted television advertising in Flanders. Flanders is a unique case study as two incumbent network providers (Telenet and Proximus) have started implementing targeted TV advertising in 2016. Proximus inserts targeted advertising in commercial breaks for Video-On-Demand (VOD) programs, whereas Telenet provides targeted advertising spots in the commercial breaks during live, linear broadcasts. Both work with a system of opt-out for audience approval: their customers can un-tick the box in their client-profile on the network-providers' website. For the empirical research, we conducted expert interviews with different actors across the television value network and conducted focus groups with different types of television viewers. Looking at the development of targeted advertising in Flanders as a moment of 'interpretive flexibility' [24], allows us not only to recreate the challenges that were faced during the development, but mainly to underline the codependency in the social arrangements between network providers, commercial broadcasters and their audience.

To conclude, we formulate recommendations for the commercial television industry and policy makers. These recommendations reflect strategies to tackle challenges that could impede the stabilization of targeted advertising.

THEORETICAL FRAMEWORK

The framework of Social Construction Of Technology (SCOT) has been used to describe the formation and stabilization of technologies of a very heterogeneous variety through a diversity of case studies (e.g. photography, household appliances). However, central to these studies is the offset that what constitutes technological change is more than just innovation in technology. Rather, explanations for the development and ultimate stabilization of technologies are sought by analyzing the strategies of **relevant social actors**. Arguably, relevant social actors either benefit from or resist technological change and will implement their power to steer and influence the outcome: "(...) *technology is stabilized if and only if the heterogeneous relations in which it is implicated, and of which it forms a part, are themselves stabilized.*" [7]

As such, the strategies of the relevant social groups involved in the development and stabilization of a new technology and the interaction between these actors are the main objects of SCOT-research [7]. Different social groups use diverse strategies to steer the development of the technology towards the most beneficial solution to their agenda. A technology thus becomes stabilized in **Social arrangements** that can be defined as the relations between relevant social groups. This means that the development of targeted television should be scrutinized as a resetting of social arrangements between different actors within the television industry (e.g. broadcasters, advertisers). The changes within the commercial television ecosystem are also changes within television as an institution: certain existing social arrangements -e.g. audience measurement techniques- concerning commercial television are being rethought and restructured. In this light, the development of targeted advertising on digital television is being defined by organizational circumstances. Within this context, the definition of what constitutes television, television advertising, television viewing and even a television audience, is under discussion. It can be seen as a moment of **'interpretive flexibility'** implying that different relevant social groups can give a different meaning to the technological artifact [24], in this case television and television advertising. Targeted television advertising is constructed by organizational strategies, collaborations and stakeholders.

The main actors involved in the development of targeted television advertising are commercial broadcasters who sell the advertising space and network providers who provide broadcasters with access to audiences and who gather data through their set-topboxes (STB). But audience practices are relevant as well, not just as part of the context but as influential behavior for the development of a media service. Audience practices are influential since commercial television functions as a two-sided market, reliant on attracting audiences and then selling them to advertisers. Although there is no shortage in studies on audience behavior (e.g. [1, 9, 20, 26, 31]) advertising effectiveness (e.g. [4, 11, 12, 13]) and advertising avoidance (e.g. [14, 16, 29, 33, 34, 35]) the audience is usually approached as (a collection of) end-users. In line with the SCOT-framework, we position the audience as a relevant actor for the development and stabilization of targeted advertising. Instead of assessing audience behavior and perception separately at the end of the process, we underline the interplay between industry strategies, audience practices and technological change before and during the development of targeted advertising.

In the following sections of the theoretical framework, we discuss the alternating relationships within the television broadcasting sector, changing audience practices and the pivotal relationship between audience and television industry in light of the development of targeted advertising.

The changing television industry

Traditionally, the roles in the TV value network were clear-cut. **Television network providers** provided the connection between broadcasters and audience by delivering the TV-signal into people's homes. Broadcasters made sure there was qualitative content to broadcast. This changed significantly with the introduction of digital television. Digital television can be described as a networked digital technology. It features personalization and interconnectivity and is increasingly becoming a two-way interactive medium [8]. As part of the digitization process, network providers started working with set-topboxes (STB). These digital devices had the advantage of increased capacity and thus allowed an increase in number of television channels brought to people's homes, as well as the development of new services, such as Video On Demand (VOD) and Electronic Programming Guides (EPG). This means network providers, through the STB, have become content aggregators as well [15]. This is a form of vertical integration, which affects cooperation between different actors in the sector [2, 23]. Network providers decrease their need to cooperate with certain other actors, such as broadcasters, while strengthening their own position.

Digitization has increased competition for **television broadcasters**. Because of the activities of network providers in content aggregation and the exponential increase in available TV-channels compared to the analogue TV-system, the current TV offer has seen an exponential growth. In addition, digital convergence has allowed players such as Netflix to create over-the-top (OTT) services that offer content on a variety of devices. Although commercial broadcasters can generate income from multiple sources (network providers, subscriptions, copyrights etc.), their current business model strongly relies on the commodification of audiences, i.e. television broadcasters selling audience attention to advertisers in order to be able to invest in the production or acquisition of programs. The increasing supply of content leads to a

specialization of media, which means that there are more TV channels and content-providers that target more specific groups, leading to a differentiation and fragmentation of the audience [5]. At the moment, large, aggregated and linear TV audiences are still at the core of the commercial television business model. Consequently, the advertising model for television is under pressure. Old issues such as the 'waste'[1] of traditional television advertising resurface and traditional television advertisings' effectiveness is questioned. Of course, digital technologies also provide opportunities for commercial television broadcasters to administer their own content across different platforms or in OTT services. This way the potential audience for television content actually expands [21]. However, economies of scale are increasingly important, as successful content platforms need to attract a large audience to be commercially viable. Fragmentation of audiences and increased competition are factors that impede the success of local commercial broadcasters.

Other relationships between the players in the television market are also under pressure, since they are each faced with their limitations, challenges and opportunities [30]. **Media planners and advertisers** are trying to find new ways to reach their target audience fitting the functionalities and affordances of digital television [17]. At the same time, the STB allowed network providers to monitor audience behavior more accurately. As STB's function like hard drives, the interaction of audiences (or should we say: users) is registered and can be used for measurement purposes. Although STBs owned by different providers have the downside that they provide non-standardized data [21, 30], the data holds important information for all parties involved in TV advertising. Audience measurement will be addressed below, for now it is important to underline that network providers have adopted additional roles in the digital television value network such as content aggregation and audience measurement, leading to a position of power compared to commercial broadcasters when it comes to targeted advertising. To define television viewers' profiles, network providers can use the behavioral data of the STB and add personal data from clients such as geographical location and even combine these with third party data, such as loyalty card data. However, to translate these preferences into targeted advertisements in meaningful TV content, network providers and broadcasters need to work together [21]. And in addition to the powerful role of network providers in this relationship, 'tailoring' advertisements based on viewers' behavior and preferences, using behavioral, personal and/or third party data raises privacy questions about the ownership and sharing of data.

Changing audience practices

In this section, we discuss the relevant behavior of the TV audience with specific attention for its importance within

---

[1] i.e. the amount of people reached that were not part of the intended target group.

43

the commercial television value network. In a general sense, television audiences differ from traditional, analogue audiences in 2 ways: they have become more fragmented and more autonomous. **Audience autonomy** refers to the increased control media users have over their media consumption [25]. Digital TV-services such as time-shifted viewing, ad skipping and VOD give the audience the opportunity to avoid advertising but also to compose its own programming, although within certain boundaries [28, 36]. Digital devices and convergence also allow media users to access TV content through mobile phones, laptops or tablets. This relates to the **fragmentation of audiences**, as different platforms can be used to access content (i.e. inter-media fragmentation) and individual platforms can offer more (and different) content (i.e. intra-media fragmentation). This increased control is undermining the traditional way of audience conceptualization and offers a different perspective on audiences as active and interacting users [25].

Advertising avoidance is an important aspect of audience practices that needs to be addressed when discussing advertising innovations such as targeted TV advertising. Advertising avoidance is not a new concept, and negative externalities are part of the television business model: *"Viewers are interested in programming with little advertising; hence advertisers exert a negative external effect on viewers. Conversely, advertisers are interested in a large number of viewers; hence viewers exert a positive external effect on advertisers."* [27]. The traditional classification of advertising avoidance strategies divides these into mechanical (i.e. zapping[2] or zipping[3] during commercials); cognitive (i.e. focusing on something else during commercials) and physical (i.e. leaving the room during commercials) [33]. When it comes to digital television, especially the zipping and multi-screen usage are interesting to look at. Although video recorders also allowed viewers to record content and fast-forward through commercial breaks, the STBs make it easier for viewers to do so. There is no hardcopy involved and it can be done by using the remote control. And although zipping as a practice is not new, the STB can measure when advertising is being fast-forwarded. In terms of cognitive avoidance, media users now have more screens in their homes and combine usage of different screens at the same time. An international study by Accenture in 2015[4] showed that 87% of users combine multiple devices while watching television. The combination between TV and smartphone is most popular, but also laptop and tablet are often used in combination. These alternative devices are also increasingly used to watch video content[5].

Targeted advertising: the pivotal relation between audience and television industry

Increased competition, the functionalities of the STB, audience autonomy, fragmentation and advertising avoidance increasingly challenge the advertising model of commercial television. Audience measurement is essential in this regard. The planning of media content and advertising campaigns as well as the calculation of their Return On Investment (ROI) depend on accurate audience measurement [3]. Not just the way audiences consume media has changed, the way media industries are looking at and are measuring audiences has altered as well. The industry has the opportunity to measure feedback and preferences through digital media [25]. The behavior of audience members who use digital devices such as the STB is instantaneous and visible. Since viewers leave traces of their preferences using digital interfaces, the television industry could figure out how to create a better viewing experience using these viewer interactions [30].

Interesting discussions in the academic field relate to whether audience fragmentation and autonomy signify a change in the relation between audience and media. On the one hand, it can be described as the commodification of audiences and media users (e.g. [32]) or the institutionalization of audiences through audience measurement (e.g. [1]). On the other hand, increased control can be framed as 'empowerment' of media users and audiences as they can control their own content consumption and interaction (e.g. [9, 20]). In previous work, we argue that by looking at audiences as actors in the process of changing technology, increased audience autonomy in a television context can be seen as both empowerment of audiences as media users and further commodification of the audience as media users. When audience behavior changes, (commercial) television broadcasters are likely to follow and adapt their strategies in order to maintain market share. Thus, the audience takes a particularly interesting place in media industries, both as a customer for commercial broadcasters as well as a product being sold to advertisers. It is both visible and institutionalized as well as elusive and autonomous [22]. Consequently, we argue that audience members can be seen as relevant actors for the development of targeted advertising on television.

In a technical sense, targeted television advertising can be presented as a logical next step in a digitized television market. But as we have shown in the previous section, digitization and the development of targeted advertising

---

[2] I.e. changing channels during the advertising break
[3] I.e. fast-forwarding through the commercial break
[4] Online survey conducted in 2014, with 24.000 consumers in 24 countries: Australia, Brazil, Canada, China, Czech Republic, France, Germany, India, Indonesia, Italy, Japan, Mexico, Netherlands, Poland, Russia, Saudi Arabia, South Africa, South Korea, Spain, Sweden, Turkey, United Arab Emirates, United Kingdom and the United States. The sample in each country is representative of the online population, respondents range in age from 14 to +55.

[5] Accenture rapport Digital Video and the Connected Consumer:
https://www.accenture.com/t20150914T152334__w__/us-en/_acnmedia/Accenture/Conversion-Assets/DotCom/Documents/Global/PDF/Dualpub_20/Accenture-Digital-Video-Connected-Consumer.pdf#zoom=50

also involves different social arrangements that need to be addressed. Commercial broadcasters and network providers are key actors that need to work together to make targeted television advertising a reality. But negative externalities as well as relevant privacy issues imply that the television audience needs to be involved as well. Therefore, we argue that television viewers are a relevant social group in the development of targeted advertising. In the empirical section below, we discuss the challenges and opportunities for targeted television advertising and include the perspective of television viewers.

METHODOLOGY

This research focuses on the Flemish rather than the Belgian TV sector as from a regulatory perspective, the broadcasting market in Belgium has been divided into two separate, independent markets: a Walloon (South of Belgium) and a Flemish (North of Belgium) broadcasting market. As we wanted to focus on both the vision of the industry and the viewers, we conducted expert interviews with media professionals and focus group interviews with TV-viewers.

In the first part of the research, 13 professionals active in the television industry in Flanders were interviewed between 2012 and 2017 (see overview in table 1). Different **stakeholders and media experts** were selected to provide variation and to acquire more nuanced insights, as experts are not objective [18]. The first interviews allowed us to gain a broad understanding of digital marketing opportunities associated with the digitization of television as well as more specific insights in the changing value network and the dynamics between actors (network providers, broadcasters, media agencies). Later interviews focused more specifically on targeted advertising.

Table 1: Overview Interviews Flemish Television Industry

Interviews		
Year	**Company**	**Interviewee function**
2012	SBS Belgium (*commercial broadcaster*)	Commercial Director
2012	Medialaan (*commercial broadcaster*)	Commercial Director
2012	Telenet (*network provider*)	Vice President of Content Management
2012	Belgian Association of Direct Marketing[6] (*umbrella organization*)	Director Strategic Manager

2012	Katrien Berte	Media-expert
2012	Jo Caudron	Media-expert
2013	Havas Media (*media agency*)	CEO
2013	Paratel (*technology application developer*)	General Manager
2016	Proximus (*network provider*)	Head of Consumer Innovation
2016	Palm Breweries (*targeted television advertiser*)	Marketing Director
2017	Telenet[7] (*network provider*)	Director Advanced Advertising Product Manager Advanced Advertising

To keep a close eye on the full process and to be kept up-to-date with the latest developments, additional follow up-meetings with representatives from Telenet and SBS Belgium took place between 2015 and 2017. Several consultations took place that were not recorded or organized as interviews but served the purpose of following up on the development of targeted television advertising and validating research outcomes and methodological set-up. The main contact persons are listed in table 2.

Table 2: Overview Follow Up Consultations

Follow up		
Year	**Company**	**Point of Contact function**
2015 - 2017	SBS Belgium (*commercial broadcaster*)	Director Business Intelligence Head of Innovative Advertising
2015 - 2017	Telenet (*network provider*)	Director Advanced Advertising

---

[6] Double interview

[7] Double interview

To gain insights in the practices, perception and strategies of **television viewers**, we conducted a series of focus groups in the beginning of 2016. 6 focus groups with a total of 48 respondents were held across Flanders to obtain geographical dispersion. Purposeful sampling was used to ensure the focus groups were internally balanced in terms of gender, age, television viewing patterns and attitude towards advertising. 31 men and 17 women between 21 and 59 years old took part in the focus groups, the average age of participants being 32. Their viewing patterns were diverse, ranging from the average 1-3hours of television content[8] a day, to a heavy +3 hours a day or less than 1 hour a day. A limited number of respondents had a predominantly live viewing pattern (n=3). In contrast, others indicated that they where innovative in gaining access to their desired content by building their own systems and using special (legal as well as illegal) software (n=3). In general, participants used widespread services such as time-shifted viewing via the STB, OTT-subscriptions or streaming websites on a regular basis, ranging from daily to once a week. The main discussion topics during the focus groups included current television viewing practices, advertising avoidance practices and the perception of traditional television advertising formats. Then examples and probes were used to enable discussion on new advertising formats, such as targeted advertising.

RESULTS AND DISCUSSION: SOCIAL ARRANGEMENTS IN THE FLEMISH TELEVISION INDUSTRY

Power struggles and customer ownership as hurdles before the development of targeted advertising

In the expert interviews it became clear that the discussion and collaboration on targeted television advertising has known many delays. This is mainly due to power struggles and discussion on customer ownership between network providers and commercial broadcasters. The plans to implement targeted advertising already started in 2012, but the implementation itself only started in 2016. Difficulties in negotiations were mentioned in all the expert interviews conducted in 2012 and 2013. These negotiations were not all directly linked to targeted advertising, but they defined the context for the interaction between the same stakeholders on the topic of targeted advertising. Specifically, network providers enabling zipping –i.e. fast forwarding advertisements– without consulting broadcasters was a big issue. In this discussion, broadcasters are either asking for compensation by making this a service that viewers have to pay for or, if they have to, for cancellation of the ability to fast-forward commercials: "(…) *we will have to renegotiate* [pricing]. [Making zipping impossible] *will be hard but if we have to, we will.*" [Medialaan, expert interview, 2012]

Another argument stressed the traditional roles of broadcasters and network providers and customer-ownership: "*We invest in content, the viewer is attracted to our content and uses the platform of the network provider to access (that content). It is not the network providers' job to alter that content (...) The customer is actually more ours than theirs.*" [SBS Belgium, expert interview, 2012] The argument stresses that advertising (both traditional and targeted) requires good quality content that attracts viewers of a specific profile. For Flemish commercial broadcaster this is their specific core business and strength.

Network providers argued that it was too late to change or cancel this service and referred to customer loyalty: "*We've addressed this multiple times: broadcasters, stop whining about the PVR (Personal Video Recorder). We will not tell our customers that they cannot record content any more. If we do not do it, someone else will.*" [Telenet, expert interview, 2012] Eventually, broadcasters challenged the zipping-functionality in the Flemish parliament, contesting the possibility of zipping by highlighting that the Flemish media decree (article 185-186)[9] stipulates signal integrity: broadcasters own the broadcasting signal and distributors are only allowed to transmit this signal, not alter it. The Flemish parliament endorsed broadcasters, and a contractual agreement between network providers and broadcasters was reached, specifying remuneration for zipping.

When the controversy on zipping died down, collaboration on targeted advertising could take shape. To develop targeted advertising, working together is a necessity in the Flemish market, as network providers are the owners of the STB-data but local commercial broadcasters provide the content and advertising space that viewers want. Network providers could not launch targeted advertising (or any advertising-related activity for that matter) on their own, or they would put their relationship with commercial broadcasters at risk [Telenet, expert interview, 2012]. In 2014, a partnership evolved between commercial broadcasting company SBS Belgium and network provider Telenet, who bought 50% of the share of the holding that owns SBS Belgium. Although Telenet had to guarantee that the take-over would not jeopardize the contracts with other broadcasters, they started working on targeted advertising together[10]. For Proximus, the natural Flemish commercial partner was Medialaan[11]. Between Telenet and SBS Belgium, collaboration is considered 'demand-driven'. This means that to develop a targeted commercial advertisers

---

[8] Including content viewed via the TV-set, OTT-services, streaming websites, (free) apps, pay TV, etc.

[9] See:
http://www.vlaamseregulatormedia.be/sites/default/files/geconsolideerde_tekst_van_het_mediadecreet_van_27_maart_2009_-_bijgewerkt_tot_3_februari_2017.pdf

[10] See also:
http://deredactie.be/cm/vrtnieuws/cultuur%2Ben%2Bmedia/media/1.2000794

[11] Proximus also works with Flemish public broadcaster VRT, Walloon public broadcaster RTBF and Walloon commercial broadcaster RTL.

will contact commercial broadcaster SBS with a specific profile request after which the commercial broadcaster sends the request to network provider Telenet. Telenet then deliberates on how to fulfill the request and feeds back to SBS Belgium [Telenet, expert interview, 2017].

An important issue in the development of targeted advertising is privacy regulation and data sharing. To avoid infringement of the current privacy-regulation and to allow targeting advertising based on the network providers' profile data the explicit consent of viewers is needed. The solution implemented by network providers Telenet and Proximus was adding an opt-out option on online customer profiles. Customers can un-tick the box in their client-profile on the network-providers' website. Although this is not completely in line with privacy regulation -which requires opt-in rather than opt-out- and minister of media Sven Gatz has already announced an investigation[12], the first targeted advertising spots on television became a fact in Belgium in 2016. However, it is unclear whether the collaboration between broadcasters and network providers and their usage of customer data comply to the General Data Protection Regulation (GDPR), effective of May 2018. The privacy-issue is thus far from solved.

Current challenges and opportunities for targeted advertising

Commercial broadcasters work together with network providers because they hope that targeted advertising will reverse their decreasing advertising revenues. The main advantages for commercial broadcasters are (1) the ability to **address specific target groups**, thus reducing 'waste' and (2) attracting smaller, **local advertisers** to television as audiences can be segmented based on location. Also, collaboration between local network providers and commercial broadcasters is seen as a necessity to be able to compete with international players like Netflix, Google and Facebook [Havas Media, expert, interview, 2013; Telenet, expert interview, 2017]. Creating personalized profiles for Flemish media users allows them to develop an alternative for advertisers, who increasingly reach Belgian audiences through international platforms [37] that have scale-advantages compared to Flemish media companies.

At the same time, network providers and commercial broadcasters face challenges in terms of scale, privacy and technology:

- **Scale:** Targeted advertising is relevant in markets such as the US and UK, as they serve big audiences. This makes narrowing audience segments a merit. But Belgium is already a small market, which is divided into a Flemish and a Walloon market, with separate media and divided by language barriers. This raises questions on the profitability of targeted advertising in small markets.

- **Privacy:** Sharing data between different actors within an industry and developing a remuneration model that benefits broadcasters and network providers is not a straightforward task. Collaboration is necessary, but to what extend are commercial partners willing to share interesting data? And how does this challenge the viewers' privacy? How can compliance to changing privacy regulation be accomplished?

- **Technology:** Rather than developing individual profiles, like users do on social media, STBs collect data at the household level. As such, the precision of personalization on television is unclear. Is it useful to segment at the household level? And is this an advantage compared to traditional television advertising?

Audience practices and perceptions of targeted TV advertising

The most recent Digimeter report (2017)[13] discusses TV viewing practices of the Flemish TV-audience. While TV remains the preferred screen to watch video content (66,4% watches TV on the TV-screen on a daily basis), the smartphone becomes more and more popular as a medium to watch video fragments. 33,1% watches content on the smartphone on a daily basis. For youngsters between 15-19 years old, the smartphone has even become more popular than the TV-set. This is important since advertisers indeed have difficulties reaching youngsters via the TV-set and hope they can regain control over this audience segment by providing them with targeted (and thus more relevant) advertising. Watching linear television is still a daily practice for 56,6% of the population. Almost 30% watches time-shifted television daily. In Flanders, time-shifted viewing allows viewers to zip through the commercial break. 73,5% claims to do this monthly. These TV-related practices will evidently impact the development of targeted advertising[14]. For example, if youngsters keep avoiding television as a medium, advertisers will have to develop other strategies to reach them.

From the focus group discussions, it seems that targeted advertising is not necessarily a problem for Flemish television viewers. Personalization is obviously an added value, as the lack of relevant advertising on television is a frustration that surfaced in many of the discussions. Most of the participants are open to more relevant advertising both by omission -irrelevant messages are left out- and by insertion -relevant messages are added-.

---

[12] See also:
http://www.standaard.be/cnt/dmf20170112_02670164

[13] available at http://www.imec-int.com/nl/digimeter
[14] Survey conducted yearly on a representative set of at least 1.500 Flemish inhabitants (+15 years old). From August to September 2016, 2.164 individuals completed the survey.

"... all those [irrelevant] ads about soccer or something, I find it worse. Because it's even more obvious, like 'that's not for me, I have no use for it'... and now [with targeted advertising] it's like, yes, maybe about shoes, that you think 'Oh, I'm still looking for shoes' and that you happen to find nice ones." (Daisy, age 21)

Additionally, targeted television advertising could provide a solution for another recurring frustration: the repetition of the same advertising spots. Targeted advertising techniques allow network providers not only to determine which signal goes out to which STB, but can also measure and control how many times an advertisement was shown.

"I also have the impression that the first time that I see an advertisement, that I just: 'ok, now we're going to watch it', but it's repeated so often." (Steve, age 39)

However, targeted television advertising is no silver bullet. Television viewers underlined remaining issues of originality and duration as well as the frustration of interruption of the content you are watching.

"I also have the idea that you are more annoyed with this [type of] advertisement because of the interruption of your program, rather than because of the commercial itself." (Elly, age 26)

Even though respondents recognized the necessity of advertising for the viability of the commercial broadcasting companies, it seems that audience autonomy has an influence on the way advertising is perceived and experienced. Respondents underlined that advertising is something they can decide to avoid, making it their own decision.

"But that is also something recent, we are used to be able to zap and avoid everything we don't want to see. And to select what we do like to watch. And advertising is usually not something we want to see". (Jane, age 32)

When it comes to privacy issues, several questions and issues were put forward in the discussion. Here too, autonomy and control play an important role. Different degrees of control were mentioned in the discussions. At the most basic level, consent was mentioned.

"I wouldn't necessarily want to see it but I would euhm yeah, have the possibility myself to have it removed. If I'm like, 'look, that's enough. I don't want all of that personalized advertising anymore.'" (Derek, age 30)

One step higher is transparency, or the right to view the data network providers are using to target viewers:

"As long as I know, I agree and that's why I want to know it, which methods are used." (Steve, age 39)

Finally, some respondents addressed even more control, by requesting a profile they could manage themselves, where they could specifically insert and manage their current interests. Although we have to question whether many television viewers would (want to) spend time updating a profile that's mainly there for advertising purposes, it's an interesting observation to make:

"As long as you have a say, I like it because you can modify it, you can adapt it, you can say like ok, two weeks ago I was interested in a car but not anymore because I bought one. I compared all the cars, now I want to change it, now I'm looking for something else." (Josh, age 24)

Often overlooked in privacy issues is privacy towards others. Especially because television is considered a family medium, concerns rise for contextual appropriate advertising -e.g. less naughty advertising when you're watching with the kids- as well as concerns for over-sharing with relatives and even visitors -e.g. the present you found for mother's day is visible on the television screen for the whole family to see-. Although the example used during the focus groups focused on family-oriented and rather general products, respondents were quick to question the feasibility of targeting advertising at a household level. Behavioral, personal and third party data are considered private to the person, not the household. Respondents also preferred to have no targeting towards children in the household. This is of course also a legal constraint.

"[…] if you're watching alone as an adult couple, then there can be some cheeky commercials, and when you're watching with the kids that you think 'keep it appropriate'. Some of the perfume commercials are already a bit risky to me, when I have to watch them with my 5 year old nephew. Those are things they don't want to see." (Karl, age 27)

CONCLUSION

In this paper we departed from the SCOT-framework to assess the development and stabilization of targeted television advertising. In order to understand how and by which means targeted television advertising is developed, we have argued that the social arrangements between relevant social actors are key. Targeted television advertising is defined by network providers and commercial broadcasters who need to work together to make the technology functional and to adapt processes to allow the shift in audience measurement from aggregated to personal data. As commercial television is a two-sided market, the television audience was defined as a relevant social group as well. To fully understand how targeted advertising takes shape, understanding audience practices and their evaluation of television advertising and targeted TV advertising is fundamental.

To successfully implement targeted TV advertising in Flanders, it is essential to take the role of the TV audience in the development of the technology into account. Based on our research, the following recommendations can be made for the commercial television industry and policy makers:

- **Consent:** Explicit consent is already part of the current privacy regulation. Our research indicated that consent is important to television viewers as well. Therefore, it is relevant to stress that network providers -who manage the data- should offer users an opt-in that can be adapted when deemed necessary. If the viewer has had it with targeted advertising, it's paramount that he or she can disconnect in a straightforward manner. Policy makers should enforce compliance to the current privacy legislation.

- **Transparency:** Being transparent about the data that are used is not just important from a legal perspective. Respondents indicated they like to know on what basis they're being profiled. Having the right to view the data that are used to build your profile is therefore a necessity. Broadcasters and network providers could increase transparency by making targeted advertising interactive as well, allowing viewers to check 'why I get to see this ad' for example by pushing the red button or scanning the advertisement with a mobile app.

- **Profile management:** For some respondents, there should also be an option to have a say in the type of products they receive targeted advertising for. Although we can question whether viewers would actually update a profile for advertising purposes, it might be worth considering what type of user would like to assess their own profile and whether these preferences are useful for advertisers. If deemed worthwhile, network providers could invest in accessible and user-friendly client profiles that can be managed by those viewers who are interested and willing to actively engage and to tailor their interests.

- **Privacy of the family:** television remains a family medium and as advertising is concerned, a line is drawn when it comes to targeting children. In addition to concerns about the feasibility of targeting at a household level, families are concerned about the appropriateness of advertising based on behavioral, personal and third party data. As with traditional television, advertisers should remain ethical and should take into account a variety of viewers and viewing contexts when developing targeted advertising spots.

ACKNOWLEDGEMENTS

We would like to thank the respondents for their enthusiastic participation in the focus groups, as well as the experts who were willing to reserve time in their schedules and share their insights with us.

REFERENCES

1. Ang, I. (2006) *Desperately seeking the audience.* Londen: Routledge.

2. Ballon, P. (2007) Business modelling revisited: the configuration of control and value. *Info*, 9(5): 6-19.

3. Barnes, B. & Thomson, L. (1994) Power to the people(meter): Audience measurement technology and media specialization, in: ETTEMA J., WHITNEY D., (eds.) *Audiencemaking: How the media create the audience.* California: Sage.

4. Bellman S., Schweda A. & Varan D (2009) A comparison of three interactive television ad formats, *Journal of Interactive Advertising*, 10(1): 14-34

5. Bermejo, F. (2009) Audience manufacture in historical perspective: from broadcasting to Google, *New Media & Society*, 11(1-2): 133-154.

6. Bijker, W. E. (1987) The social construction of Bakelite: Toward a theory of invention. In: BIJKER, W., HUGES, T., PINCH, T., (eds.) *The social construction of technological systems.* Cambrige: the MIT Press.

7. Bijker, W. E. & Law, J. (Eds.). (1997). *Shaping Technology/ Building Society: Studies in Sociotechnical Change.* Cambridge: The MIT Press.

8. Carlson, M. (2006) Tapping into TiVo: digital video recorders and the transition from schedules to surveillance television, *New Media Society*, 8(1): 97-115.

9. Castells, M. (2009) *Communication power.* Oxford: Oxford University.

10. Cauberghe, V. & de Pelsemacker, P. (2006) Opportunities and thresholds for advertising on interactive digital TV: a view from advertising professionals, *Journal of Interactive Advertising*, 7(1):2-23.

11. Cauberghe, V. & De Pelsmacker, P. (2008), The Advertising Impact of an Interactive TV Program on the Recall of an Embedded Commercial, *Journal of Advertising Research*, 48(3): 352-362.

12. Cauberghe, V. & De Pelsmacker, P. (2008). The Impact of Banners on Digital Television: The Role of Program Interactivity and Product Involvement. *CyberPsychology & Behavior*, 11(1): 91-94.

13. Cauberghe, V., Geuens, M. & De Pelsmacker, P. (2011) Context Effects of TV Programme-induced Interactivity and Telepresence on Advertising

Responses. *International Journal of Advertising*, 30(4): 641-663.

14. Cronin, J. J. & Menelly, N. E. (1992) Discrimination vs. avoidance:"zipping" of television commercials. *Journal of Advertising*, 21(2): 1-7.

15. Donders, K. & Evens, T. (2010) *Broadcasting and its distribution in Flanders, Denmark and the United States: an explorative and future-oriented analyses – A research report for SBS Belgium* (working paper), Belgium, Vrije Universiteit Brussel.

16. Duff, R. I. & Faber R. J. (2011) Missing the mark: Advertising Avoidance and Distractor Devaluation, *Journal of Advertising*, 40(2): 51-62.

17. Griffiths, A. (2003) *Digital Television Strategies. Business challenges and opportunities.* Wales: Palgrave Macmillan.

18. Harvey, W.S. (2011) Strategies for conducting elite interviews, *Qualitative Research*, 11(4):431-441.

19. Jaffe, J. (2005). *Life after the 30-second spot: Energize your brand with a bold mix of alternatives to traditional advertising.* Hoboken: John Wiley & Sons.

20. Jenkins, H. (2006) *Convergence Culture. Where old and new media collide*, New York: New York University Press.

21. Jennes, I. & Pierson, J. (2013) Innovation in TV advertising in Flanders, in: Storsul T., Krumsvik A.H., (eds.). *Media Innovations. A multidisciplinary study of change.* Nordicom: Göteborg.

22. Jennes I., Pierson J. & Van den Broeck W. (2014), User Empowerment and Audience Commodification in a Commercial Television Context, *Journal of Media Innovations*, 1(1): 71-87.

23. Küng, L. (2008) *Strategic management in the media. Theory to practice.* London: Sage

24. Law, J. & Callon, M. (1997). The Life and Death of an Aircraft: A Network Analysis of Technical Change, in: Bijker, W. E., & Law, J. (eds.) *Shaping Technology/ Building Society: Studies in Sociotechnical Change.* Cambridge: The MIT Press.

25. Napoli, Ph. M. (2008) *Toward a model of audience evolution: new technologies and the transformation of media audiences* (working paper), New York, Fordham University.

26. Napoli, Ph. M. (2011) *Audience evolution: New Technologies and the Transformation of Media Audiences.* New York: Columbia University Press.

27. Peitz M & Valletti TM (2008). Content and Advertising in the Media: Pay-tv versus Free-to-air, *International Journal of Industrial Organization*, 26: 949-965.

28. Pyungho, K. & Harmeet, S. (2002) A Machine-like New Medium: Theoretical Examination of Interactive TV, *Media Culture & Society*, 24: 217-233.

29. Rojas-Méndez I. J., Davies G. & Madran C. (2009) Universal differences in advertising avoidance behaviour : A cross-cultural study, *Journal of Business research*, 2009(62): 947-954.

30. Seles, S. (2010*) Turn On Tune In Cash Out: Maximizing the Value of Television Audiences*, Massachusetts: Massachusetts Institute of Technology.

31. Slot, M. (2007) Changing User Roles in ICT Developments; The Case of Digital Television, *Telematics and Informatics*, 24(4): 303-314.

32. Smythe, D. (1977) Communications: Blindspot of Western Marxism, *Canadian Journal of Political and Social Theory*, 1(3): 1-28.

33. Speck, P.S. & Elliott, M.T. (1997), Predictors of Advertising Avoidance in Print and Broadcast Media, *Journal of Advertising*, 14(3): 61-76.

34. Stühmeier T. & Wenzel T. (2011) Getting Beer During Commercials: Adverse Effects of Ad-avoidance, *Information Economics & policy*, 2011(23), 98-106

35. Teixera S. T., Wedel M. & Pieters R. (2010) Moment-to-moment optimal branding in TV commercials: preventing avoidance by pulsing, *Marketing Science*, 29(5): 783-804.

36. Van den Broeck, W. & Pierson, J. (2008) *Digital television in Europe,* Brussels: VUBPRESS.

37. Wellens, G., Neels, L., Wauters, D. & Caudron, J. (2014) *Het nieuwe TV kijken: een positieve kijk op televisie in Vlaanderen: het model Vlaanderen INC*, Tielt: LannooCampus.

Let's Play My Way: Investigating Audience Influence in User-Generated Gaming Live-Streams

Pascal Lessel[1,i], Michael Mauderer[2,ii], Christian Wolff[3,i], Antonio Krüger[1,i]

[1]DFKI GmbH, [2]Department of Computing, [3]Saarland University

[i]Saarland Informatics Campus, [ii]University of Dundee

pascal.lessel@dfki.de, mmauderer@dundee.ac.uk, s9ccwolf@stud.uni-saarland.de, krueger@dfki.de

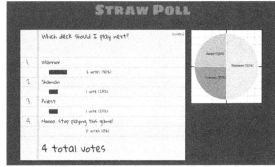

Figure 1. Left: Screenshot (taken from `https://www.twitch.tv/gronkhtv`) of the Twitch user interface, with the stream in the left area and the viewer chat on the right. Right: External poll application (taken from `https://strawpoll.me`), often used in live streams.

ABSTRACT

We investigate how the audience of gaming live-streams can influence the content. We conducted two case studies on streams in which audience influence is central and in which the audience can directly participate: First, we review an existing format of the Rocket Beans TV channel and describe how the audience can influence its course of action. With this, we illustrate current practices for integrating the audience. Second, we report the results of our investigation of a "Twitch Plays Pokémon" (TPP)-like setting in which the audience shares the control of the main character through aggregated chat messages. We explored a wider range of techniques than the original TPP offered and found that this can help the audience to organize itself in more nuanced ways. From both case studies, we synthesize results that are of relevance for streams that want to give the audience more influence.

Author Keywords

Interactive streams; co-presence; audience experience; Twitch Plays Pokémon; Rocket Beans TV; viewer participation

ACM Classification Keywords

H.5.m. Information Interfaces and Presentation (e.g. HCI): Miscellaneous

Permission to make digital or hard copies of all or part of this work for personal or classroom use is granted without fee provided that copies are not made or distributed for profit or commercial advantage and that copies bear this notice and the full citation on the first page. Copyrights for components of this work owned by others than ACM must be honored. Abstracting with credit is permitted. To copy otherwise, or republish, to post on servers or to redistribute to lists, requires prior specific permission and/or a fee. Request permissions from Permissions@acm.org.

TVX '17, June 14–16, 2017, Hilversum, Netherlands

© 2017 ACM. ISBN 978-1-4503-4529-3/17/06...$15.00

DOI: http://dx.doi.org/10.1145/3077548.3077556

INTRODUCTION

Twitch [37] is a streaming platform for distributing user-generated live video content. Twitch focuses mainly on gaming (which attracts a large audience [20, 48]). During such a stream, the audience can interact with the content creator (also called "broadcaster" or "streamer") through a live chat (see Figure 1, left). This provides a communication channel between content creator and audience and poses the question of how the audience can influence the creator to adapt the content which is currently streamed. In streams, where viewer numbers are large, the chat that Twitch provides as a communication channel is problematic for receiving an overview of what the audience wants [30]. Third-party tools exist that can assist the streamer, e.g. polling tools such as StrawPoll [11] (see Figure 1, right). Also, a new streaming platform, Beam.pro [2], integrates more sophisticated options directly into the platform, to make the audience integration easier.

While there are different options to facilitate audience interaction, it is currently unclear how streamers use them in gaming live-streams and whether they are sufficient. This paper addresses this question by presenting two case studies that illustrate representative examples in which audience influence is important: First, we analyze an existing Twitch live-stream format which regularly attracts more than 30,000 viewers and claims to be highly interactive. We reviewed more than 20 hours of this format for elements that involved the audience and considered how they influenced the content. Second, we investigate "Twitch Plays Pokémon", a so-called social experience on Twitch (e.g. [19]). Here, viewers simultaneously play the game's main character via chat commands, without any streamer in between. Thus, the audience alone decides how the stream proceeds. In a small-scale study, we analyzed what the audience's perception of such an experience is and whether it is beneficial to have an enhanced interface for self-organization to reach a better consensus. With case study 1, we provide an analysis of what is done (conceptually and technologically) today, if the audience is integrated. With case study 2, we illustrate novel techniques, which allow for better audience self-administration. We discuss how both studies relate and how the results can improve streams that have the goal to empower the audience with more influence.

RELATED WORK

Understanding audience interactions helps to shape performance and enrich the experience [45]. Because of space restrictions, we limit ourselves to notable examples and we focus on technology-mediated interaction, not purely social interactions, e.g., as can happen through verbal interaction or physical intervention in live theater performances [23].

TV, Theater, Dance and Sports

Even as pure consumers of TV/radio shows, the audience began to form a relationship with the persona or actor [22], a phenomenon called para-social interaction, which appears in web video as well [8]. The theory of this interaction allows one to classify different types of relationships [18]. Horton and Strauss [23] identify roles for interacting parties in TV content, e.g., studio/home audience and audience performers (e.g., volunteers from the studio audience), which can also be seen in web video. Considering these could lead to insights about which relationships could be enabled or bolstered through the addition of interactions between audience and performers. Especially the differences in how a TV performer can interact with a home audience as opposed to a studio audience are also applicable to streams where part of the audience is present during the stream and others will consume the video after the recording has been finished. Integrating the home audience has been a part of the field of social TV [6] with the goal to provide additional information [1, 10] and new communication channels [1, 60]. Ursu et al. investigated how TV storytelling can become more interactive [57] and found elements for viewer participation that are also transferred to web videos: voting in contests, content suggestions between episodes and the option to evaluate user-generated content for developing a story.

Physical co-location of audience and performance (e.g., at theater, dance or sports events) allows easy interaction, and a large variety of augmented interactions have been introduced for co-located events. Some systems allow communication among the audience or between the audience and the performers, e.g., polling systems based on mobile devices [15] that collect explicit information about the audience's opinion regarding the performance or sensing the audience [17, 58] to infer the audience's reactions. Recently, in interviews with performers, Webb et al. [59] found that the interaction with audiences is an important topic for them, which is why systems that allow interactions that shape the performance, by considering the audience itself seem beneficial, as they deliver an engaging, tailored experience [12, 46]. Providing

users/viewers with more autonomy is also beneficial from a motivational theory point of view. Work such as [29] builds on the self-determination theory (SDT) [13] and has already shown that empowering users with options on how they can shape their own experience is beneficial for motivation, because of the autonomy aspect of the SDT. As our case studies also consider how the audience can influence performances, such theories are highly relevant for live-streaming as well.

Web Video

The advent of the Internet has opened up an easy-to-use return channel for communication between content creator and audience. While first approaches with similar systems have been made in the context of social TV, previous iterations of the concept had to rely on phone hotlines, text messages or custom setups [5, 24]. The Internet, however, allowed easier communications as well as ways to distribute content itself, e.g., video streaming or on-demand video [7, 51].

Research on video streaming of games has become relevant recently. Works such as [25, 35, 37] use corresponding streaming APIs to reason about, for example, viewer/channel distributions or predictions of the number of chat messages in relation to viewer numbers. The audience itself is often a relevant part in research on these platforms: Postigo describes how digital labor as a streamer on YouTube happens and discusses the importance of the community integration in this domain [38]. Cheung and Huang investigated the game *StarCraft* in the area of e-sports, and identified nine personas and what entertains spectators [9]. They found a broad range of reasons why people are interested in watching. Even though they only focused on the *StarCraft* community, it is not unreasonable that the motivations can also be valid for other categories of gaming videos, and depending on this motivation, will require a different amount of influence people can have on produced content. Smith et al. [48] conducted an analysis of gaming streaming communities, by specifically focusing on "Let's Plays" (the content creator plays a game and shares his play-through with others for entertainment purposes) and using the aforementioned personas. They also state that through social functions such as live chats, viewers have the chance to become active and that this is an incentive for them to watch a stream. Hamilton et al. focused on which kinds of communities are built around live-streams on Twitch [20] by interviewing content creators and viewers. They reported that content creators use enhanced participatory options already: viewers can play against the content creator in competitive games, they can provide answers through the chat that are used in a streamed quiz game, and polls are used to make decisions in games, or for answering unrelated questions and showing fan-art in the stream. It was also emphasized that this helped viewers to identify with the stream and to become regulars. Additionally, in terms of McLuhan's consideration of hot and cool media [34], the authors state that they see the live-streaming platform as a hybrid form, with the combination of the (cool) chat and the (hot) live video.

How streamer-viewer communication can be improved is an ongoing and current research area. In TwitchViz [36], for example, a system is presented that allows the streamer to analyze chat messages, which should help streamers to better understand their audience for subsequent streams (as at the time, no live integration was available). Rivulet [21] is a tool for multi-stream experiences, but provides further options for the audience to better interact with the streamer (e.g. a push-to-talk option), besides just the chat. Another recent example is Helpstone [30]; here, Lessel et al. decided to focus on the game *Hearthstone* and as a case study implemented and evaluated a tool that provides new communication channels. The goal was to enable viewers to better articulate hints and feedback to the streamer, especially for large viewer numbers. They found that viewers appreciate more sophisticated interaction options (especially direct interaction on the video stream), rather than only writing into the chat, and that these options can raise the perception of influence the audience can exert.

CASE STUDY SELECTION

An audience can exert direct and indirect influence [45]. A simple example of the latter in online video is a high view count, which is desirable for every streamer. Thus, a streamer could base the decision to stream one game over another by checking variations in the view numbers. Even though [20] mentions and [30] considers direct audience influence options, this was not yet (to our knowledge) investigated in streams in which audience influence is a central component. Similar to Lessel et al. [30], we approach this topic with case studies.

In case study 1, we considered a stream with a large audience in which a pen & paper role-playing game is played and the content creators claim that the audience influence is important. In comparison to a video game, the "game engine", "programming" and "storytelling" is represented by a human; thus, in contrast to programmed video games, the only limiting factor is the imagination of the people playing this game. By analyzing such a format we have the chance to see what is possible if the underlying content does not restrict the interaction. With this case study, our goal was to analyze the current practices in a large channel to make interactive audience options available, i.e. which approaches are possible with current technology. It is of particular interest whether the audience integration options in typical Twitch gaming streams (in which the audience influence is not central) mentioned in [20] are also found here. Even though pen & paper role-playing games are not "mainstream" for Twitch, several channels are providing such formats; thus they can still be considered as relevant.

In case study 2, we first introduce the "social experiment Twitch Plays Pokémon", a setting in which the audience alone decides on the course of the stream, as no streamer is present in it. This provides the basis for understanding this setup, which also attracted a large number of viewers. This experiment received extensive media attention and today several "Twitch Plays" streams are available. To complement the results of case study 1, in which options that are already used today were analyzed, case study 2 had the goal to investigate how viewers perceive new options, which enable them to come to a better consensus for self-administration and enrich the experience. We created our own prototype with several influence options for the audience in the "Twitch Plays Pokémon" setting and conducted a study with it to learn how these are perceived.

Figure 2. Setup of the B.E.A.R.D.S. pen & paper session, with the "Twitter Wall" on the left. Picture taken from Episode 6, https://www.youtube.com/watch?v=crNKgbLIor0, retr. 17/04/2017

After presenting the results from the case studies, we discuss how both streaming situations are similar, and how our insights contribute to the understanding of audience influence in live-streaming. Our selection does not cover any of the Twitch "mainstream" channels (i.e., "Let's Plays" of known games), as it appears that in these streams audience influence is often only considered as byproduct (see also [20]); thus they do not fit our goal to examine large channels with a focus on audience interaction (although analyzing such "mainstream" channels specifically is an interesting next step for future work).

CASE STUDY 1: ROCKET BEANS TV PEN & PAPER

The goal of this study was to analyze a streaming format which attracts a large number of viewers and claims to be highly interactive by giving the audience participatory options. This allows us to get a first impression of which actions are taken when the goal is to provide the viewership with more influence over what is happening during the stream.

Rocket Beans TV [47] was a German Twitch channel broadcasting 24/7 (today it broadcasts over YouTube). In 2014, they launched a pen & paper role-playing game format, in which the audience is encouraged to participate through various means. On average every two months a new episode was produced (with a much higher frequency today). The format attracts more than 30,000 viewers and is among the top formats on this channel [44]. In a pen & paper role-playing game [56] one player (the "game master") represents the game world/narrator and can flexibly react to player actions. Players interact within this world in the form of an improvisational theater and can explore the story and the world the game master has prepared. Usually there exist rules to handle character creation and actions inside this world (e.g. fights), and dice are often used to make it more interesting by introducing randomness.

Stream Content

Their pen & paper session consists of four players and a game master sitting around a table; the scenery is arranged to thematically fit the role-playing setting (see Figure 2) and in the episodes considered a post-apocalyptic and a Viking setting were used. Viewers can chat via the Twitch chat (which is not shown to the players, thus only allowing information exchange

Question	Options
What will the group encounter at the bottom of the stairs?	A zombie eating the guard Frank
	The guard Frank still searching for the key
	Another prisoner
	A popcorn machine
What happens in the night?	They will be wakened by scary sounds
	Their shelter begins to burn
	Someone calls one of them
What does Steven do?	He eats a leg
	He and a guest are drinking tea

Table 1. Examples of polls and the available answer options

between viewers), but can also post via Twitter. Tweets are shown in the studio on the "Twitter Wall", which, in contrast to the chat, allows pictures to be shared with the players. During a stream, information overlays, music and sound effects that fit the current situation are added and pre-made clips and pictures are used to visualize certain aspects.

Audience Participation

We reviewed the first six episodes (around 24 hours of video), i.e. all episodes of Season One and one of Season Two[1,2]. The review analyzed elements involving the audience, following an open coding scheme by using a thematic based analysis. We annotated direct (e.g. the community is encouraged to vote or otherwise directly addressed) and indirect (e.g. the camera shows the Twitter Wall, or elements that were formerly created by viewers are shown) social interactions, with a timestamp and a short description. This transcript was later used to derive categories which were discussed by two of the authors. We counted 209 direct and 293 indirect interactions. We clustered these into 21 categories. The number of instances per category varies (with smaller categories such as *viewers providing hints on the game rules* to large categories such as *direct acknowledgements of user contributions*). We related categories and they led to the following overall themes:

Voting

A core element in this format is voting. In Episodes 1–5, this was conducted via StrawPolls (see Figure 1, right), an external web page. Until Episode 6, usually these polls were published just before advertisements were shown. This gave the audience time to vote, without missing any story-related content in the stream (as the transition to the external page was necessary). Due to synchronization problems with the progress in the story and the need to display advertisements at specific times, this was later relaxed and polls were also used directly during the session. In Episode 6, the Twitch chat was used for voting: The question and answer options (which could be entered as commands in the chat) were displayed as a stream overlay. In general, by voting the audience could decide how scenes should proceed (see Table 1). The voting results were visualized and the most popular answers were used by the game master. In total, 24 polls were conducted and on average 9533 (SD=5338) votes were given. Not considering the first episode, in which the format was tested, and the sixth episode, in which only registered users were able to

[1]This were all existing episodes at the time of the analysis. No new audience influence concepts were introduced across both seasons.
[2]Videos are available on the Rocket Beans TV YouTube Channel https://www.youtube.com/user/ROCKETBEANSTV, retr. 17/04/2017.

vote via the chat, the number increased to 13118 (SD=1563). Five times they used polls for which they only provided the question and viewers had the chance to tweet possible answer options. These were screened by people working with Rocket Beans TV and they generated a poll based on selected answers. Such polls are more difficult for the game master, as he needs to improvise, while for pre-defined answers, scenarios for each outcome could be derived beforehand. As this is still moderated, the audience influence remains limited. In contrast to these live polls, the community also had the chance to participate in a poll with pre-defined answers between the two seasons to decide which setting should be played next.

Direct influence on the setting and story

Viewers had the chance to send illustrations and descriptive texts of items the players found within the story. Small cards with representations of the fictive items were given to the player of the character owning the item. The viewer incentive, besides getting directly acknowledged in the stream, was that items were usually available across several episodes and thus were potentially shown multiple times. Before Episode 6, the audience was asked to send pictures and video material fitting the setting. Selected elements were shown during the episode, and even though they were not relevant for influencing the course of action, they were part of the content shown in the stream. However, the audience also had the chance to influence the story: in Episode 2, the audience was spontaneously invited to generate a name for a building in the game. This was picked up for the second season, where story elements could be generated collaboratively [26]. They could create them freely, or could provide explanations and content for aspects that were already marked by the game master. Parts of the content were approved by the game master and then used in the game. The viewers could thereby influence the imaginary world, although the decision on what would be integrated was again not audience-driven. Additionally, the audience received tasks to be carried out during the stream that were directly interwoven with the story and the world (i.e., if a task was not completed, the situation would worsen for the players): In Episode 5, the viewers were told to post photos on Twitter showing a German landmark with themselves disguised as zombies in front of it. In Episode 6, the audience represented the inhabitants of a town, and their task was to decide whether they are convinced by a speech given by the players. They were to respond via Twitter by sending "thumbs up or down".

Communication channel for the audience

Players often read tweets on the Twitter Wall, especially when they were less engaged in a game situation. They even praised the community engagement several times. The Twitter Wall is often implicitly shown when the camera position focuses on specific players, or explicitly, either because the content seemed interesting/fitting for the stage direction or because the players were discussing parts of it. Thus the wall was directly influencing the content of the stream. Images from the wall were shown and discussed, and comments, either from during or between episodes, were often read and discussed by the players. The name of the contributor was mentioned or shown in the stream, and the players also acknowledged good contributions directly. The players used suggestions by the audience to alter their behavior in the game, e.g. by asking other story-relevant questions in-game or re-interpreting rules because of a viewer hint. Additionally, help from the audience was also explicitly encouraged by the game master whenever riddles were encountered by the players.

Discussion

This case study revealed different kinds of audience participation that are used in a stream that has the goal to incorporate interactive elements. We restricted ourselves to the elements that are shown directly in the stream, not social media sources around the streaming experience that were not directly involved (Facebook, Reddit, etc.). This study showed various ways to integrate the audience that exist already. Nonetheless, all the elements we found are at some point moderated, either by the game master, the players or the team behind the scenes, so they do not offer the audience direct (unfiltered) influence. Through the Twitter Wall, viewers have a direct channel in the stream, which is influencing the course of action during the stream. Through the integration of user-generated content, polls and other ways to shape the story, the audience has some kind of shared authorship. It can also be seen that single viewers' suggestions are directly incorporated (e.g. user-generated content such as images) and polls suggest what the majority of the viewers want to happen in the story, i.e., they provide influence over the content of the stream in a nearly-real-time fashion. Besides these synchronous actions during the stream, there are also elements that alter asynchronously how the content will change in the future (e.g. co-story creation).

We found means for audience influence that were also observed by Hamilton et al. [20] in streams which could be considered more "mainstream". The difference with our findings is that all options we report were integrated in one stream, while it remained unclear to what degree they were available in the channels considered by Hamilton. Elements such as the co-story creation option and directly shaping the experience that unfolds in the stream were not found in this work. One explanation is that in these channels digital games were played that do not easily allow for such adaptations. The high interest the community shows here is a hint that games/streams should offer more of these options. The large overlap of elements here and in the streams considered by Hamilton et al. hints that there are only a few common concepts for when the audience should be integrated into the streaming experience today.

We do not know yet how these options are perceived by the audience. Maybe the technological considerations are the limiting factor (i.e., concepts for more audience integration simply cannot be realized with the current setups) or the audience itself is satisfied already (i.e., making it unnecessary to develop more). The work of Lessel et al. [30] indicates that the latter is not true. As our case study only analyzed video content, we were not able to collect viewers' opinions on the different interactive elements. For future studies, we will create a similar setting in which we will also interview viewers after they have watched such a stream and ask how they experienced it. Nonetheless, this case study has contributed insights into a particular stream offering integration options for their viewers and revealed that many options are already at the streamer's

Figure 3. A TPP situation showing a fight and the viewer commands

disposal. In our second case study, we investigate alternatives not yet used in streams and let viewers assess the usefulness of these elements.

CASE STUDY 2: TWITCH PLAYS POKEMON

We first give an overview of the "Twitch Plays" phenomenon by elaborating on its first installment. We then present a system that built upon TPP and use it to explore options that are of relevance for streams that want to empower their audience.

The "Twitch Plays" phenomenon

In February 2014 "Twitch Plays Pokémon" (TPP) launched on Twitch and the game "Pokémon Red" was streamed. In this game, the player's avatar collects creatures and fights against others in a turn-based manner. The game's goal is to win fights against specific non-player characters. The novelty in this channel was that the audience alone played the game simultaneously via chat commands that mapped to game commands (e.g. typing in "down" moves the avatar downwards; see Figure 3). Every registered user on Twitch could participate and more than 1.1 million people entered 122 million commands [39]. At the peak, 121,000 people played simultaneously. The game was finished in 16 days, despite players hindering progress ("trolls"), the "Twitch lag" [61], the (initial) decision that every command was carried out ("anarchy" mode) and difficult game areas. Beneficially for this, the "democracy" mode (only commands entered by the most players within a time-frame were carried out) was introduced [33]. The mode could be switched by the audience [27].

TPP provides a completely different experience than playing a multiplayer online game: all players share control over one character. TPP lived through more than one instance; after the first game was finished it continued successfully with other Pokémon games. And more TPP-like channels appeared with different games, e.g. Hearthstone [54], a round-based trading card game, or Dark Souls [53] a (real time) action role-playing game. But other non-gaming areas were also explored. For example, in "Twitch Installs Arch Linux" [52], the audience (successfully) installed a Linux operating system. Twitch also provided its own section for such channels [16]. These examples show that this is an emerging phenomenon falling into the purview of several research areas, such as computer-mediated communication and crowdsourcing. We crawled ten days of viewer count data in April 2016 from streams that appeared on the aforementioned TP section, to

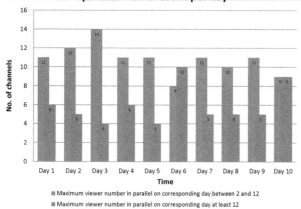

"Twitch plays..." channel and their maximum parallel viewer count per day

Figure 4. Maximum parallel viewer count per day for TP channels.

Figure 5. Screenshot of our web application.

learn how frequented these channels are. Every 20 minutes, we checked the viewer count in channels listed there. 58 channels appeared, and the massive numbers seen during the first instance of TPP were not reached by TPP itself or any other TPP-like stream. The channel with the most viewers in parallel had 7689 viewers on one day and was a notable exception. TPP had 322 viewers in parallel at the peak and apparently, there are two classes of channels (see Figure 4): a few channels that attract a larger number of viewers, and channels that have a small viewership in parallel (< 13).

For our second case study, we were interested in how such an experience is perceived, how far the audience can administrate itself and how this can be facilitated. In contrast to the first case study, in which we reviewed an existing stream, here, we analyze potential future options for live-streams. To explore these aspects, we created a system with a TPP-experience to be able to manipulate different elements: As the "democracy" mode in TPP was introduced to make progress faster [33], we were interested in exploring further modes. Work on crowd input aggregation [28, 42] has already investigated different options ("aggregators"), partially in game settings as well [32], but not yet in a setting similar to TPP. As the audience changes over time, goals may change as well, which is why the audience should also have the option to alter the aggregator used. We wanted to add further options for self-administration to learn how the audience perceives these. We framed them as gamification elements [14], as these are becoming more common in live-streaming channels these days: The streaming platform Beam.pro integrates a gamification concept for viewers directly into their platform, and external tools exist that allow streamers on other platforms to use game elements in their streams. Moreover, in the absence of a streamer in TPP-like channels, adding more sources of motivation to engage channel visitors to participate seems relevant. As gamification is also used for this kind of goal (see for example [29]), it seems reasonable to investigate the perception of such elements directly in a TPP setting as well. Both the aggregators and gamificaton elements have the goal to raise engagement (as positively applied in social TV approaches such as [1]) and the level of audience self-administration.

System

A server and a web application were developed in order to be able to manipulate the setup more easily than it could be using Twitch. As a basis, we adapted elements used there, i.e. the chat and the streaming capability, as well as the option to enter commands into the chat that are interpreted in the game (see Figure 5). We added an option to directly use keystrokes to carry out commands (instead of using the chat) and added more aggregators and gamification elements:

Aggregators

For the aggregators (see Table 2) we provided a mode in which all commands are executed ("Mob"), one in which non-experts have more weight ("Proletarian"), a mode in which the audience can give certain viewers more influence ("Expertise Weighted Vote"), modes in which the best conforming decision is selected ("Majority Vote", "Crowd Weighted Vote") and modes in which an individual decides ("Active", "Leader"). Every user can change the desired mode, but only the most often selected becomes active and is shown on the webpage.

Gamification elements

We use two values, called *influence* and *reputation*. While reputation is a permanent value (used in "Expertise Weighted Vote"), influence is used for buying items. Every user can "up-vote" other users, e.g. after they have provided good suggestions. The amount of up-votes a user can spend is limited, but refreshes over time. Every up-vote generates influence and reputation for this user. Influence can be spent on these items:

- *Agenda*: A user-generated short-term goal (e.g., "Go to city X") can be established, which might be beneficial for motivation [31]. It is shown to the audience and they can vote on whether the goal has been reached or not, or state that they do not want to pursue this goal. If a decision has reached a majority (among all logged-in users), or the majority has cast their vote, the agenda ends. Participating users gain a small amount of influence independent from the outcome, in order to prevent incentives to manipulate agenda votes for influence gain. Only one agenda can be active and no agenda items can be bought during this time.

Aggregator name	Aggregator functionality
Mob	"Anarchy" mode in TPP and Mob/Multi in [28]. Every vote is processed and carried out.
Majority Vote	"Democracy" mode in TPP. Time frames are considered and the most-selected command is used.
Crowd Weighted Vote	Based on [28]. Crowd Weighted Vote is an iterative aggregator that provides a weighted majority vote, where the user's weight is based on their conformity to the crowd. The weight of all users is continuously adapted based on their voting and the most popular vote, i.e. increased (decreased) if the choice is (not) congruent with the most popular vote.
Active	Based on [28]. If this aggregator is chosen, one user is randomly selected and takes control over the game. As long as the user provides inputs, he remains in control (if the aggregator is not changed).
Leader	Based on "Legion Leader" [28]. Leader combines Active and Crowd Weighted Vote; a user is selected not randomly, but based on his or her conformity to the crowd.
Expertise Weighted Vote	A weighted majority vote with weights based on the expertise of the users (often used in crowd-based systems [42]). In our case, the individual expertise is generated by the crowd itself, as users can receive up-votes (which improves the "Reputation") for their actions, i.e. the crowd can identify people they want to provide with more weight in decisions.
Proletarian	The inverse of the Expertise Weighted Vote, i.e. the crowd can empower the non-experts.

Table 2. The aggregators used and an explanation of how they work.

- *User Spotlight*: One detrimental factor in user motivation within a crowd is the invisibility of one's own contributions [3]. This item tries to motivate users by highlighting their actions for all others. The featured person is chosen randomly and showcased for a fixed period of time, after which the next one is selected. Players can cumulatively increase their chance of being chosen by buying this item.

- *Repay*: This item distributes its influence cost evenly among peer players. The concept behind this item is motivated by the variety of player types. Loparev et al. introduced a passive game mode (control mode) which allowed users to aid their fellow players without directly influencing the game state [32]. Additionally, in cases of a skewed distribution of influence, which for example might occur when one or a few players are favored by the crowd due to their expertise, this item can be used to re-balance.

We evaluated this system in a user study, to learn how both the aggregators and the gamification elements are perceived and used by an audience and what further expectations users might have. Moreover, we were interested in assessing the overall perception of a TPP-like setting. It can be expected that the dynamics in such streams differ, the more viewers take part. As it was shown that more TPP-like channels attract only a smaller viewership, we aimed also for a smaller group of participants in parallel for this first evaluation.

Method

We used our system in a LAN setup to minimize streaming delay; all participants were physically separated, a list of usernames was handed out, and it was forbidden for them to reveal their identity. This was meant to mimic the TPP setting, in which participants probably do not know each other. After a pre-session questionnaire (assessing demographics and subjective experience with computer games and TP settings), every participant received access to the "Pokémon Red" game and had ten minutes to get familiar with it. An interactive explanation of how the aggregators work followed: The participants were able to define voting options and values, and could see what a selected aggregator outputs. The user interface was also explained. In the experiment the subjects controlled the avatar (as in TPP). This part was separated into four phases, representing different conditions. The first two phases did not use

gamification, restricting the user interface to the login button, stream window, chat, mode vote option (without "Expertise Weighted Vote" and "Proletarian") and direct input option. In order to avoid demotivation, the phases without gamification had to happen before gamification was introduced, since taking away features could have a negative impact on the user experience [50]. The four phases used were:

1. *Easy, no gamification (ENG):* This phase started in an area in which navigation and fights are easy.

2. *Difficult, no gamification (DNG):* This phase starts in a difficult game area ("the Rock Tunnel") since the screen will turn almost black, only showing silhouettes of the walls. Using a special ability of the avatar, players can illuminate their surroundings. Combined with a more challenging navigation task, this situation demands coordination from the players. In TPP it took 9 hours to complete this task [40].

3. *Easy, with gamification (EWG):* Reusing or resetting known scenarios could frustrate players who have their achieved progress reset; thus, for the gamification conditions we needed to ensure the use of other states fulfilling the requirements. Thus, we selected a similar but different state compared to ENG, i.e. easy navigation and easy fights.

4. *Difficult, with gamification (DWG):* The phase started in the difficult game area called "Spinning Hell". A high amount of floor tiles move (spin) the character in different directions, making navigation through the maze hard. This area led to the introduction of the "democracy" mode in TPP, because progress in "anarchy" mode proved impossible [40].

Every phase took 15 minutes of game time. At the beginning of each phase, participants receive information about the available creatures, items, special abilities and the story state. No requirements regarding method of play were given. Between phases they were asked to answer questions regarding their enjoyment, perceived progress, difficulty and usefulness of the available features on a 7-point scale. The last questionnaire contained an additional section including an assessment of the framework. Additionally, a post-session interview was conducted to gather further qualitative feedback. Besides these qualitative measures, we also recorded interactions with the interface and video-taped the game play. The chat was also recorded but led to no conclusive data.

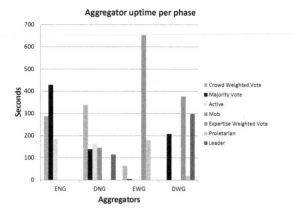

Figure 6. The different aggregators and their uptime.

Participants
Eight German subjects participated (one female) and all were between 21 and 30 years old. People of this age represent the largest user group on Twitch Germany (42%) [41]. Also, the gender imbalance is representative; as only 9% of the German Twitch viewers are women [41]. Six participants were students, two were employed, and all deemed themselves quite experienced with video games (Mode x_D=7; Median Mdn=8.5) on a ten-point scale. One had participated in at least one TPP session; six had already seen footage or heard of it.

Results
The participants were able to solve tasks such as lighting and successfully proceeding within the "Rock Tunnel", navigating parts of the "Spinning Hell" and winning fights against non-player characters throughout all phases, i.e. the group achieved progress. One explanation for this could be that we had no destructive forces amongst the participants ("trolls") and a low participant count, in contrast to TPP. Nonetheless, the participants evaluated their progress as low throughout all phases: lowest in EWG and DWG (both: x_D=1; Mdn=1.5) and highest in DNG (x_D=3; Mdn=4.5). As situations occurred in which advancement was slowed, mostly due to dissent on how to proceed, this could be an explanation. An example failure occurred in EWG where the group steered the character back and forth for minutes. We observed that participants with a lower overall system interaction per minute count, tended to do social actions (chatting, upvoting, polls etc.) instead of issuing commands. This indicates that our audience was also not uniform (fitting into [9]) and different roles might be available in the audience, altering how they interact. This should be analyzed in future work on this topic.

Self-Administration Through Aggregators
In every phase, we started with the "Majority vote" aggregator. In ENG, the first mode change occurred after 63 seconds; in the later phases the first mode change occurred after 4 seconds on average. The ability to change the aggregator was deemed fairly important by our subjects (medians per phase: 4.5; 5.5; 2; 4.5) and they disagreed with the statement that all aggregators were equally important (1.5; 4; 1; 1). Figure 6 shows the measured usage times. The most used aggregator was "Expertise Weighted Vote" with an overall uptime of 1028 seconds, while "Mob" (145 sec) and "Proletarian" (198

sec) were barely used. Considering the assessment of the aggregators, "Crowd Weighted Vote" was always mentioned as important (and got 65 up-votes in EWG and 39 in DWG) and in the difficult phases, aggregators that provide individuals with more weight ("Expertise Weighted Vote") or single user options ("Active", "Leader") were highlighted. While it could be argued that although "Leader" was chosen in DNG, all other aggregators in this phase had more uptime than "Leader", a closer look at the game footage provides more insight. DNG has two major tasks: lighting the rock tunnel (once lighted it stays lighted) and navigating it. In TPP, the first task was never completed (they navigated without seeing the whole map) and thus the overall difficulty of this scenario was quite high. In our study, the participants managed to solve the first task at the four minute mark; during this time "Leader" had its total uptime of 115s. The set of aggregators was rated as complete (x_D=6; Mdn=6) and as containing useless ones (x_D=6; Mdn=6): "Proletarian" was named thrice, "Mob" twice and "Active" once, which coincides with their uptimes. The participants were indifferent to the statement that aggregators provide a good option to self-administer the group (3.5; 4.5; 3; 4), even though they had the feeling that their decisions were in line with the group decisions (5; 4.5; 4; 5.5).

Perception and Self-Administration Through Gamification
The participants agreed only slightly with the statement that they had fun (asked on a single scale) overall (x_D=4; Mdn=5). Breaking it down to the single phases, we see that in ENG and DNG the perceived fun (x_D=3; Mdn=3.5; x_D=2; Mdn=3.5) was low. This could hint that playing games that are not designed primarily for an "unmoderated stream" needs further incentives to be fun. After adding the gamification elements, the self-reports for the perceived fun improved in EWG (x_D=6; Mdn=6) and in DWG (x_D=6; Mdn=5.5), even though the perceived progress was lowest in these phases, as stated. There was a sig. difference in these measurements, as a Friedman ANOVA showed: $\chi^2(3)$=10.87, p=0.012. Post-hoc analysis with Wilcoxon signed-rank tests was conducted with a Bonferroni correction applied, but revealed no sig. differences between the phases. When asked about whether or not gamification elements improved the user interface, users evaluated them clearly as beneficial (x_D=7; Mdn=7) and also that these elements added to their enjoyment (x_D=6; Mdn=6 in EWG and x_D=6; Mdn=5 in DWG). Additionally, these features were deemed helpful regarding self-administration (x_D=6; Mdn=6 in EWG and x_D=4; Mdn=4 in DWG) and added subjectively to a positive group feeling (x_d=6, Mdn=6 in both phases). Overall, 20 spotlight, 15 repay and 11 agenda items were bought. Not surprisingly, the sample also agreed with the statement that gamification is a good idea in this setting overall (x_D=7; Mdn=6). And even though the offered functions were assessed as helpful (4.5; 4.5; 6; 5), apparently they were not enough (6; 5; 5; 5). An issue that was revealed in the interviews was that more shop items would be reasonable, e.g. sub-agendas or an item that provides the leader role for a short time. Two participants also wished for options with more impact: These participants had a lot of up-votes and wanted to spend their influence further. The experience could be improved by adding more statistics, social information and the option to share re-

sponsibilities. The most common demand was a static display of the current leader visible to everyone. Additional demands concerned seeing how much influence or reputation users have, and one subject also wanted a display of how much weight the users have in each voting phase.

Discussion
Our study was the first controlled exploration of the TPP phenomenon. The perceived game progress was low, even with the additional elements offered. The perceived fun was low in the no-gamification settings, but higher in the gamification settings. This might explain why TPP-like streams are rare today and considering Figure 4, why viewer counts in many such streams are low. Considering the content of the original TPP setting, the significantly higher numbers can be explained by the novelty, but also the "fandom" that was created (cf. [43]).

Considering that the audience needs to organize itself in the absence of a moderator, the results indicate that simple majority polls are not sufficient. The audience judged the ability to change the input aggregators as fairly important, and made use of it, as changes occurred during each phase. Depending on the situation, the audience reduced the average player influence for the sake of progress and coordination, either by selecting single-user aggregators ("Leader" or "Active") or empowering a group of individuals ("Expertise Weighted Vote"). This indicates that the audience does not always want everyone to contribute equally, for example to achieve faster progress. The conformity-driven aggregator "Crowd Weighted Vote" was selected in the first two phases but was almost not used at all later. Potentially, as in later phases the "Expertise Weighted Vote" aggregator was available, it appeared more suitable. What can be derived from this is that a fixed aggregator seems insufficient. Demands vary depending on the situation, and there should be different options offered to fit these situations. Using all inputs or only plurality votes, as is being done today in these streams, is probably not enough.

A surprising result was that aggregators were not perceived as useful for the self-administration of the group, even though they were actually used. First, this could be a result of integrating (as stated by the participants) useless aggregators. Potentially, this could have altered the perception of the aggregators overall. Second, it could be that aggregating single-user commands is necessary to make progress, but will still lead to a different feeling than in a single-player game, in which one user has full control. It is most likely that not every decision of a viewer is carried out in a TPP setting (independent of the aggregator), which might lead to such an impression overall. In contrast, considering the introduced gamification elements, we learned that these add to the experience and provide a better feeling of self-administration. The participants requested additional elements, not only for entertainment, but also to better influence the decisions and how the game proceeds. Integrating their suggestions and experimenting with these elements are interesting further research directions. It would also be interesting to see how these are perceived long-term.

Our study had limitations: first, even though in line with the Twitch demographics, the lab study with its small and gender-biased sample. As many available TPP-channels have a similar

small audience, our study still provided actionable results. A second limitation was the short time frame the participants had to interact with the game phases. We decided to see this as acceptable, as it is currently unclear how long people interact with a TPP-like setting in general. 15 minutes appears to be a compromise for the participants to report their initial perception. Third, the user study itself had no players hindering progress, in contrast to the original TPP setting. Even though we think that the available aggregators will moderate effects that are introduced with trolls, our study can draw no definite conclusions for this. To account for these limitations we will start a live-stream in-the-wild (with a different setting, as another TPP channel might provoke undesirable viewer responses as long as the original TPP channel is still available). Work such as [25] shows that most channels on Twitch attract only a few viewers; i.e., launching a channel does not automatically mean that a large viewer-base simultaneously can be reached, which is why we decided against this for this first study. Fourth, the decision to do this study within-subject (instead of using a between-subject design/without a control group that plays through the four scenarios without gamification) could have led to learning effects (while cycling through the difficulties) and thus the impact on the gamification elements could have been overestimated by the participants (even though we found that less likely based on the qualitative answers). Fifth, our study used the relatively simple (considering interacting and navigating) Pokémon Red game. The results should be seen as applicable for this genre and not necessarily other genres, as these might demand faster interaction cycles (e.g., shooters), thereby posing different challenges. Those could be reviewed similarly in the future. Sixth (as this was not the main focus), follow-up studies should deploy more sophisticated measurements for the concept of fun and player experience, and not only a single scale question (cf. [4]).

COMPARISON OF STUDIES & LESSONS LEARNED
The selection of streams for our case studies was guided by our goal to consider channels which attract large viewer numbers and see the audience influence as central. Each case study provided actionable results, and even though the selected streams appear different, the results show that properties for audience influence are similar and can influence each other:

Moderated influence – In both studies we see that an individual contribution is not necessarily integrated in the stream; thus the individual alone has no direct influence option. This leads to viewer actions that are simply "thrown away". In CS1, the moderating factor is humans; in CS2 it is an aggregation system. Both studies showed that an individual can (to a certain extent) increase the chance of their contribution being used: in CS1 by providing high quality material (for example a good story element); in CS2, by changing the aggregation system towards one that gives this viewer more influence or by buying elements from the shop. As reported in CS2, it seems impossible to let every viewer contribute unfiltered (cf. the initial attempt to do this in TPP was a failure in terms of progress in the game), but CS2 also showed that more sophisticated, viewer-changeable aggregation mechanisms (than the used plurality vote in CS1) are relevant for the audience and should also be considered in current streams.

Emergence of new experiences – Considering self-determination theory [13], both case studies provided insights in streams that give the audience more autonomy. The stream in CS1 belonged to one of the top formats of the channel we looked at, and the feedback of our participants of CS2 hint that having more autonomy and options in streams seems interesting (even for passive viewers [30]). Merging the results of CS1 and CS2, we could easily imagine new interaction forms that vary with the degree of autonomy and thus shape new experiences: The streamers could keep some form of meta-control and, for example, decide during the stream how the community is allowed to interact. Sometimes the audience could receive full control similar to CS2 (and the streamer would only comment), or could simply choose an aggregator for upcoming polls. We saw in CS2 that there are occasions in which the audience let individuals decide on the course of action; in such new instances this individual could be the content producer; the same is true for CS1, in which the viewers were able to provide game content. Games such as ChoiceChamber [49] are also instances of such new experiences. Twitch tries to encourage these new experiences by their "Stream First" approach [55]. In general, what this also shows is that research on different types of streams can also shape other types. Moreover, this kind of research helps to better understand the need for autonomy in live-streaming.

Engagement in streams – Both studies revealed that different forms of engagement are used to keep viewers motivated. In CS1, the knowledge that one's own contribution gets acknowledged by the content producers might be a reason why so many viewer-generated elements are created. In CS2, we learned that additional gamification elements (for example through the Spotlight item, which is similar to the acknowledgements mentioned before) dramatically increased the fun the participants had during the experiment. Thus, in both cases, engaging viewers to contribute with more than the material which is streamed is relevant. And we see that both studies provided approaches for how this can be achieved, and that the social component is crucial. As discussed, the original TPP setting had the benefit of the large "fandom" that was created around it [43]. Considering the gamification elements, we learned that the participants of CS2 demanded further options. In the context of gaming live-streams it seems reasonable to assume that the audience is already open to game-like elements. Thus, based on the results of CS2 it seems that besides these social elements, sophisticated gamification elements will increase the viewer engagement further.

Different viewer roles exist – Both studies provided hints that not every viewer wants to exert influence. This is in line with the research [9, 30]. In CS1 we saw, for example, that the participation rate in polls is lower than the actual viewer numbers, and in CS2 we learned that some participants focused more on social than game-related interactions. We follow the argumentation of Lessel et al., that viewers who do not want to exert direct influence might still profit when an channel provides more influence options, as the experience for them can also be improved, even though they remain passive [30]. We reason that this should be accounted for, e.g., the influence activities should remain voluntary.

Lack of expressive options – The case studies showed that the chat as medium in live-streaming platforms is not expressive enough by itself and additional efforts or third-party tools are necessary to give the audience more influence: Besides the chat as polling platform in CS1 (which is often done today), all other communication channels used were not directly integrated on Twitch. In CS2, on the other hand, many of the offered functions would not have been smoothly integrable into the Twitch platform. This raises the question of how many channels would be interested in giving the audience more power but refrain because of the required time investment to set up these elements. Obviously, this becomes more important the more viewers a channel attracts. A content creator can ask a question and could review the most frequent answer through a chat with ten participants, but this becomes impossible for larger numbers [20]. Although the platforms provide APIs, they are not yet powerful enough to provide more sophisticated interfaces than text chat. Even though links to external pages are possible, it is unclear whether this is accepted by viewers. The platform Beam [2] allows streamers to alter their channel page with input elements for the audience, which is a step in the right direction according to our findings.

CONCLUSION

We conducted two case studies on streams that have audience influence as a central element for their viewer experience. In the first study, we presented an existing format that tightly integrates the audience's opinion using existing communication channels and that uses different techniques to involve the audience. Our second study investigated a setting similar to the "Twitch Plays Pokémon" stream, but provides more options for the audience to organize itself. From this, we learned that more influence options are appreciated and considered as important. By relating both studies, we learned that even though the stream approach looks different, attitudes towards audience influence are similar. To our knowledge, our paper is the first that investigates this, and our results provide a starting point for further research. Our findings are also relevant for other domains, for example, computer-mediated communication, and are not only applicable to live-streaming.

Besides the options already mentioned throughout the paper, several directions for future work can be followed: our studies focused on technology based on cool media [34], which leads to the question how audience influence can be realized by using hot media and how this changes the experience for the audience and the streamer. Also, an in-the-wild study of a TPP setting enhanced with our findings could be conducted, to learn about individual differences but also to see differences from the small-scale study. Finally, research into different formats and game genres will be helpful to learn whether specific formats/games require specific audience influence options and will also help to generalize the findings on a larger scale. Moreover, this would help in creating a taxonomy in this domain. We only briefly mentioned the different characteristics of the underlying streams (e.g., moderated/unmoderated, synchronous/asynchronous). Such a taxonomy should consider these and relate them to potential effects on the audience influence capabilities. Finally, investigating how content creators perceive the options for their audience is also relevant.

REFERENCES

1. Santosh Basapur, Hiren Mandalia, Shirley Chaysinh, Young Lee, Narayanan Venkitaraman, and Crysta Metcalf. 2012. FANFEEDS: Evaluation of Socially Generated Information Feed on Second Screen as a TV Show Companion. In *Proc. EuroITV 2012*. ACM, New York, NY, USA, 87–96. DOI: http://dx.doi.org/10.1145/2325616.2325636

2. Beam Interactive Inc. 2017. Beam.pro. (2017). https://beam.pro, retr. 17/04/2017.

3. Gerard Beenen, Kimberly Ling, Xiaoqing Wang, Klarissa Chang, Dan Frankowski, Paul Resnick, and Robert E Kraut. 2004. Using Social Psychology to Motivate Contributions to Online Communities. In *Proc. CSCW 2004*. ACM, New York, NY, USA, 212–221. DOI: http://dx.doi.org/10.1145/1031607.1031642

4. Jason T Bowey, Max V Birk, and Regan L Mandryk. 2015. Manipulating Leaderboards to Induce Player Experience. In *Proc. CHI PLAY '15*. ACM, New York, NY, USA, 115–120.

5. Pablo Cesar and Konstantinos Chorianopoulos. 2009. The Evolution of TV Systems, Content, and Users Toward Interactivity. *Found. Trends Hum.-Comput. Interact.* 2, 4 (April 2009), 373–395. DOI: http://dx.doi.org/10.1561/1100000008

6. Pablo Cesar and David Geerts. 2011. Understanding Social TV: A Survey. *Proc. NEM Summit 2011* (2011), 94–99.

7. Meeyoung Cha, Haewoon Kwak, Pablo Rodriguez, Yong-Yeol Ahn, and Sue Moon. 2007. I Tube, You Tube, Everybody Tubes: Analyzing the World's Largest User Generated Content Video System. In *Proc. IMC 2007*. ACM, New York, NY, USA, 1–14. DOI: http://dx.doi.org/10.1145/1298306.1298309

8. Chih-Ping Chen. 2016. Forming Digital Self and Parasocial Relationships on YouTube. *Journal of Consumer Culture* 16, 1 (2016), 232–254. DOI: http://dx.doi.org/10.1177/1469540514521081

9. Gifford Cheung and Jeff Huang. 2011. Starcraft from the Stands: Understanding the Game Spectator. In *Proc. CHI 2011*. ACM, New York, NY, USA, 763–772. DOI: http://dx.doi.org/10.1145/1978942.1979053

10. Konstantinos Chorianopoulos. 2007. Content-Enriched Communication—Supporting the Social Uses of TV. *Journal-Communications Network* 6, 1 (2007), 23.

11. Curse Inc. 2017. StrawPoll. (2017). https://strawpoll.me, retr. 17/04/2017.

12. Luke Dahl, Jorge Herrera, and Carr Wilkerson. 2011. TweetDreams: Making Music with the Audience and the World Using Real-Time Twitter Data. In *Proc. NIME 2011*. 272–275.

13. Edward L Deci and Richard M Ryan. 2011. Self-Determination Theory. *Handbook of Theories of Social Psychology* 1 (2011), 416–433.

14. Sebastian Deterding, Dan Dixon, Rilla Khaled, and Lennart Nacke. 2011. From Game Design Elements to Gamefulness: Defining "Gamification". In *Proc. MindTrek 2011*. ACM, New York, NY, USA, 9–15. DOI: http://dx.doi.org/10.1145/2181037.2181040

15. Christopher Drackett, Victoria Fong, Judy Ko, Saki Tanaka, and Salma Ting. 2004. Global Garden: A Vision of the Universal Scoring Device. In *CHI 2004 Extended Abstracts*. ACM, New York, NY, USA, 1646–1650. DOI: http://dx.doi.org/10.1145/985921.986179

16. Brooke Van Dusen. 2016. Announcing the "Twitch Plays" Game Category. (2016). http://blog.twitch.tv/2016/01/twitchplays-game, retr. 17/04/2017.

17. Yuan-Yi Fan and Rene Weber. 2012. Capturing Audience Experience via Mobile Biometrics. *Proc. ICAD 2012* (2012), 214–217. http://hdl.handle.net/1853/44416

18. David C Giles. 2002. Parasocial Interaction: A Review of the Literature and a Model for Future Research. *Media Psychology* 4, 3 (2002), 279–305. DOI: http://dx.doi.org/10.1207/S1532785XMEP0403_04

19. Guinness World Records. 2015. Most Participants on a Single-Player Online Videogame. Internet. (2015). http://www.guinnessworldrecords.com/world-records/most-participants-on-a-single-player-online-videogame, retr. 17/04/2017.

20. William A Hamilton, Oliver Garretson, and Andruid Kerne. 2014. Streaming on Twitch: Fostering Participatory Communities of Play Within Live Mixed Media. In *Proc. CHI 2014*. ACM, New York, NY, USA, 1315–1324. DOI: http://dx.doi.org/10.1145/2556288.2557048

21. William A. Hamilton, John Tang, Gina Venolia, Kori Inkpen, Jakob Zillner, and Derek Huang. 2016. Rivulet: Exploring Participation in Live Events Through Multi-Stream Experiences. In *Proc. TVX 2016*. ACM, New York, NY, USA, 31–42. DOI: http://dx.doi.org/10.1145/2932206.2932211

22. Donald Horton and R Richard Wohl. 1956. Mass Communication and Para-Social Interaction: Observations on Intimacy at a Distance. *Psychiatry* 19, 3 (1956), 215–229. DOI: http://dx.doi.org/10.1007/978-3-658-09923-7_7

23. Donald Horton and Anselm Strauss. 1957. Interaction in Audience-Participation Shows. *Amer. J. Sociology* 62, 6 (1957), 579–587. DOI: http://dx.doi.org/10.1086/222106

24. Jens F Jensen. 2008. Interactive Television—A Brief Media History. In *Changing Television Environments*. Springer, 1–10. DOI: http://dx.doi.org/10.1007/978-3-540-69478-6_1

25. Mehdi Kaytoue, Arlei Silva, Loïc Cerf, Wagner Meira, Jr., and Chedy Raïssi. 2012. Watch Me Playing, I Am a Professional: A First Study on Video Game Live Streaming. In *Proc. WWW 2012 Companion*. ACM, New York, NY, USA, 1181–1188. DOI: http://dx.doi.org/10.1145/2187980.2188259

26. Deniz Kökden. 2017. BEARDS Wiki. (2017). https://www.beardswiki.de/index.php, retr. 17/04/2017.

27. Harris Kyriakou. 2015. Twitch Plays Pokémon: An Exploratory Analysis of Crowd Collaboration. Internet. (2015). http://www.innqui.com/wp-content/uploads/2015/11/Twitch-Draft.pdf, retr. 17/04/2017.

28. Walter S Lasecki, Kyle I Murray, Samuel White, Robert C Miller, and Jeffrey P Bigham. 2011. Real-Time Crowd Control of Existing Interfaces. In *Proc. UIST 2011*. ACM, New York, NY, USA, 23–32. DOI: http://dx.doi.org/10.1145/2047196.2047200

29. Pascal Lessel, Maximilian Altmeyer, Marc Müller, Christian Wolff, and Antonio Krüger. 2016. "Don't Whip Me With Your Games": Investigating "Bottom-Up" Gamification. In *Proc. CHI 2016*. ACM, New York, NY, USA, 2026–2037. DOI: http://dx.doi.org/10.1145/2858036.2858463

30. Pascal Lessel, Alexander Vielhauer, and Antonio Krüger. 2017. Expanding Video Game Live-Streams with Enhanced Communication Channels: A Case Study. In *Proc. CHI 2017*. to appear. DOI: http://dx.doi.org/10.1145/3025453.3025708

31. Edwin A Locke and Gary P Latham. 2002. Building a Practically Useful Theory of Goal Setting and Task Motivation: A 35-Year Odyssey. *American Psychologist* 57, 9 (2002), 705.

32. Anna Loparev, Walter S Lasecki, Kyle I Murray, and Jeffrey P Bigham. 2014. Introducing Shared Character Control to Existing Video Games. In *Proc. FDG 2014*.

33. Michael Margel. 2014. Twitch Plays Pokemon: An Analysis of Social Dynamics in Crowdsourced Games. Internet. (2014). http://www.cs.utoronto.ca/~mmargel/2720/paper.pdf, retr. 17/04/2017.

34. Marshall McLuhan. 2003. *Understanding Media: The Extensions of Man*. Gingko Press. https://books.google.de/books?id=m7poAAAAIAAJ

35. Gustavo Nascimento, Manoel Ribeiro, Loïc Cerf, Natalia Cesario, Mehdi Kaytoue, Chedy Raïssi, Thiago Vasconcelos, and Wagner Meira Jr. 2014. Modeling and Analyzing the Video Game Live-Streaming Community. In *9th Latin American Web Congress*. 1–9. DOI: http://dx.doi.org/10.1109/LAWeb.2014.9

36. Rui Pan, Lyn Bartram, and Carman Neustaedter. 2016. TwitchViz: A Visualization Tool for Twitch Chatrooms. In *CHI 2016 Extended Abstracts*. ACM, New York, NY, USA, 1959–1965. DOI: http://dx.doi.org/10.1145/2851581.2892427

37. Karine Pires and Gwendal Simon. 2015. YouTube Live and Twitch: A Tour of User-generated Live Streaming Systems. In *Proc. MMSys 2015*. ACM, New York, NY, USA, 225–230. DOI: http://dx.doi.org/10.1145/2713168.2713195

38. Hector Postigo. 2016. The Socio-Technical Architecture of Digital Labor: Converting Play Into YouTube Money. *New Media & Society* 18, 2 (2016), 332–349. DOI: http://dx.doi.org/10.1177/1461444814541527

39. Sam Prell. 2014. Twitch Plays Pokemon Final Stats: 1.1 Million Players, 36 Million Views. Internet. (2014). http://www.engadget.com/2014/03/01/twitch-plays-pokemon-final-stats-1-1-million-players-36-millio, retr. 17/04/2017.

40. Reddit (Pureownege75). 2014. The History of Twitch Plays Pokemon. Internet. (2014). http://www.reddit.com/r/twitchplayspokemon/comments/1y94r8/the_history_of_twitch_plays_pokemon, retr. 17/04/2017.

41. Quantcast. 2017. Twitch.tv Statistics Germany. Internet. (2017). https://www.quantcast.com/twitch.tv?country=DE, retr. 27/01/2017.

42. Nguyen Quoc Viet Hung, Nguyen Thanh Tam, LamNgoc Tran, and Karl Aberer. 2013. An Evaluation of Aggregation Techniques in Crowdsourcing. In *Web Information Systems Engineering (WISE 2013)*, Xuemin Lin, Yannis Manolopoulos, Divesh Srivastava, and Guangyan Huang (Eds.). Lecture Notes in Computer Science, Vol. 8181. Springer Berlin Heidelberg, 1–15. DOI:http://dx.doi.org/10.1007/978-3-642-41154-0_1

43. Dennis Ramirez, Jenny Saucerman, and Jeremy Dietmeier. 2014. Twitch Plays Pokemon: A Case Study in Big G Games. In *Proc. DiGRA 2014*. 3–12.

44. Reddit (roundabout10). 2016. Detaillierte, ehrliche Analyse der Twitch-Zuschauerzahlen. (2016). https://www.reddit.com/r/rocketbeans/comments/3m28pe/detaillierte_ehrliche_analyse_der, retr. 17/04/2017.

45. Stuart Reeves, Steve Benford, Claire O'Malley, and Mike Fraser. 2005. Designing the Spectator Experience. In *Proc. CHI 2005*. ACM, New York, NY, USA, 741–750. DOI:http://dx.doi.org/10.1145/1054972.1055074

46. Charles Roberts and Tobias Hollerer. 2011. Composition for Conductor and Audience: New Uses for Mobile Devices in the Concert Hall. In *Proc. UIST 2011 Adjunct*. ACM, New York, NY, USA, 65–66. DOI: http://dx.doi.org/10.1145/2046396.2046425

47. Rocket Beans Entertainment GmbH. 2017. Rocket Beans TV. (2017). https://www.rocketbeans.tv, retr. 17/04/2017.

48. Thomas Smith, Marianna Obrist, and Peter Wright. 2013. Live-Streaming Changes the (Video) Game. In *Proc. EuroITV 2013*. ACM, New York, NY, USA, 131–138. DOI:http://dx.doi.org/10.1145/2465958.2465971

49. Studio Bean. 2016. Choice Chamber. (2016). http://choicechamber.com/, retr. 17/04/2017.

50. Jennifer Thom, David Millen, and Joan DiMicco. 2012. Removing Gamification from an Enterprise SNS. In *Proc. CSCW 2012*. ACM, New York, NY, USA, 1067–1070. DOI:http://dx.doi.org/10.1145/2145204.2145362

51. Andrew Tolson. 2010. A New Authenticity? Communicative Practices on YouTube. *Critical Discourse Studies* 7, 4 (2010), 277–289.

52. TwitchInstallsArchLinux. 2016. Twitch Installs Arch Linux. (2016). https://www.twitch.tv/twitchinstallsarchlinux, retr. 17/04/2017.

53. TwitchPlaysDark. 2016. Twitch Plays Dark Souls. (2016). https://www.twitch.tv/twitchplaysdark, retr. 17/04/2017.

54. TwitchPlaysHearthS. 2016. Twitch Plays Hearthstone. (2016). https://www.twitch.tv/twitchplayshearths, retr. 17/04/2017.

55. Twitch.tv Inc. 2016. Stream First. (2016). https://dev.twitch.tv/stream-first, retr. 17/04/2017.

56. Anders Tychsen. 2006. Role Playing Games: Comparative Analysis Across Two Media Platforms. In *Proc. IE 2006*. Murdoch University, Murdoch University, Australia, Australia, 75–82. http://dl.acm.org/citation.cfm?id=1231894.1231906

57. Marian F Ursu, Maureen Thomas, Ian Kegel, Doug Williams, Mika Tuomola, Inger Lindstedt, Terence Wright, Andra Leurdijk, Vilmos Zsombori, Julia Sussner, Ulf Myrestam, and Nina Hall. 2008. Interactive TV Narratives: Opportunities, Progress, and Challenges. *ACM Trans. Multimedia Comput. Commun. Appl.* 4, 4 (Nov. 2008), 25:1–25:39. DOI: http://dx.doi.org/10.1145/1412196.1412198

58. Chen Wang, Erik N Geelhoed, Phil P Stenton, and Pablo Cesar. 2014. Sensing a Live Audience. In *Proc. CHI 2014*. ACM, New York, NY, USA, 1909–1912. DOI: http://dx.doi.org/10.1145/2556288.2557154

59. Andrew M. Webb, Chen Wang, Andruid Kerne, and Pablo Cesar. 2016. Distributed Liveness: Understanding How New Technologies Transform Performance Experiences. In *Proc. CSCW 2016*. ACM, New York, NY, USA, 432–437. DOI: http://dx.doi.org/10.1145/2818048.2819974

60. Justin D Weisz, Sara Kiesler, Hui Zhang, Yuqing Ren, Robert E Kraut, and Joseph A Konstan. 2007. Watching Together: Integrating Text Chat with Video. In *Proc. CHI 2007*. ACM, New York, NY, USA, 877–886. DOI: http://dx.doi.org/10.1145/1240624.1240756

61. Cong Zhang and Jiangchuan Liu. 2015. On Crowdsourced Interactive Live Streaming: A Twitch.tv-Based Measurement Study. In *Proc. NOSSDAV 2015*. ACM, New York, NY, USA, 55–60. DOI: http://dx.doi.org/10.1145/2736084.2736091

User Experience of Panoramic Video in CAVE-like and Head Mounted Display Viewing Conditions

Adam Philpot
Middlesex University
London, UK
a.philpot@mdx.ac.uk

Maxine Glancy
BBC Research &
Development
Salford, UK
maxine.glancy@bbc.co.uk

Peter J Passmore
Middlesex University
London, UK
p.passmore@mdx.ac.uk

Andrew Wood
BBC Research &
Development
London, UK
andrew.wood1@bbc.co.uk

Bob Fields
Middlesex University
London, UK
b.fields@mdx.ac.uk

ABSTRACT
Panoramic 360 video is a rapidly growing part of interactive TV viewing experience due to the increase of both production by consumers and professionals and the availability of consumer headsets used to view it. Recent years have also seen proposals for the development of home systems that could ultimately approximate CAVE-like experiences. The question arises as to the nature of the user experience of viewing panoramic video in head mounted displays compared to CAVE-like systems. User preference seems hard to predict. Accordingly, this study took a qualitative approach to describing user experience of viewing a panoramic video on both platforms, using a thematic analysis. Sixteen users tried both viewing conditions and equal numbers expressed preferences for each display system. The differences in user experience by viewing condition are discussed in detail via themes emerging from the analysis.

ACM Classification Keywords
H.5.2 User Interfaces: Evaluation/methodology; H5.1.1 Multimedia Information Systems: Video

Author Keywords
panoramic video; CAVE; HMD; user experience

INTRODUCTION
Panoramic (also referred to as 360 degree) videos are produced using an array of cameras and video stitching software. The majority of panoramic videos currently available are monoscopic and typically viewed on computers, hand held phones

Permission to make digital or hard copies of all or part of this work for personal or classroom use is granted without fee provided that copies are not made or distributed for profit or commercial advantage and that copies bear this notice and the full citation on the first page. Copyrights for components of this work owned by others than ACM must be honored. Abstracting with credit is permitted. To copy otherwise, or republish, to post on servers or to redistribute to lists, requires prior specific permission and/or a fee. Request permissions from permissions@acm.org.

TVX '17, June 14-16, 2017, Hilversum, Netherlands
© 2017 ACM. ISBN 978-1-4503-4529-3/17/06. . . $15.00
DOI: http://dx.doi.org/10.1145/3077548.3077550

or Head Mounted Displays (HMDs). The increasing availability of consumer and professional panoramic video cameras means that the amount of panoramic content is growing rapidly along with the sale of consumer HMDs used to view them. For example, Samsung [22] recently announced that over five million Gear VR headsets have been sold and over ten million hours of video has been watched. A large amount of these videos can be assumed to be panoramic (Samsung has not released a breakdown of this content, some of it may have been watching ordinary videos in 360 virtual cinemas). Compared to traditional TV, panoramic video viewed on a HMD is interactive, as the user has the ability to rotate their view to look anywhere around them. It is also reported to be more immersive than traditional TV, and to engender a sense of presence. The advent of easy to use consumer 360 cameras has lowered the threshold to producing content. At the same time, media companies are increasing production of 360 content; the New York Times is producing a new 360 video every day [27].

While HMDs are becoming cheap, CAVE-like systems are expensive and require dedicated space. However, in recent years, with developments in projection mapping and Augmented Reality (AR), a number of systems have been developed that could be used to approximate CAVE-like systems in the home, for example Microsoft's Illumiroom [13] and RoomAlive projects [12], and Razer's Project Ariana [21]. Furthermore, inside out tracking AR systems, like Microsoft HoloLens and Intel's Project Alloy, can simulate projection mapping, and could (with wider field of view) also approximate CAVE-like systems. Consequently it is of interest to compare user experience in HMDs and CAVE-like systems.

HMD and CAVE-like Systems
While a HMD is an effective solution for viewing 360 video, indeed, 360 video experiences are seen as a way to entice consumers to buy such devices, there are a number of different ways of viewing panoramic video. At the top end of Virtual

Figure 1. A flyer for the panoramic video (left), viewed in a CAVE-like environment (right).

Reality (VR) applications, CAVE-like systems that use projection onto purpose built planar surfaces (essentially rooms), are often considered the most sophisticated viewing systems.

A HMD and a CAVE differ in a number of respects. Firstly, the resolution differs between the displays with a current HMD roughly one megapixel per eye and a CAVE typically more than double that per screen; however, it is the resolution of the panoramic video (typically 4K) that currently limits resolution respectively. The HMD is completely immersive as the viewer is entirely surrounded by video, whereas in a 4-sided CAVE, video is only projected onto the front, left and right walls, and the floor. The Field Of View (FOV) in the CAVE is that of human vision, roughly 180 degrees, whereas on a typical current HMD it is much less (e.g. the Gear VR has roughly 95 degrees FOV). In terms of embodiment in the HMD, concerning panoramic video, there is typically no representation of body; while in the CAVE, embodiment is natural, as the viewer can see their own body. In terms of comfort, the HMDs are bulky to wear, have to be strapped to the head, and may feel uncomfortable. In terms of viewing position, the HMD naturally places the viewer in the centre of the viewing sphere, which is harder to do in the CAVE and may lead to an unnatural viewpoint. Also, in terms of physiology, in the CAVE, vision is normal, whereas for the HMD, accommodation and vergence are decoupled, leading to possible discomfort [8]. For HMDs, the user is typically alone in the virtual world (although work in social VR is rapidly progressing), while in the CAVE, the space is big enough to naturally accommodate a number of viewers at the same time.

Therefore HMDs and CAVEs differ in many ways, and there are many reasons that a viewer may prefer one system over the other; making it hard to predict which systems users will prefer. The aim of this study was to discover, in detail, how the user experience of these viewing conditions differ, allowing viewers to express themselves in their own words.

RELATED WORK

Cinematic Virtual Reality refers to cinematic experiences in Virtual Reality which range from monoscopic 360 degree panoramic video, to various forms of stereoscopic 360 video, including those derived from computational photography (such as Google Jump), to emerging forms of navigable video. Content may be filmed, computer generated, or a mixture of both. The development of Light Field capture systems such as the Lytro Immerge [10] and playback systems such as Nozon Presenz [20] suggest that navigable six degrees of freedom video is on the horizon. However, monoscopic panoramic video currently predominates.

While CAVE systems have been around for some time [4], they are expensive and require dedicated room scale spaces to accommodate a permanent installation. There are a range of intermediate systems that could achieve some of the functionality of a CAVE and possibly be available to consumers to use in the home. The Ambilight system, an ambient lighting system [24], used low resolution projections around a TV to extend projection beyond a TV set into a room. The BBC's Surround Video system [18], projected a simultaneously filmed wide angle view onto the walls surrounding a television, to produce a more immersive experience. More recently, a higher resolution system, SurroundVideo+, featuring a TV with projected peripheral content in a three walled CAVE-like system [16], was used in user studies along with a TV and HMD conditions. Microsoft's IllumiRoom took the surround video concept a step further by using 3D scanning with the kinect and projection mapping to project images onto the walls around a games console [13] in a home environment. The Illumiroom was followed up by the RoomAlive project, which used multiple projectors and six kinects to produce higher definition room scale projection [12]. Razer has recently demonstrated Project Ariana, which also uses 3D scanning, a pair of 3D cameras - to scan the room geometry, detect lighting and the monitor, and use projection mapping to project graphics onto the surrounding environment [21].

Apart from projection based systems, recently developed, inside out, Augmented Reality (AR) systems like Microsoft's HoloLens [17], or Intel's Alloy system [11], could ultimately (with wider FOV) also be used to simulate CAVE systems in real world environments. These systems build up 3D models of the environment so that graphics can be 'pinned' to the geometry in the environment.

Comparative Studies

There have been a range of comparative studies including HMDs or CAVEs over a range of scenarios, with varying results. In [23] collaboration between CAVE-like environments, was compared to collaboration with a CAVE and a desktop environment, on a Rubik's cube type puzzle. They found the best task performance with the CAVE-like system collaboration. Another study [1] investigated comparing human behaviour between a HMD and a four-sided Spatially Immersive Display (SID), looking at natural turning (head movement) compared to manual turning (display rotation). They found that subjects have a significant preference for real turns in the HMD, and for virtual turns in the SID. In [7] performance on an oil well planning task was compared on a stereo enabled desktop display, and a CAVE-like system, with the latter system found to facilitate faster and more accurate performance. In [26] an experimental comparison of interaction in the real world and a CAVE virtual environment was carried out, varying interaction with and without virtual hands and comparing two manipulation tasks. They found users took longer and made more errors in the CAVE environment. In an analysis of Virtual Reality Induced Symptoms and Effects (VRISE) [25] results indicated that 60-70% of participants experience an increase in symptoms pre-post exposure for HMD, projection screen and reality theatre viewing conditions. Their most notable finding of inter- and intra-participant variability highlights the variability of individual susceptibility to VRISE. In a study on anxiety [14] showed that anxiety produced by fear of heights was higher in a CAVE compared to in a HMD. In [15] performance on a modified Stroop task under low and high stress conditions, was compared for desktop, HMD and CAVE-like viewing conditions. The CAVE-like system induced the greatest sense of presence. One study looked at how viewing of high or low emotional impact videos, viewed on a HMD compared to a tablet, affected the viewers pro-environmental attitude and behaviour [5]. They found that the increased immersion and higher emotional impact of the HMD appeared to increase self-reported measures, but that higher immersion did not increase pro-environmental behaviour significantly. In [3] the higher resolution successor to the CAVE, the CAVE2, was compared to the HMD for collaborative sense making, in particular, the collaborative analysis of network connectivity. They found that participants using HMDs were faster than for CAVE2, and no different for accuracy or communication.

The current study aims to add to the body of comparative work by examining user experience of 360 video in HMDs and CAVE-like systems.

METHODS

Aim and Experimental Conditions

The aim of the study was to compare the user experience of a monoscopic 360 video viewed either in a CAVE or HMD. An eight minute documentary profile of an artist was used. The video was a character led study of the artist's exploration of beekeeping and music making. The video was viewed either on a Samsung Gear VR using a Samsung Note 4 phone, hereafter referred to as the HMD condition, or on a CAVE-like system comprising three walls and a floor, hereafter referred to as the CAVE condition. The CAVE system used was the ReaCToR system at University College London (http://vr.cs.ucl.ac.uk/facilities/immersive-displays-lab/).

Subjects

The study was carried out with sixteen participants comprising twelve male and four female subjects in the age range from nineteen to fifty two. The subjects were BBC employees along with three university students. Each subject viewed the video once per condition, and the order of viewing for any two conditions was alternated to counter order effects (seven viewed the CAVE condition first, nine viewed the HMD condition first). All subjects had tried VR before but none had experience of a CAVE system previously. Subjects were volunteers that were recruited via email to employees of the BBC, and members of a university based human computer interaction interest group.

Procedure

For the HMD condition, viewers sat in an office swivel chair. For the CAVE condition viewers sat on an inflatable white sofa, aligned with the (missing) back wall of the space, see Figure 1.

Subjects were first shown a short panoramic video clip about London Chinatown to orient them to the task and to familiarise them with the viewing scenario. Subjects then viewed the main video *The Resistance of Honey* using their assigned viewing mode. Following this, a semi-structured interview was used to elicit conversation about the viewing experience. Guideline questions that could be used in the interview included: "How do/did you feel after/while watching the video? Did you find any differences to 'normal' videos that you watch on your phone, PC or TV? What's good about watching videos this way? What's bad about watching videos this way? Can you recall any moments that made you feel inclined to look around more? How much did the video hold your attention or focus?" A final question was: "Which viewing condition did you prefer and why?" . These questions were the same for each participant and allowed expansion on replies of interest. The participants were video recorded and observed throughout the study.

Following the second viewing and interview, the participant was asked to complete six questions in the form of a Likert scale for each condition undertaken. The subjects were asked to circle the number: from 1 (not at all) to 5 (very much), that best matched their response to each statement. The questions and the median and mean responses to the questions are shown in the Results section in Table 2.

The general procedure was thus: users completed a pre-trial consent form, underwent orientation for the first platform, the user watched the documentary using the first platform, was interviewed about the first platform, underwent orientation for the second platform, the user watched the documentary using the second platform, was interviewed on the second platform, and finally, the user completed the Likert scale questionnaire for each viewing condition.

Thematic Analysis

The thematic analysis methodology of Braun and Clarke [2] was used for the analysis of the data collected during the study. The overall aim of the analysis is to capture, as a collection of 'themes', an understanding of what is really going on in the mass of data captured in the full set of interview transcripts. The data consisted of sixteen transcribed interviews from the video recordings. The transcriptions were loaded into NVivo 10, a qualitative data analysis computer software package. The software was used to code relevant sentences in the transcripts and in the analysis phase for querying the data when coded, (e.g. example query: display all sentences coded with both the presence and the HMD themes). Transcripts were coded using an open coding procedure, during which the coding scheme was inductively defined and refined as the coding proceeded, very much in the spirit of Grounded Theory's *constant comparative* method [9, 6]. A starting point for the analytic process was a set of seven codes found to be relevant in a previous study [19]. These codes are shown in the left hand column of Table 1 and are referred to as the Established Themes in subsequent discussion.

Items of the interview data were considered in turn, and compared to the emerging coding scheme, to find existing codes that apply, to refine the definition of previously generated codes, or to produce new codes as appropriate. Thus, while reading the text, 'nodes' (as they are termed in NVivo) or themes, were created as necessary and sentences assigned to them. The nodes were created according to the judgement of one of the authors and refined and modified during the coding process. Subsequent words or sentences were allocated to the newly formed nodes, with new nodes created as and when the author felt they were needed. Five of the sixteen transcripts were also coded by a second author, and discrepancies between the two sets of nodes were resolved through discussion. The analysis resulted in the initial set of seven codes being extended by the addition of a further seven new codes, and the combined collection provided a structure for the discussion in the following sections.

RESULTS - ESTABLISHED THEMES

As a starting point to guide the thematic analysis, we used the Established Themes described in the previous section. In this section, we concentrate on themes for which user experience is similar for both conditions, under these themes, the two experiences are only subtly different. In the next section we will discuss themes that discriminate between user experience of the two viewing conditions, which are referred to as the Discriminating Themes, and which are displayed in the right hand column of Table 1.

The following text contains quotes from users and are labelled thus [User ID, the condition they are talking about, H or C - short for HMD or CAVE] e.g. [P99,H].

Presence

Both CAVE and HMD viewers referenced presence in various ways. Some were more explicit than others, with some users

Established Themes	Discriminating Themes
Presence.	The size of images.
Certainty (about what should be attended to).	Embodiment.
Comfort.	Peripheral Vision.
Attention.	Projection of image on self.
Concentration on story.	Physical surfaces particularly the floor.
Engagement.	Cube effects.
Social ease.	Confined or Trapped.

Table 1. Themes

suggesting presence through their use of words by describing parts of the video as when they were 'in' the bee hive, studio or park.

A number of users referred to the environment and/or video as being immersive, or feeling immersed in the video or environment. It was quite similar for both conditions with neither appearing to be more immersive than the other. Attributes which contributed to the user's immersion included feeling as though they were a part of the environment: *"You are in a more real environment and that made you feel you are actually in there; in the display."*[P12,H], and *"Definitely, the actual sense of being sat down watching something happening and being sat in that moment."*[P11,C]. Many users' comments referred to being 'in' particular scenes of the video which contributed to their increased sense of immersion and presence.

Some users felt that the HMD was more immersive than the CAVE: *"It's probably more immersive because you're actually sitting within and obviously there's the 360 element."*[P6,H], and *"Here [CAVE] I had a good overview, but it just wasn't as immersive."*[P15,C].

Some users mentioned the height of the camera in specific scenes of the video. When the camera position was high up, some users mentioned feeling tall while another felt a sense of vertigo, and when the camera position was lower some users felt small: *"You're in the bee keepers hut and you're very tall, and then you're outside and you're at the vent where bees are coming out, and you're really small again."*[P8,H].

One particular scene, where the camera is positioned between the Bee Man and a table, and the Bee Man is working with some electronics, provoked many comments, mainly from HMD viewers, both positive and negative: *"Then I was thinking, it feels like I'm in his lap or something, that feels weird."*[P7,H], and *"One really good bit was, it was kind of a first-person perspective where he was fiddling with the controls so I could see his hands and see all the different electronic bits."*[P15,H].

Some users referred to feeling like a 'fly on the wall': *"I was just looking and it felt like I was a fly on the wall up in the ceiling."*[P7,H]. Some users remarked on the size that they felt within the scene also relating that their reduced size made them feel more a part of the scene, for example, feeling small in the scene when viewing in the CAVE: *"There's a marked difference in this environment, because you feel like you're shrunk down and you're much more in the scene.*"[P14,C].

Certainty (about what should be attended to)

Users in both conditions expressed concerns about whether they were looking in the correct direction or where the focus of the action was and whether they were missing anything by looking somewhere else. CAVE users did not express a fear of missing out directly, but hinted at the fact that there may be other things to look at while watching one area of the video: "*It wasn't like I was focused on one point, I could kind of just glance left and right and still see a bit of what was going on.*"[P8,C]. Whereas HMD users were slightly more specific with mentioning that they could miss information somewhere else; while looking in a particular direction, or when looking around the environment: "*I was wondering if anything else is going on at the time, whether I was looking at the right thing.*"[P11,H].

Many users sited a scene change as a good time to look around. This was to familiarise themselves with their surroundings and to explore the environment: "*I think when the scene changed, I'd look around to get to understand where I am, so to speak.*"[P13,C]. Once the scene remained the same for a period of time, some users said that they felt that it was a good time to look around, also when they found themselves not so interested by a particular part of the video: "*I think essentially, whenever a shot was kind of in the same place, not moving for 10 or 15 seconds, that's when I start looking around.*"[P16,C]. Some users said that while the character/Bee Man was talking, they felt that they could listen and look around at the same time without fear of missing anything: "*I was listening to what he was saying, and looking at what he was doing, just looking around the environment as he was talking.*"[P9,C]. Additionally, the fixed voice to camera affords users to look around confidently.

Comfort

Some CAVE users remarked about how relaxing and comfortable it was to view the video in the CAVE. This could be attributed to the fact that they were sitting on a soft sofa (as opposed to a swivel chair in the HMD condition) and they can relate to the situation as the way that they usually watch videos: "*[I preferred] The CAVE, because I generally felt more relaxed. I felt more comfortable, it was nice to be surrounded and it was atmospheric. This one [HMD] just felt not as comfortable.*"[P1,H]. Some users directly compared the relaxation of the CAVE to the HMD: "*Sitting on a sofa without a head thing on is a bit more comfortable.*"[P13,H], and "*Compared to the headset, it was more relaxed because it's not so... There's nothing pressed up against your face.*"[P14,C].

None of the users exhibited any signs of cyber sickness, though two users mentioned that they felt slightly disoriented when removing the HMD. However, they soon adjusted to the actual world, with no lasting implications: "*Once I'd taken the headset off, I feel a bit sort of um, my mind feels a little bit kind of lost for a moment, just trying to re-orientate myself as you come out of it.*"[P8,H].

Some users found the HMD quite uncomfortable due to its weight pressing on the face, some eye strain due to the closeness of the screen to the eye and feeling slightly claustrophobic: "*Comfortable, though the weight of the actual headgear at times felt a bit uncomfortable.*"[P13,H], and "*My eyes were beginning to strain a bit. There was slight discomfort.*"[P3,H].

Attention

Both CAVE and HMD viewers appeared to be aware that most of the 'action' in the video took place in the forward viewing direction of the camera (in front), as in traditional documentary. This provided a reference point of where to return one's view following looking around or exploring the environment: "*Especially in a piece like this where most of the action takes place in front of you, so you know to go back to looking forward.*"[P14,H], and "*The bulk of the activity still happened in front of you.*"[P13,C]. In the CAVE condition, the use of a fixed seat (as opposed to a swivel chair in the HMD condition) encouraged this, and also discouraged viewers from turning and looking behind them; it was not essential to view behind, considering that the majority of the action was taking place in front of the camera: "*When I was in the CAVE, probably because my chair was fixed, I was looking in front of me.*"[P9,H.

Some users noticed the absence of the ceiling and the back wall when viewing in the CAVE and others liked the fact that they could look all the way round and up when viewing using the HMD: "*Well you missed the ceiling and the back, but they don't matter at all.*"[P10,C], "*I preferred the head set, because I could look all the way around.*"[P5,H] and "*In the CAVE, I knew there wasn't a back wall, so I didn't look right around.*"[P1,H].

Concentration on Story

Some users were able to recall specific information about the video at will when speaking about their experience. This occurred both following the first and second viewings regardless of condition: "*No I can't remember, but I remember a whole load of stuff about him being allergic to animals and stuff like that.*"[P15,H], and "*The fact the guy made music from bees, and then there were all these alternative ways that he was finding to make the music from the bees, yeah, I found that quite interesting.*"[P8,C].

Two users mentioned that they were sometimes following the visuals as opposed to what the Bee Man was saying: "*When I had the headset on, I wasn't listening as much to what he said because it's visually more immersive, so you don't listen, you're too busy looking round.*"[P6,C]. Whereas others were able to concentrate on the narrative as well as look around: "*I was listening to what he was saying and looking at what he was doing, just looking around the environment as he was talking.*"[P9,C].

Engagement

Twelve of the sixteen participants mentioned that they either had some interest in the video or found elements of the video interesting; if a user has no interest in the subject however, they did not engage with the content of the video: "*Nice to be surrounded by things and the story is interesting."*[P1,C], and *"You'd never put bees with music making, so that alone is interesting."*[P3,H]. Conversely, some users were not interested in the video. The video was described as many things, ranging from unique, quirky and interesting to dark, sinister and weird. This eclectic collection of descriptors contributed to the interest and range of user responses exhibited towards the content of the video: *"I thought it was very silence of the lambs stroke Aphex Twin a little bit sinister."*[P6,C], and *"I felt that it was a little bit quirky. Towards creepy because they never got their hats off."*[P7,H].

Some users commented that sound was good to help create atmosphere and also blocked out the surrounding noise allowing enhanced engagement and focus: *"And especially with the sound it goes a long way because it tends to block out what you are hearing in the room you're in or where you are."*[P14,H]. The video production included a lot of work on the sound to attempt to achieve an enhanced viewer experience.

Social Ease
There was not much said by users; however it appears that users would not watch videos with other people while wearing HMDs as they found it quite a solitary, isolated experience: *"But all wearing your headsets in the living room in isolation, so it's an immersive experience, but you're quite isolated."*[P3,H]. The CAVE was also described as *"less for social watching."*[P1,C], but two users believed that one could watch a video in a CAVE with others and have an immersive experience: *"And being able to sit with someone else and watch a movie and still have the immersive experience, that would be really cool."*[P11,C]. It is not unthinkable that a sofa can be shared and, ultimately, the viewing experience in a CAVE. Users were specifically asked if they could imagine viewing with other people in the CAVE, surprisingly not many considered that they would.

RESULTS - DISTINGUISHING THEMES

The Size of Images
Some users liked the apparently larger scale of image in the CAVE (though the image size on the retina should have been the same for both conditions): *"I enjoyed the size of it, the ability to be able to look at really small details whilst still, because the main image is so big you can't miss it."*[P16,C].

Embodiment
Some users mentioned that they felt disembodied, more so when using the HMD. The fact that when they looked down and did not see their legs or any kind of body representation was quite strange for some users: *"It's a disembodied experience; I wasn't a person sitting in space, I was an undefined body voyeur."*[P4,H], and *"When I looked down I realised I wasn't standing there."*[P5,H]. One user quite liked the experience: *"That's what was interesting, I felt disembodied a load of the time. I really liked instances, where, again going back to disembodied, so put in places that weren't to scale with my body."*[P4,H].

One user reported feeling disoriented due to feeling like they were 'Hovering in mid-air': *"Initially it was disorientation, when you look down it's like you are hovering in mid-air."*[P5,H].

Peripheral Vision
Some CAVE users liked the wider field of view and that the image was 'everywhere': *"The wider view, so you could see more at the same time from a better perspective."*[P12,C], and *"What I like, more in theory than in actual, is the idea that nothing ends in my field of vision, which is great."*[P4,C].

Some users really liked seeing things in their peripheral vision: *"I like the use of my peripheral vision. The use of my ability to use my peripheral vision."*[P9,C], and *"You can see, I suppose, the interesting difference in the headset; you seem to be restricted to your line of vision you have to look around to see it, but here you can catch it more easily out of your peripheral vision."*[P14,C]. HMD viewers did not mention peripheral vision.

In the CAVE some users were distracted by things happening in the background, such as a car moving past or other people walking by: *"Times he might be talking about stuff that's interesting but I'd be distracted by a car."*[P3,C]. This is related to having a wide field of view as in real life. One does not have to contend with this in usual TV viewing. One user pointed out that it was more visually stimulating and therefore found that they gave more attention to looking than listening: *"When I had the headset on, I wasn't listening as much to what he said because it's visually more immersive, so you don't listen, you're too busy looking round."*[P6,C]. HMD users were distracted by the ability to look around the environment, and while doing so, to not pay attention to what was happening in the video: *"Sometimes you were so consumed by the fact you were in this world, and you could look around, that it's easy to be distracted."*[P3,H]. Some users mentioned that they were not distracted by external influences due to wearing the HMD: *"It's not like you can be distracted by anything else going on outside of the screen, the screen is all you can see."*[P14,H].

Projection of Image on Self
The projection of the image onto the user in the CAVE provoked various comments. Some users found it quite pleasant and interesting; one user did not like it. Some users found that it increased the immersion, made them feel physically involved and added to the experience: *"What really did it was the projection on the floor and on you as well, it was noticeable and interesting."*[P3,C].

The projection of the image upon the user raised some interest with one or two users commenting to this effect. It did not increase engagement, but did add 'something' to the experience, one user commenting that: *"You notice it's on your legs therefore you sort of, there's an element of feeling physically involved."*[P6,C]. One user particularly did not like being projected upon stating: *"And I didn't feel like I liked it projected upon me, like the flowers or the bee hive upon me, it was like, 'eh?'."*[P7,C].

Physical Surfaces Particularly the Floor

Some users noticed that the image on the floor made a difference to their viewing experience and liked it; in one part of the video the electronics were projected onto the floor and they looked down to see that: *"Oh yeah yeah the floor especially that bit with the table when he was doing the, building some electronics stuff. So yeah that was based on the bottom, so definitely, I looked at the bottom part."*[P12,C]. However, one user found it strange that they had to look down to the floor to see what was happening and one user did not like the image projected onto the floor: *"No, I think it was a little strange, for instance, looking down to the floor to see, to focus on the activity when he was pulling out the honeycomb."*[P13,C]. The user observations could be attributed to the novelty of the CAVE, as it is something different to the 'normal' way of viewing, on a TV, phone etc.

Cube Effects.

Something that CAVE viewers remarked upon was the visibility of the angles in the room where each wall met each other and the floor, at 90 degree angles: *"Things that let it down were you could see the joins between the wall and the floor, and that made it slightly less than the headset."*[P5,C], and *"With the CAVE, you've got these clear lines between it, which kind of throw you off a little bit with it."*[P8,C].

The video had scenes inside a shed, and other rooms, and some users felt that the fact that these scenes did not map to the walls and floor in the room via the projection was problematic: *"So the nature of the environment means for example the walls of the beehive didn't look straight because of where it was dissected by the lines of the room."*[P13,C], and *"Sometimes the wall was on the floor."*[P9,C]. Some users suggested a solution could be to project onto a dome or curved walls: *"I guess if it was a dome, it would be fantastic."*[P7,C].

Confined or Trapped

One user found that being cut off from the actual world when viewing the video using the HMD was a good thing: *"Specifically 360 video, you are so much more part of the experience because you, there's no getting away from it the same way."*[P14,H]. Whereas others found it unpleasant and in one instance claustrophobic: *"It's a bit claustrophobic at times compared to a normal usual screen."*[P16,H], and *"And the bee hive, it was so close that I wanted to get some distance."*[P7,H]. One user liked the fact that the HMD does not have any 'sides' like a TV screen: *"Just the fact that you can explore the environment more instead of being confined to the sides of a screen."*[P10,H].

RESULTS - PREFERENCE

Users were asked which condition (C or H) they preferred and why, at the end of their second viewing. Seven users preferred the HMD and seven users preferred the CAVE; two users could not decide and have been assigned the preference of 'BOTH'. In the following section users are denoted by their participant number with their preference following in parentheses.

Although users P5(H), P6(H) and P13(H) preferred viewing the video using the HMD, they all remarked that the CAVE was more comfortable. They found the HMD uncomfortable, simply due to the fact that they were wearing it, and in the CAVE they were not: *"The CAVE experience was more comfortable, because I didn't have this thing on my head."*[P5], *"But the headset's quite uncomfortable, so this [CAVE] is comfier."*[P6], and *"sitting on a sofa without a head thing on is a bit more comfortable."*[P13].

Users P1(C), P3(C) and P6(H) specifically mentioned the discomfort of the HMD: *"This one (H) just felt not as comfortable."*[P1], *"It's more immersive, you felt you were there. But with that comes discomfort."*[P3], and *"But the headset's quite uncomfortable."*[P6]. Also, pertaining to discomfort when using the HMD, two users, P3(C) and P16(C), both mentioned the feeling of claustrophobia when viewing using the HMD: *"It's less claustrophobic in the CAVE."*[P3], and *"The full immersion of the headset I found actually quite overbearing and claustrophobic."*[P16].

As well as the comfort and discomfort of the two conditions, three users, P1(C), P8(C) and P16(C) felt relaxed in the CAVE setting. This was not attributed to anything in particular; however the inflatable sofa could have been an influential factor: *"The CAVE because I generally felt more relaxed."*[P1], *"I was more relaxed in it. I felt I could just chill out and I didn't have this thing stuck to my face and that was more relaxing."*[P8].

Presence and Immersion was quite prominent in the reasons for some users' preference. Users P2(C), P3(C), P5(H), P6(H), P10(C), P12(H), P14(BOTH) and P15(H) all either specifically mentioned, or alluded to, presence and/or immersion as a key factor in their preference of condition: *"Gives a greater sense that you are there."*[P2], *"The headset felt far more as if you were 'in', it's more immersive, you felt you were there."*[P3], *"The headset, just because it's more immersive, more interesting."*[P6], *"Again it feels a lot more immersive."*[P10], *"You are in a more real environment and that made you feel you are actually in there; in the display."*[P12], *"I certainly felt more immersed in the headset."*[P14], and *"It's an immersive experience."*[P15]. Clearly, both conditions provide presence and immersion to the user which ultimately contribute to a pleasurable experience.

There were two users P11(BOTH) and P14(BOTH), who could not decide which they preferred, citing the dependency on what type of content they viewed in each condition as the crux of their indecision: *"For this particular bit of content the headset. But I would say, with different content, like a movie, probably this [CAVE]."*[P11], and *"Depends on content."*[P14].

Overall, the fact that the users were split equally in their preference of condition, in this instance, did not highlight whether one is preferred over the other. Although just two users mentioned content when speaking about their preference, it is likely to be quite influential in a viewer's experience when watching panoramic video using various conditions. The comfort and relaxation associated with the CAVE contributed to users' preference, but was not a distinguishing factor. The outstanding attribute relating to preference of condition in this study appears to have been whether the viewer experiences

Statement	CAVE Median	HMD Median	CAVE Mean	HMD Mean	P Value
S1 I felt like I was there, in the scenes of the video.	3	4	3.25	3.94	0.044
S2 I felt I could interact with the displayed environment.	2	2.5	2.31	2.56	0.43
S3 I paid more attention to the displayed environment than I did to my own thoughts (e.g., personal preoccupations, daydreams etc.).	3	4	3.31	3.88	0.169
S4 I felt as though I was in the same space as the character and/or objects.	3	4	3.25	3.81	0.147
S5 How much did you enjoy the content of the clip?	4	4	3.69	3.63	0.705
S6 How much did you enjoy the way you viewed the clip?	4	4	4.06	3.88	0.417

Table 2. Median and mean values for the responses to the instructions "Please circle the number; from 1 (not at all) to 5 (very much), that best matches your response to each statement". The last column is the P value from Related Samples Wilcoxon Signed Rank Tests (n=16) on responses to the six statements. Only S1 was significant at P=0.05 level.

presence and immersion when watching panoramic video in a CAVE or using a HMD.

RESULTS - QUESTIONNAIRE

After completing the two viewing conditions, subjects were asked to rate their responses to six questions on a Likert scale of five points ranging from agree 'not at all' to agree 'very much'. The responses to these questions are summarised in Table 2. The results per viewing condition were aggregated ignoring order and the medians and means were calculated as measures of central tendency. The median and mean results are generally similar for the two conditions.

The Wilcoxon Signed Rank test was chosen to analyse the results, as it makes no assumption of normality or equal variance in the distributions. Related Samples Wilcoxon Signed Rank Tests were thus performed on responses to the six statements. A significant difference between the two viewing conditions was only found for the first statement concerning presence. HMD viewers rated higher agreement with this statement than CAVE viewers, suggesting the sense of presence was higher for the HMD condition. This may be due to the fact that in the CAVE condition the video was not completely 360 degrees around the viewer and due to the anomalies affecting the illusion shown in Figure 2.

S4 also related to presence, and while the P value was lower than for the other statements apart from S1, it was not significant.

S2 queried how much viewers felt they could interact with the environment, as interaction is limited to changing viewpoint, it is not surprising that both conditions scored low. S3 queried how much viewers paid attention to the display, again this was a little higher for the HMD than for the CAVE condition but not a significant difference.

S5 asked how much viewers enjoyed the video, and for this group it was generally rated positively with means and medians above three. In order to look at the format of the presentation, S6 asked whether viewers enjoyed the way they had viewed the content, and again, they gave generally positive responses with means and medians values above three for both CAVE and HMD conditions.

DISCUSSION

Drawing Comparisons

Clearly, a comparison of CAVE and HMD is only relevant for content that may be shown in a CAVE missing the ceiling and back wall. However, casual sampling of 360 content shows that many videos do not fully use 360 most of the time. Furthermore, it is a consideration that making people look around a lot could be tiring. Given the position of the sofa, and the fact that the CAVE system had no projection on the ceiling or back wall, viewers could view the remaining walls and floor by looking around, without the need to rotate the seating. However the restriction in the freedom to move around and to sit comfortably possibly caused biases which are not part of the systems compared.

That presence is an overriding feature of panoramic video is evident in user discussion around that concept, and it is also largely supported by responses to the questionnaire. It is interesting that subjects tended to cite presence and immersive factors as reasons for their preference of viewing condition, regardless of which it was.

There are some obvious differences between the two viewing conditions, such as in peripheral vision and sense of embodiment, as noted in the introduction. Thus, it was not surprising when these terms came up during the interviews, and that they eventually emerged as themes. However, even though obvious differences came up, it was still difficult to predict which of the two viewing conditions the users would prefer.

The discriminating themes found in this study have identified issues which could be addressed to improve the user experience of watching monoscopic panoramic video within a CAVE-like environment. Careful consideration should be paid to the video environment mapping to the physical space i.e. the walls of the CAVE, and care in technical post-production i.e. stitching.

There were some references to both embodiment and disembodiment when viewing the video in both conditions. The fact that the viewer has no reference to themselves within the video environment, when watching using the HMD, was pleasant to some users and off-putting to others. In respect to viewing panoramic videos using the HMD, there may be advantages to representing the viewer as part of the video in order to ease the negative sense of disembodiment.

A range of differences between viewing conditions are thus evident in the reports of participants. In the remainder of this section, a framework is presented that aims to make sense of the differences, organising themes into clusters, based on how they appear to influence the users' experience of panoramic video.

Towards a Framework

The thematic analysis research method adopted here sought, through the careful examination and coding of interview data, to arrive at an understanding of the key concepts at work when people draw comparisons between the two viewing platforms. In common with methods like Grounded Theory, the current research aims to make connections between themes produced, looking for common patterns, aiming to identify which, of all the issues raised, are the key ones – analogous to the Grounded Theory notion of a *core category* or *core variable* that can help to explain the majority of the variability observed in the data.

Looking at the discussions of themes, the concepts that appear most central are those to do with presence and immersion – the words and the theme crop up in much of what people say (both in the analysis of themes and in the participants explanations of their preference for one system over another). Many of the other themes described above are not explicitly about presence, but are still connected in some way (for example, the comments relating to projection of image on self refer to the significance of such projections in helping to create or diminish peoples sense of being there, being involved, and so on). Identification of Presence as a central theme is supported by the qualitative analysis, in which the Likert item S1, relating to peoples' sense of 'being there' – closely connected to presence, produced a significant difference between viewing platforms.

Having identified the central theme of Presence, the relationships between the remaining themes and Presence can be considered, producing clusters of themes that stand in a similar relation to the central theme of Presence. The emergent framework, illustrated in Figure 2, identifies clusters of themes that capture the ways that presence can be influenced, positively or negatively. Three clusters have been identified: Anomalies affecting the illusion, Affect and feeling, and Cognitive and perceptual effects.

CONCLUSIONS

This study has added to the body of knowledge concerning the user experience of panoramic video by considering the differences between viewing in a HMD and viewing in a CAVE-like environment. A set of themes that were previously applied to comparing HMD and phone and screen viewing were used to compare viewing in the HMD and CAVE conditions. However,

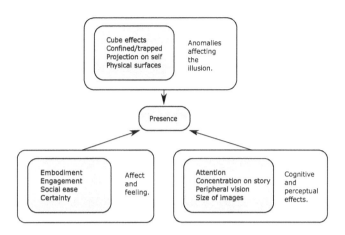

Figure 2. A framework for understanding user experience of panoramic video in a HMD and CAVE.

consideration of these themes did not discriminate between viewing experiences for these two viewing conditions, and the user responses in relation to these themes was very similar. Consequently, a set of themes which do discriminate between the two was identified and elucidated. We also asked which viewing condition users preferred, and their opinion was split equally between the two options. Presence is a major feature of 360 video, compared to traditional film, and it appears that the users reported sense of presence was the deciding factor in choosing a preference. The emergent themes that summarise what participants reported when asked to describe various aspects of their experience of panoramic video on the two platforms, have been organised into a framework that puts Presence centre-stage, and aims to identify the clusters of sub-themes that influence the experience of being present in the panoramic video scene. Future work will develop this research in three directions:

- Development of the theoretical framework further, for instance, to better understand how the minor themes influence Presence.

- Exploration of how cinematic conventions are used in the production of panoramic video, and how viewers understand and orient towards directorial elements. Such an exploration will allow us to develop an understanding of how a filmic literacy is emerging for this novel medium.

- Identification of consequences of the findings for the production of panoramic video content. This could take the form of 'design advice' or guidelines, or could lead to an empirically informed evaluative critique of emerging guidance.

ACKNOWLEDGMENTS
We would like to thank Anthony Steed for facilitating access to the University College London ReaCToR system, and to David Swapp and Drew MacQuarrie for assistance in using the equipment.

REFERENCES

1. Doug A Bowman, Ameya Datey, Young Sam Ryu, Umer Farooq, and Omar Vasnaik. 2002. Empirical Comparison of Human Behavior and Performance with Different Display Devices for Virtual Environments. In *Proceedings of the Human Factors and Ergonomics Society Annual Meeting*. 2134–2138.

2. Virginia Braun and Victoria Clarke. 2006. Using thematic analysis in psychology. *Qualitative Research in Psychology* 3, 2 (jan 2006), 77–101. DOI: http://dx.doi.org/10.1191/1478088706qp063oa

3. Maxime Cordeil, Tim Dwyer, Karsten Klein, Bireswar Laha, Kim Marriott, and Bruce H. Thomas. 2017. Immersive Collaborative Analysis of Network Connectivity: CAVE-style or Head-Mounted Display? *IEEE Transactions on Visualization and Computer Graphics* 23, 1 (jan 2017), 441–450. DOI: http://dx.doi.org/10.1109/TVCG.2016.2599107

4. Carolina Cruz-Neira, Daniel J. Sandin, Thomas A. DeFanti, Robert V. Kenyon, and John C. Hart. 1992. The CAVE: audio visual experience automatic virtual environment. *Commun. ACM* 35, 6 (jun 1992), 64–72. DOI: http://dx.doi.org/10.1145/129888.129892

5. Diana Fonseca and Martin Kraus. 2016. A comparison of head-mounted and hand-held displays for 360 degree videos with focus on attitude and behavior change. In *Proceedings of the 20th International Academic Mindtrek Conference on - AcademicMindtrek '16*. ACM Press, New York, New York, USA, 287–296. DOI: http://dx.doi.org/10.1145/2994310.2994334

6. Barney G. Glaser. 1965. The Constant Comparative Method of Qualitative Analysis. *Social Problems* 12, 4 (apr 1965), 436–445. DOI: http://dx.doi.org/10.2307/798843

7. K. Gruchalla. Immersive well-path editing: investigating the added value of immersion. In *IEEE Virtual Reality 2004*. IEEE, 157–164. DOI: http://dx.doi.org/10.1109/VR.2004.1310069

8. David M Hoffman, Ahna R Girshick, Kurt Akeley, and Martin S Banks. 2008. Vergence-accommodation conflicts hinder visual performance and cause visual fatigue. *Journal of vision* 8, 3 (2008), 33.1–30. DOI: http://dx.doi.org/10.1167/8.3.33

9. Judith A. Holton. The Coding Process and Its Challenges. In *The SAGE Handbook of Grounded Theory*. SAGE Publications Ltd, 1 Oliver's Yard, 55 City Road, London England EC1Y 1SP United Kingdom, 265–289. DOI: http://dx.doi.org/10.4135/9781848607941.n13

10. Lytro Immerge. 2017. Lytro Immerge. (Jan 2017). Retrieved Janurary 9, 2017 from https://www.lytro.com/press/releases/

11. Intel. 2017. Intel Alloy. (Jan. 2017). Retrieved Janurary 9, 2017 from https://newsroom.intel.com/press-kits/project-alloy/#news-coverage

12. Brett Jones, Lior Shapira, Rajinder Sodhi, Michael Murdock, Ravish Mehra, Hrvoje Benko, Andrew Wilson, Eyal Ofek, Blair MacIntyre, and Nikunj Raghuvanshi. 2014. RoomAlive. In *Proceedings of the 27th annual ACM symposium on User interface software and technology - UIST '14*. ACM Press, New York, New York, USA, 637–644. DOI: http://dx.doi.org/10.1145/2642918.2647383

13. Brett R. Jones, Hrvoje Benko, Eyal Ofek, and Andrew D. Wilson. 2013. IllumiRoom. In *Proceedings of the SIGCHI Conference on Human Factors in Computing Systems - CHI '13*. ACM Press, New York, New York, USA, 869–878. DOI: http://dx.doi.org/10.1145/2470654.2466112

14. M. Carmen Juan and David Pérez. 2009. Comparison of the Levels of Presence and Anxiety in an Acrophobic Environment Viewed via HMD or CAVE. *Presence: Teleoperators and Virtual Environments* 18, 3 (jun 2009), 232–248. DOI: http://dx.doi.org/10.1162/pres.18.3.232

15. Kwanguk Kim, M. Zachary Rosenthal, David Zielinski, and Rachel Brady. 2012. Comparison of desktop, head mounted display, and six wall fully immersive systems using a stressful task. In *2012 IEEE Virtual Reality (VR)*. IEEE, 143–144. DOI: http://dx.doi.org/10.1109/VR.2012.6180922

16. Andrew MacQuarrie and Anthony Steed. 2017. Cinematic virtual reality: Evaluating the effect of display type on the viewing experience for panoramic video. In *2017 IEEE Virtual Reality (VR)*. IEEE, 45–54. DOI: http://dx.doi.org/10.1109/VR.2017.7892230

17. Microsoft. 2017. Microsoft Hololens. (Jan 2017). Retrieved Janurary 12, 2017 from https://www.microsoft.com/microsoft-hololens//

18. Peter Mills, Alia Sheikh, Graham Thomas, and Paul Debenham. 2011. Surround video.. In *Proceedings of the 2011 Networked and Electronic Media Summit*. 55–63.

19. Peter J Passmore, Maxine Glancy, Adam Philpot, Amelia Roscoe, Andrew Wood, and Bob Fields. 2016. Effects of Viewing Condition on User Experience of Panoramic Video. In *ICAT-EGVE 2016 - International Conference on Artificial Reality and Telexistence and Eurographics Symposium on Virtual Environments*, Dirk Reiners, Daisuke Iwai, and Frank Steinicke (Eds.). The Eurographics Association. DOI: http://dx.doi.org/10.2312/egve.20161428

20. Nozon Presenz. 2017. Nozon Presenze. (Jan 2017). Retrieved Janurary 9, 2017 from http://www.nozon.com/presenz

21. Razer. 2017. Project Ariana. (Jan 2017). Retrieved Janurary 9, 2017 from http://www.razerzone.com/project-ariana

22. Samsung. 2017. Samsung sold 5 million Gear VR headsets. (Jan 2017). Retrieved Janurary 9, 2017 from http://www.roadtovr.com/samsung-sold-5-million-gear-vr-headsets/

23. Ralph Schroeder, Anthony Steed, Ann-Sofie Axelsson, Ilona Heldal, Åsa Abelin, Josef Wideström, Alexander Nilsson, and Mel Slater. 2001. Collaborating in networked immersive spaces: as good as being there together? *Computers & Graphics* 25, 5 (oct 2001), 781–788. DOI: `http://dx.doi.org/10.1016/S0097-8493(01)00120-0`

24. P Seuntiens, I Vogels, and A Van Keersop. 2007. Visual experience of 3D-TV with pixelated ambilight.. In *Proceedings of PRESENCE 2007*.

25. Sarah Sharples, Sue Cobb, Amanda Moody, and John R. Wilson. 2008. Virtual reality induced symptoms and effects (VRISE): Comparison of head mounted display (HMD), desktop and projection display systems. *Displays* 29, 2 (mar 2008), 58–69. DOI: `http://dx.doi.org/10.1016/j.displa.2007.09.005`

26. Alistair Sutcliffe, Brian Gault, Terence Fernando, and Kevin Tan. 2006. Investigating interaction in CAVE virtual environments. *ACM Transactions on Computer-Human Interaction* 13, 2 (jun 2006), 235–267. DOI: `http://dx.doi.org/10.1145/1165734.1165738`

27. New York Times. 2017. The Daily 360. (Jan 2017). Retrieved Janurary 14, 2017 from `https://www.nytimes.com/video/the-daily-360`

Integrating Mid-Air Haptics into Movie Experiences

Damien Ablart[†], **Carlos Velasco**[‡], **Marianna Obrist**[†]
†SCHI Lab, School of Engineering and Informatics, University of Sussex, UK
‡Department of Marketing, BI Norwegian Business School
da292@sussex.ac.uk, carlos.velasco@bi.no, m.obrist@sussex.ac.uk

ABSTRACT

"Seeing is believing, but feeling is the truth". This idiom from the seventieth century English clergyman Thomas Fuller gains new momentum in light of an increased proliferation of haptic technologies that allow people to have various kinds of 'touch' and 'touchless' interactions. Here, we report on the process of creating and integrating touchless feedback (i.e. mid-air haptic stimuli) into short movie experiences (i.e. one-minute movie format). Based on a systematic evaluation of user's experiences of those haptically enhanced movies, we show evidence for the positive effect of haptic feedback during the first viewing experience, but also for a repeated viewing after two weeks. This opens up a promising design space for content creators and researchers interested in sensory augmentation of audiovisual content. We discuss our findings and the use of mid-air haptics technologies with respect to its effect on users' emotions, changes in the viewing experience over time, and the effects of synchronisation.

ACM Classification Keywords

H.5.m. Information Interfaces and Presentation (e.g. HCI).

Author Keywords

Mid-Air Haptic; Touch; User Experience; Movie Experiences; Skin Conductance Response; Short Movie; Emotions.

INTRODUCTION

Audiovisual media has become omnipresent in people's everyday lives and has a significant impact on their feelings and emotions [2, 19]. Over the last few years, the sense of touch has gained attention as a means to enhance users' experiences, particularly to create more immersive media experiences. For example, Surround Haptics provides smooth tactile motions on the back through a system that is integrated in a seat [13], a tactile jacket that triggers vibrations to intensify emotions [16], AIREAL uses vortexes of air that delivers tactile sensations in free air [28], and Ultrahaptics that display ultrasonic waves to create tactile sensations in mid-air [5]. The first two examples require physical contact, while the latter two generate tactile sensations in the air, not requiring any physical contact between the user and the interface.

Permission to make digital or hard copies of all or part of this work for personal or classroom use is granted without fee provided that copies are not made or distributed for profit or commercial advantage and that copies bear this notice and the full citation on the first page. Copyrights for components of this work owned by others than ACM must be honored. Abstracting with credit is permitted. To copy otherwise, or republish, to post on servers or to redistribute to lists, requires prior specific permission and/or a fee. Request permissions from permissions@acm.org.
TVX 2017, June 14–16, 2017, Hilversum, The Netherlands.
Copyright © 2017 ACM ISBN 978-1-4503-4529-3/17/06 ...$15.00.
http://dx.doi.org/10.1145/3077548.3077551

In this paper, we focus on mid-air haptic technology and its effect on media experiences, as it has not been studied before. More precisely we focus on mid-air haptic feedback and their potential role in movie experiences. There is a growing body of knowledge on the perception of mid-air haptic stimuli (localisation and discrimination) [31] and the creation of shapes in mid-air [18]. However, the effects of these kinds of stimulation on human emotions has only recently been studied.

In contrast to previous studies where the haptic experience is created to match a specific emotion [16], to mirror the screen [15], or to match the specific semantic space [13], we designed a single haptic pattern to enhance viewers' experiences. By pattern, we mean a mid-air haptic creation defined by an intensity, a movement, and a frequency over time. We explored this pattern with respect to its temporal integration into movies (synchronized versus not synchronized with the peak moments in a movie). We focus on "one-minute movies", which is a content format that conveys a complete narrative in one minute and allows a comparable set of movies of the same format and length. Then, we conducted a study following three main steps: (1) selection of movies, (2) creation and integration of haptic feedback (haptic pattern) into the movie narrative (synchronised vs not synchronized) and (3) evaluation of the users' viewing experiences (emotions) in two instances (two weeks separated). For the evaluation, we used three conditions: (a) with and without haptic feedback, (b) movie-specific design versus one cross-movies design, and (c) repeated viewing after two weeks. We used a combination of measures (i.e. self-report questionnaires and skin conductance responses) to capture the effect of the haptic feedback on users viewing experiences.

The present study contributes to the growing literature of haptic experience [27] and multisensory experience design [25]. First, we demonstrate the integration of mid-air haptic feedback into audiovisual content in form of a simple haptic pattern. This approach can be further extended towards a variety of pre-defined and custom-made or even automated patterns in the future. Second, we describe a methodological procedure to study the immediate and more long-term effect of haptic feedback. Finally, we discuss future directions for research, and possible developments in the broader context of media experiences.

RELATED WORK

In this section, we discuss relevant previous work that has explored the potential of the senses to enhance movie experiences. We first present an overview of the media and the senses and we then focus on the use of mid-air haptics and the challenges of designing haptic feedback for one-minute movies.

The senses (i.e. smell, taste, and touch) are a relevant component of Human-Computer Interaction [24] and have been studied in the context of interactive media [29]. The MPEG-V ISO standard [12] and Mulsemedia [8] are good examples of the effort made to create standards for the multisensory integration into media.

The sense of smell has been studied with media, in a recent survey Murray [20] exposes various context of olfactory integration with media. On the other hand, the sense of taste has received little attention but recent works [21, 26] show interesting new interaction mechanisms that could open new ways of integrating taste with media. The sense of touch is presented in the next section.

Haptically enhanced media experiences

Touch is a powerful means to communicate emotions [10]. Indeed, researchers have aimed to reproduce its richness in haptic feedback system. Simple examples of such systems include vibrations of our mobile phones [30], video game controllers [7], and force feedback in steering wheels for racing games [11]. More specifically, Israr et al. [13] introduced the idea of Surround Haptics, a new tactile technology that uses a low-resolution grid of vibrating actuators to generate high-resolution, continuous, moving tactile strokes on the human skin. Different game events are mapped to different haptic feedback patterns. Those patterns are sent to the user through a chair embedded with vibratory actuators on the back. This is an interesting example of more immersive experiences that is based on a carefully designed video-tactile-audio gaming environment.

While the previous example of Surround Haptics requires actual physical contact with the user, new haptic technologies that promote the idea of touchless interaction for media experiences have emerged over the last years. Sodhi et al. [28], for example, developed AIREAL, a haptic technology that delivers tactile sensations in free air using vortex-based tactile actuation. An air vortex is a ring of air that can travel at high speeds over larger distances to create free air haptic experiences.

In the present research, we are particularly interested in mid-air haptic technology presented by Shinoda et al. [1], the only mid-air technology that allows the creation of real-time patterns with various frequencies and intensity. It is composed of a series of ultrasonic transducers that emit very high frequency sound waves. When all of the sound waves meet at the same location at the same time, they stimulate the human's skin creating haptic sensations in mid-air. No gloves or attachments to the user's body are required as the feeling is directly projected onto the user's hands (or body part).

Previous work using this mid-air haptic technology has provided insights into the perception and localisation of mid-air haptic stimuli [31], the creation of complex haptic patterns such as shapes [18], and most recently the mediation of emotions through mid-air haptics [23]. The challenge is still to understand how to create the right haptic experience for a given media or movies.

Designing tactile experiences for movies

Various approaches have been explored to design haptic feedback for movies. Danieau et al. [6], for instance, recorded haptic feedback experienced during specific activities (e.g. horse riding) alongside video and sound. Users experienced the movies with 3 different haptic conditions (recorded, randomly generated, and no haptic feedback) and rated them using a Quality of Experience (QoE) questionnaire. Users rated the captured haptic feedback as more immersive than random haptic feedback and the random feedback was also better than no-feedback at all. While those findings are interesting, this approach is mainly focusing on the mirroring of an action (motion) on the screen and hence the stimulation of the visual sense, rather than the sense of touch.

Lemmens et al. [16], in contrast, created patterns for a haptic jacket based on typical touch behaviours from human emotional touch communication (e.g. highly energetic movements to indicate surprise or happiness) as well as based on common wisdoms and sayings (e.g. butterflies in your stomach). Those patterns were presented together with short movies. Users reactions were assessed through physiological measurements (respiration, heart rate, skin conductance level) and questionnaires (SAM [4] and Immersion Questionnaire). The results suggested a positive effect of haptic stimuli on peoples' immersion but they used only one haptic condition per movies, making any comparison between the designed haptics and other approaches impossible.

Israr et al. [14] proposed an approach based on a systematic exploration of haptic feedback and its integration with the other senses, as well as the content and the context of use. The authors built a library that establishes a classification between haptic feedback parameters (i.e. intensity, duration, and stimulus onset asynchrony) and semantic space (e.g. rain, pulse). This library was built and evaluated by users and can be used with various kind of media [34]. Nevertheless, there is still a need to investigate the impact of using a specific pattern during a media experience as it is very likely that the main focus will be on the visual content [9] and can thus outshine the effect of the pattern used.

More creative-focused approaches have been presented. For instance, Kim and al. [15] designed an authoring tool where users can pause a movie and draw the haptic feedback on the screen, focusing of the visual elements they judge relevant. This interface is designed to work with the haptics gloves they designed. Schneider et al. [27] extended this approach in a multi-device toolkit in order to facilitate haptic experience design. The authors designed a single interface capable of supporting various kinds of devices for creating patterns by drawing on the screen. In contrast to the toolbox approach, this toolkit might challenge designers with too many possibilities in the design of tactile experiences, especially when confronted with a new device, such as mid-air technology.

This paper expands on these previous works by designing tactile experiences using mid-air haptics technology.

STUDY

In our research, we investigate the effect of mid-air haptic feedback on short movie experiences. We focus specifically on "one-minute movies", a content format that conveys a complete narrative in one minute and bridges traditional TV with online video consumption (e.g. YouTube). This particular format is featured in the annual "movie minute festival[1]" that challenges movie-makers, writers, animators, artists, designers, and creative producers to develop exciting new content.

Most importantly, this "one-minute movies" format provides us with a specific comparable timeframe for our study investigating the effect of mid-air haptic feedback on viewers' experiences. The study was divided into three main steps: (1) selecting a set of one-minute movies, (2) designing the haptic feedback, and (3) evaluating the viewer experience over time. See an overview on each step in Figure 1. In the following sections, we explain each of the three steps in detail.

Step 1: Selection of the one-minute movies

The one-minute movies for our study were selected from the international one-minute movie festival collection available on YouTube. Before the first step in the user study, we selected a total of 14 one-minute movies and invited four researchers in the field of HCI to watch and rate them using the SAM. Doing so we wanted to ensure a good spread of represented movies as well as a level of agreement with respect the perceived level of valence (positive/negative) and arousal (activation) for each movie.

Each of the four invited HCI researcher was asked to watch the 14 movies and rate them according to arousal and valence using the Self-Assessment Manikin (SAM) questionnaire [4]. We also asked them to rate their liking of the movie on a 7-point Likert scale (1 being 'didn't like it at all' to 7 'liked it a lot'). We compared the ratings for each movie and discussed them with the invited researchers with respect to the agreement on valence (if it was perceived positive, negative, or neutral) and arousal (if the movie had at least one moment of excitement, "peak moment"). The first criterion was to exclude any movies that might lead to contradicting emotional experiences and could hence be avoided for the user study. The second criterion was to inform the design of the haptic feedback along peak (arousing) moments. Based on those two criteria, two movies were excluded (one because of contradicting ratings on the valence, the other because it was perceived neutral with respect to arousal). The remaining 12 movies were used in the first step of the user study (see Figure 1).

Based on this initial pre-study step, we then recruited 22 users for our first step in the user study that lasted around 30 minutes and was rewarded with 6.5 USD. Each of the 22 users was invited to watch the 12 selected one-minute movies in a controlled lab environment. We used again the SAM questionnaire [4] to collect the arousal and valence ratings from users and asked them to rate their liking of each movie using the question "How much did you enjoy the movie?". We also

one-minute movies	Valence	Arousal
Black Hole	Neutral[0.60]	Neutral[0.58]
Chop Chop	Cheerful[0.71]	Neutral[0.53]
Grandpa	Neutral[0.47]	Neutral[0.54]
Loop	Sad[0.38]	High[0.63]
The Key	Neutral[0.63]	Low[0.41]
Wildebeest	Cheerful[0.73]	Neutral[0.59]

Table 1. List of the six selected movies for step two in our study - balancing between low and high valence and arousal movies (scaled to 0 and 1, where 0 is referring to low ratings and 1 to high ratings.

recorded the users Skin Conductance Responses (SCR) for each movie using the Shimmer2 GSR device[2].

To analyse the SCR data (18 out of 20 valid, 2 excluded due to technical problems), we first prepared the data for the analysis by (1) using a windowing function (taking the mean of values in a widow of size 9 to smooth the data and remove imperfections, (2) standardizing the raw data for each user (values from 0 to 1), (3) reducing the frequency of data from 50 Hz to 20 Hz. We then plotted all the data for each user and performed a visual analysis for each movie. All movies showed potential for the second step of the study, meaning that they all had elicited 'peak moments' (captured in the SCR responses) based on which the haptic feedback could be designed. We also took the questionnaire ratings into account in order to balance between low and high valence/arousal movies in the final selection of movies for step two. In the end, we selected six out of the 12 movies for the next step (see Table 1).

Step 2: Creation of haptic feedback

Here we describe the creation and integration of the specific mid-air haptic feedback for the six selected movies. This second step was divided into two main parts: (1) the first part is concerned with the timing of the haptic feedback and (2) the second part discusses the design of the haptic feedback (i.e. haptic pattern).

Temporal integration of the haptic feedback

In order to find the right timing for the haptic feedback (refers to the synchronisation of the haptic feedback with peak moments in a movie), a two-way manual approach was used. First, we used the SCR data (visual representation for each of the 6 selected movies, including amplitude and timing) to inform the key peak moments in the movie across users (see Figure 2). Second, we verified the 3 to 5 highest peaks revealed by the SCR data based on the narrative of the movie by comparing the timings taking into account the delay of the SCR measurements. For example, Figure 2 shows that the third peak in arousal is linked to the crocodile eating the gnu. This peak can be seen in user's SCR data at second 41, and fits the particular moment in the movie around second 39 (taking into account the 1 to 3 seconds' delay of the SCR recording). We created six synchronized haptic sequences, one for each of the short movies according to the recorded peak moments.

In addition, we create one more haptic sequence which was shared across all movies simulating an unsynchronized integration of haptic feedback. For that purpose, we defined

[1]http://www.filminute.com

[2]http://www.shimmersensing.com/

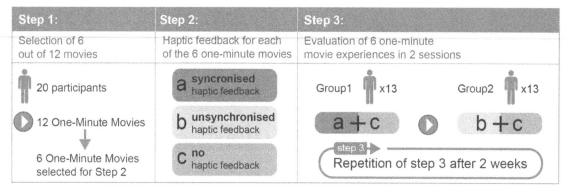

Step 1:	Step 2:	Step 3:
Selection of 6 out of 12 movies	Haptic feedback for each of the 6 one-minute movies	Evaluation of 6 one-minute movie experiences in 2 sessions

Figure 1. Overview on the study set up including the three main steps: (1) selection 6 out of 12 movies, (2) creation of the haptic feedback (i.e. haptic patterns) for the 6 selected movies, (3) evaluation of the 6 movies with and without haptic feedback in two sessions.

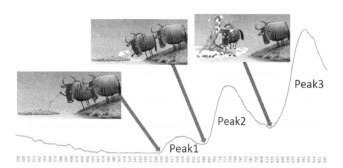

Figure 2. Example: "Wildebeest" movie. Timings and related events with the time on horizontal axis (1 unit = 20ms) and SCR in vertical axis (normalized from 0 to 1).

one pattern of peak moments at second 12, 32, 42 and 48, which resemble the other creations in terms of number of peak moments and durations.

This haptic sequence is the same for all movies. Please note that there is a small possibility that the unsynchronised condition cross with the synchronisation condition, as it was nearly impossible to avoid all 6 conditions. However, we tried to keep the same sequence across all movies to show if haptics even asynchronous has an effect or not.

Design of the haptic pattern
As described in the previous section, each haptic sequence is based on a 60 seconds' timeframe and defines the timing for integrating the haptic feedback. More precisely it sets the timestamps for the design and integration of the synchronized and not synchronized (asynchronous) haptic pattern.

The mid-air haptic pattern itself consists of a single point displayed on the hand. This point changes location every 100ms, following a pseudo-random pattern on a five by five centimetres' square surface (similar to the feeling of rain drops on the hand, however in a dry form [22]). By using this distributed pattern, we avoid focusing on a particular part of the hand, which might be perceived either more positive or negative as previous work has shown (see [23]), and would distract the focus from the temporal integration of the haptic pattern.

The frequency of the displayed point was kept constant at 200Hz and the intensity varied between 30% and 100% de-

pending on pre-defined peak moments in a movie in the synchronous condition or a random time in the asynchronous condition. This design is inspired by the idea of background sound (i.e. soundtrack) which is usually present throughout a movie and increases at important moments in the movie to emphasise the emotions and immersion. Using this approach removes the surprise effect a haptic stimulus might otherwise have if it just appears at peak moments.

Step 3: Viewer experience evaluation
The aim of this evaluation step was to understand the effect of mid-air haptics on users' viewing experience. The evaluation was repeated two weeks later to account for any novelty effects of the new mid-air haptic technology used in our stud [5].

Study design and methods
For this final step in our study, we recruited 32 users. Each user experienced the final 6 movies with and without haptic feedback. One half (i.e. 16 users) received the haptic feedback synchronised with the audiovisual content (movie specific design as described in the previous section) and the other half received the unsynchronised haptic pattern which was the same across all movies (based on pre-defined fixed timestamps across all movies). The order between with and without haptic feedback was counterbalanced across users and repeated after two weeks for each user in each of the two conditions (synchronised versus unsynchronised haptic feedback).

We used a combination of measures (i.e. SAM, Liking Scale, and SCR) to capture users feedback. Users were asked to confirm that they have no sensory impairments and to complete a short demographic questionnaire (age, gender) before starting the experiment. This study was approval by the local University Ethics committee.

Study set up and procedure
For the experiment, users seated comfortably in a chair and watch the movies on a 24" computer screen. Their right hand was positioned on a custom-made armrest that was built as a box integrating the mid-air haptic device. A hole on the top indicates where users would put their palm, so that they can perceive the haptic stimulus on their hand from below.

At the beginning, we allowed users to familiarise themselves with the haptic set up and calibrated the haptic stimulus for each user: a simple focal point was displayed in the middle of

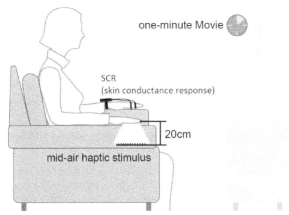

one-minute Movie

SCR
(skin conductance response)

20cm

mid-air haptic stimulus

Figure 3. The study set up showing a user with on the left hand the Shimmer2 GSR device (recording the galvanic skin response) and the right hand above the mid-air haptic device.

the hole where users put their hand. The setup ensured that users kept their hand still while watching the movies (Figure 3). On the left hand, which was resting on arm rest, users were wearing a SCR device. Users were told not to move the left hand during the experiment and to use the right hand to answer all questionnaires (displayed on the screen between each movie).

The study itself involved a succession of six movies. However, the first movie played to each user was a 3 minutes baseline video showing a series of landscapes without any animation or sounds. During that time, SCR data was collected and used as a baseline for the SCR analysis of each user. Then the six movies were played twice, with and without haptic feedback.

Before each movie, a five second black screen was displayed to give enough time to people to put their arm back above the haptic device (right armrest) and to introduce a pause between filling in the questionnaire and starting the next movie. In order to avoid any order effects, we randomised the order of the movies using a balanced latin square of size 12 (6 movies × 2 haptic conditions). After each movie, including the baseline, three main questions were asked about (1) Arousal: "How much of your emotion is activated" Self-Assessment Manikin, (2) Valence: "How did the movie made you feel?" Self-Assessment Manikin, (3) Liking: "How much did you enjoy the movie?" on the semantically Labelled Hedonic Scale (LHS) [17].

Software used

A combination of several software parts was used in the study: c++ for programming the mid-air haptic technology, the Shimmer software for the SCR recording, and c# for the presentation of the questionnaires and movies. All different parts - haptic feedback, movies, and SCR recording - needed to be synchronised in order to ensure the right integration and interpretation of the data. The synchronisation and timing between the software was assured by high precision internal media timers (precision <1ms).

For the SCR recordings, we used the Shimmer 2 sensor attached to two fingers: the index and middle finger of left hand. The settings were set to 50 Hz for the frequency of measurement and 56 kΩ to 128 kΩ for the resistance measure.

Data analysis

The data was collapsed across all movies (the baseline movie was left out from the analysis) and a $2 \times 2 \times 2$ mixed design analysis of variance (ANOVA) with haptics (off and on) and session (first and second), and group (synchronous and asynchronous) was performed on each of the rating scales and the SCR.

The raw data of the SCR were first normalized to 20 Hz, then an amplitude correction was applied which consisted of subtracting the lowest value recorded across movies and to all other values. Afterwards, the log of each value was calculated and the analyses were performed on these values [3].

RESULTS

The results of our analysis of the questionnaires and physiological recordings are presented in this section alongside with the users' information.

Users

In total, there were 54 users involved in all the steps of the study. Due to technical problems with the SCR recording, we removed a total of 8 users from the analysis. The pre-study involved 20 participants (9 female, average age 25), the group 1 which refer to the synchronised haptic condition (synchronised with the peak moments) involved 13 participants (4 males, average age 24.5), and the group 2 which refer to the cross-movies haptic condition (unsynchronised with the peak moments) involved 13 participants (5 males, average age 26).

Questionnaires ratings

A significant interaction ($p < .05$) between session and haptic stimulation was found for the valence ratings, and a significant main effect ($p < .05$) of haptic stimulation was found for the arousal ratings. Paired-samples t-tests performed on the interaction term failed to reveal a significant result ($p = .059$), nonetheless, the valence ratings appear to be higher in the first as compared to the second session, when the haptic stimulation was off (see Figure 4, 1A and 1B). Moreover, Bonferroni-corrected comparisons revealed that the users reported feeling significantly more aroused when the haptic system was on, than when it was off ($p = .014$). A visualization of all the mean ratings is presented in Figure 4.

Skin conductance responses

A summary of the results of the SCR is presented on Figure 5. Only a significant effect of session was found ($p < .001$). In particular, pairwise comparisons revealed that the users were more aroused in the first session than the second session. While no main effect of haptics was found, there was a small general tendency to obtain higher values when the haptic system was on (M = 0.48, SD = 0.29) than when it was off (M = 0.43, SD = 0.027).

DISCUSSION

We studied the possibility of augmentation of one-minute movies with mid-air haptic feedback. Our findings provide insights into how users' arousal and emotional valence are influenced by mid-air haptic stimulation, that is presented in a synchronous or asynchronous fashion alongside the movies.

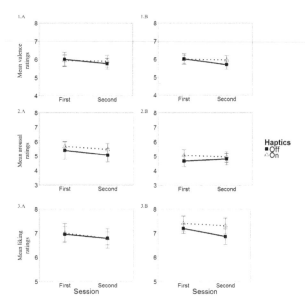

Figure 4. Summary of the questionnaire results. The numbers correspond to the different variables assessed, namely, valence (1), arousal (2), and liking (3), whilst the letters correspond to the (A) synchronous and (B) asynchronous groups. The error bars represent the standard error of the means.

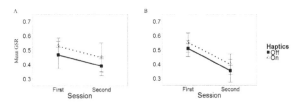

Figure 5. Summary of the SCR results. The letters correspond to the (A) synchronous and (B) asynchronous groups. The error bars represent the standard error of the means.

Below we discuss our findings and their relevance for designing haptically augmented movie experiences.

Effect of mid-air haptics on first and second time viewing experiences

Our results show that the arousal ratings are high across all conditions. This result is in line with previous work demonstrating the arousing effect of haptic feedback while watching movies [6, 16]. While a positive effect was expected for the synchronous condition, the same effect is true for the asynchronous. In other words, even when the haptic pattern does not mimic a specific movie sequence, and is placed randomly alongside the movie, users are still more aroused than with no haptic stimulation. While this is promising in particular for the novel use of mid-air haptic feedback, it is worth noticing that based on the SCR data users' arousal is dropping during the second session in both groups. This can be explained due to the fact that users already knew the movies (familiarity), and were less excited to watch them. Moreover, the novelty effect of the device is also lowered, and yet the experience with haptics is more arousing than without.

In terms of the valence ratings, a borderline significant trend was found for the interaction between Session * Haptics (see Figure 4). Post hoc analysis failed however to reach statisti-

cal significance but we observed a trend in dropped valence ratings in the second session. This might be linked to the expectation of the haptic feedback causing frustration when it is absent. Indeed, most previous work showed that adding haptic feedback to movies and and other multimedia experiences is valuable and gives a boost to the persons' experience [16, 15]. However, its sustainability over time still needs to be verified.

Effect of synchronized versus asynchronized mid-air haptic feedback

No interaction was found on the synchronisation condition (temporal integration of the haptic pattern). This could be explained by the use of a specific mid-air pattern integrated at different relevant peak moments in each movie instead of designing and using a variety of patterns (e.g. making us of different spatial distributions of focal points [23], shapes [18]). Thus, the synchronization of the haptic feedback might be less evident to users, as the pattern was generic and relevant for either synchronized and unsynchronized moments in a movie.

Most previous approaches focus on synchronised feedback [15, 16, 33] where patterns are specifically designed for a sequence. However, considering our findings, which will need further validation, it is promising that the difference between the aforesaid conditions is not significant as this gives rise to alternative design approaches, that could ultimately be simplified through providing producers and content creators with pre-defined patterns, tools to create their own patterns, or even automate the generation of haptic patterns based on the extraction of audio-visual content from a movie, as done in [32]. The synchronisation becomes less important as the emotion can be activated at different times during the sequence of a movie. Such future exploration opportunities around synchronization could become of value in relation to the MPEP-V ISO [12] standard concerned with the delivery of 'sensory information' as part of a general framework.

CONCLUSIONS

This paper provides insights into the effect of mid-air haptic feedback (a new haptic technology) on users viewing experience, specifically applied to one-minute movies. This specific content format (60 seconds narrative) allowed us to systematically investigate the design and evaluation of synchronized versus unsynchronized mid-air haptic stimuli and their effect on users perceived valence and arousal. Mid-air haptic feedback, by its ability to increase immersion, affect emotions, and contribute to the overall quality of experiences without requiring any attachment to the viewers' body, is an opportunity for interactive TV and online video. The findings are promising and open up a space for future explorations of other formats, full length movies enhanced through mid-air haptics.

ACKNOWLEDGMENTS

This project has received funding from the European Research Council (ERC) under the European Union's Horizon 2020 research and innovation programme under grant agreement No 638605.

REFERENCES

1. S. Ando and H. Shinoda. Ultrasonic emission tactile sensing. *Control Systems, IEEE*, 15(1):61–69, Feb 1995.

2. A. M. Baranowski and H. Hecht. The big picture: Effects of surround on immersion and size perception. *Perception*, 43(10):1061, 2014.

3. W. Boucsein. *Electrodermal activity*. Springer Science & Business Media, 2012.

4. M. M. Bradley and P. J. Lang. Measuring emotion: The self-assessment manikin and the semantic differential. *Journal of Behavior Therapy and Experimental Psychiatry*, 25(1):49 – 59, 1994.

5. T. Carter, S. A. Seah, B. Long, B. Drinkwater, and S. Subramanian. Ultrahaptics: Multi-point mid-air haptic feedback for touch surfaces. In *Proceedings of the 26th Annual ACM Symposium on User Interface Software and Technology*, UIST '13, pages 505–514, New York, NY, USA, 2013. ACM.

6. F. Danieau, J. Fleureau, A. Cabec, P. Kerbiriou, P. Guillotel, N. Mollet, M. Christie, and A. Lecuyer. Framework for enhancing video viewing experience with haptic effects of motion. In *Haptics Symposium (HAPTICS), 2012 IEEE*, pages 541–546, March 2012.

7. M. Faust and Y.-H. Yoo. Haptic feedback in pervasive games. In *Third International Workshop on Pervasive Gaming Applications*, volume 7, pages 1–8, 2006.

8. G. Ghinea, C. Timmerer, W. Lin, and S. R. Gulliver. Mulsemedia: State of the art, perspectives, and challenges. *ACM Trans. Multimedia Comput. Commun. Appl.*, 11(1s):17:1–17:23, Oct. 2014.

9. D. Hecht and M. Reiner. Sensory dominance in combinations of audio, visual and haptic stimuli. *Experimental brain research*, 193(2):307–314, 2009.

10. M. J. Hertenstein, R. Holmes, M. McCullough, and D. Keltner. The communication of emotion via touch. *Emotion*, 9(4):566–573, 2009.

11. S. Hwang and J. hee Ryu. The haptic steering wheel: Vibro-tactile based navigation for the driving environment. In *2010 8th IEEE International Conference on Pervasive Computing and Communications Workshops (PERCOM Workshops)*, pages 660–665, March 2010.

12. Information technology – Media context and control. Standard, International Organization for Standardization, Geneva, CH, Jan. 2014.

13. A. Israr, S.-C. Kim, J. Stec, and I. Poupyrev. Surround haptics: Tactile feedback for immersive gaming experiences. In *CHI '12 Extended Abstracts on Human Factors in Computing Systems*, CHI EA '12, pages 1087–1090, New York, NY, USA, 2012. ACM.

14. A. Israr, S. Zhao, K. Schwalje, R. Klatzky, and J. Lehman. Feel effects: Enriching storytelling with haptic feedback. *ACM Trans. Appl. Percept.*, 11(3):11:1–11:17, Sept. 2014.

15. Y. Kim, J. Cha, I. Oakley, and J. Ryu. Exploring tactile movies: An initial tactile glove design and concept evaluation. *IEEE MultiMedia*, PP(99):1–1, 2015.

16. P. Lemmens, F. Crompvoets, D. Brokken, J. van den Eerenbeemd, and G.-J. de Vries. A body-conforming tactile jacket to enrich movie viewing. In *EuroHaptics conference, 2009 and Symposium on Haptic Interfaces for Virtual Environment and Teleoperator Systems. World Haptics 2009. Third Joint*, pages 7–12, New York, NY, USA, March 2009. IEEE.

17. J. Lim, A. Wood, and B. G. Green. Derivation and evaluation of a labeled hedonic scale. *Chemical senses*, 34(9):739–751, 2009.

18. B. Long, S. A. Seah, T. Carter, and S. Subramanian. Rendering volumetric haptic shapes in mid-air using ultrasound. *ACM Trans. Graph.*, 33(6):181:1–181:10, Nov. 2014.

19. R. B. Lull and B. J. Bushman. Immersed in violence: Presence mediates the effect of 3d violent video gameplay on angry feelings. 2014.

20. N. Murray, B. Lee, Y. Qiao, and G.-M. Muntean. Olfaction-enhanced multimedia: A survey of application domains, displays, and research challenges. *ACM Comput. Surv.*, 48(4):56:1–56:34, May 2016.

21. H. Nakamura and H. Miyashita. Augmented gustation using electricity. In *Proceedings of the 2Nd Augmented Human International Conference*, AH '11, pages 34:1–34:2, New York, NY, USA, 2011. ACM.

22. M. Obrist, S. A. Seah, and S. Subramanian. Talking about tactile experiences. In *Proceedings of the SIGCHI Conference on Human Factors in Computing Systems*, CHI '13, pages 1659–1668, New York, NY, USA, 2013. ACM.

23. M. Obrist, S. Subramanian, E. Gatti, B. Long, and T. Carter. Emotions mediated through mid-air haptics. In *Proceedings of the 33rd Annual ACM Conference on Human Factors in Computing Systems*, CHI '15, pages 2053–2062, New York, NY, USA, 2015. ACM.

24. M. Obrist, C. Velasco, C. Vi, N. Ranasinghe, A. Israr, A. Cheok, C. Spence, and P. Gopalakrishnakone. Sensing the future of hci: Touch, taste, and smell user interfaces. *interactions*, 23(5):40–49, Aug. 2016.

25. M. Obrist, C. Velasco, C. T. Vi, N. Ranasinghe, A. Israr, A. D. Cheok, C. Spence, and P. Gopalakrishnakone. Touch, taste, & smell user interfaces: The future of multisensory hci. In *Proceedings of the 2016 CHI Conference Extended Abstracts on Human Factors in Computing Systems*, CHI EA '16, pages 3285–3292, New York, NY, USA, 2016. ACM.

26. N. Ranasinghe and E. Y.-L. Do. Digital lollipop: Studying electrical stimulation on the human tongue to simulate taste sensations. *ACM Transactions on Multimedia Computing, Communications, and Applications (TOMM)*, 13(1):5, 2016.

27. O. S. Schneider, A. Israr, and K. E. MacLean. Tactile animation by direct manipulation of grid displays. In *Proceedings of the 28th Annual ACM Symposium on User Interface Software & Technology*, UIST '15, pages 21–30, New York, NY, USA, 2015. ACM.

28. R. Sodhi, I. Poupyrev, M. Glisson, and A. Israr. Aireal: Interactive tactile experiences in free air. *ACM Trans. Graph.*, 32(4):134:1–134:10, July 2013.

29. C. Timmerer, M. Waltl, B. Rainer, and N. Murray. *Sensory Experience: Quality of Experience Beyond Audio-Visual*, pages 351–365. Springer International Publishing, Cham, 2014.

30. S. u. Rehman, J. Sun, L. Liu, and H. Li. Turn your mobile into the ball: Rendering live football game using vibration. *IEEE Transactions on Multimedia*, 10(6):1022–1033, Oct 2008.

31. G. Wilson, T. Carter, S. Subramanian, and S. A. Brewster. Perception of ultrasonic haptic feedback on the hand: Localisation and apparent motion. In *Proceedings of the SIGCHI Conference on Human Factors in Computing Systems*, CHI '14, pages 1133–1142, New York, NY, USA, 2014. ACM.

32. Y.-H. Yang, Y.-C. Lin, Y.-F. Su, and H. H. Chen. A regression approach to music emotion recognition. *IEEE Transactions on audio, speech, and language processing*, 16(2):448–457, 2008.

33. Z. Yuan, G. Ghinea, and G. M. Muntean. Quality of experience study for multiple sensorial media delivery. In *2014 International Wireless Communications and Mobile Computing Conference (IWCMC)*, pages 1142–1146, Aug 2014.

34. S. Zhao, O. Schneider, R. Klatzky, J. Lehman, and A. Israr. Feelcraft: Crafting tactile experiences for media using a feel effect library. In *Proceedings of the Adjunct Publication of the 27th Annual ACM Symposium on User Interface Software and Technology*, UIST' 14 Adjunct, pages 51–52, New York, NY, USA, 2014. ACM.

Project Orpheus

A Research Study into 360° Cinematic VR

Mirjam Vosmeer
Amsterdam University
of Applied Sciences
Amsterdam, The Netherlands
m.s.vosmeer@hva.nl

Ben Schouten
Amsterdam University
of Applied Sciences
Amsterdam, The Netherlands
b.a.m.schouten@hva.nl

ABSTRACT

When creating content for virtual reality, filmmakers find that they need to re-evaluate the tools they have traditionally used to tell their stories, and explore the new possibilities that this particular medium has to offer. To determine how storytelling- and filmmaking tools function in VR, the concept of presence is currently being re-evaluated for its possibilities to be used as a measurement of the relative effectiveness of these tools. The research project *Project Orpheus* is presented as a case study into trans-medial storytelling, exploring how the impact of a traditional television show may be reinforced by an immersive VR experience. The movie was subsequently used to conduct a small qualitative study into the use of 3D sound to guide the viewers attention in VR.

Author Keywords

Cinematic VR; virtual reality; surround video; Oculus Rift; VR; transmedial storytelling; presence; immersion

ACM Classification Keywords

H.5.1 [Multimedia Information Systems] Artificial, Augmented and Virtual Realities. H.1.2 [User/Machine Systems] Human Factors

INTRODUCTION

After Facebook paid 2 billion dollar to take over the company Oculus VR in March 2014 [7], the head-mounted display named Oculus Rift became world famous practically overnight. In the summer of 2017, there is hardly a technology festival, ICT conference or communication symposium left in the world that does not offer a range of demo sessions on the wonders of virtual reality (VR). While this term has already been in use for several decades, traditionally referring to all kinds of experiences that are linked to internet, videogames or cyberspace, it currently seems to be used specifically to

Permission to make digital or hard copies of all or part of this work for personal or classroom use is granted without fee provided that copies are not made or distributed for profit or commercial advantage and that copies bear this notice and the full citation on the first page. Copyrights for components of this work owned by others than ACM must be honored. Abstracting with credit is permitted. To copy otherwise, or republish, to post on servers or to redistribute to lists, requires prior specific permission and/or a fee. Request permissions from Permissions@acm.org.

TVX '17, June 14-16, 2017, Hilversum, Netherlands
© 2017 Association for Computing Machinery.
ACM ISBN 978-1-4503-4529-3/17/06…$15.00
http://dx.doi.org/10.1145/3077548.3077559

those kind of experiences in which the user is immersed in a virtual 360° environment, using a head-mounted display such as Oculus Rift.

Since 2014, a range of other displays have been introduced that offer similar experiences such as the Samsung Gear VR, the HTC Vive, or the basic but surprisingly effective cardboard viewers. As technological developments are moving ahead with dazzling speed, continuously examining new features, the need for engaging or useful content that can be viewed in 360° environments expands accordingly. Interested parties from all kinds of backgrounds eagerly follow the latest explorations into VR to determine how it may be used for their specific purposes and projects are set up to investigate the ways in which audiences may be engaged. In October 2015, for instance, the New York Times presented a collaborative project with Google, offering a series of virtual reality documentary movies, for which a million NYT subscribers had been provided with a Google Cardboard viewer, to be able to *'Put yourself at the center of our stories in an immersive virtual reality experience'* [14].

Also in academic literature, the use and evaluation of VR systems and applications is rapidly gaining attention. Based on a systematic literature review, Berntsen et al concluded that the main categories for studies regarding VR are health, exploration and presentation entertainment [1]. Within the field of healthcare, Diemer et al reviewed the possibilities that VR offers for the investigation of pathological processes in mental disorders, concluding that especially the treatment of anxiety disorders may benefit from the use of VR [6].

But while the technology races ahead and VR companies are being overflown with requests to create 'immersive' VR experiences for all kinds of purposes, the knowledge on how to produce high quality narrative VR content is developing at a somewhat slower pace. Especially the kind of VR experience that is referred to as *cinematic VR* or *surround video*, in which the VR world is not computer-generated but filmed in a real life environment, poses all kinds of intriguing questions that VR developers all over the world are just starting to unravel.

Researchers from both academic and industrial backgrounds are currently exploring the specific qualities of

VR, and studying the ways in which users (or patients, or clients, or customers) may indeed be affected by a message that is brought to them through an environment of which they feel they are being a part of, instead of just observing it on a flat screen [5, 9, 10, 23]. At the same time, filmmakers are busy sorting out the new possibilities that 360° movies offer for storytelling – and trying to find ways to work around the complications that they are also suddenly confronted with. Not only does the production of a movie in 360° degrees involve problems with for instance set dressing, lighting and directing of the actors, also scriptwriters, editors and sound designers are facing new challenges that are inherent to the medium. On a theoretical level, one of the most intriguing issues in this field is the changing relationship between the user and the movie, and how the concept of *presence* is currently being investigated for its possibilities to function as a key concept into the evaluation of storytelling for VR.

In this paper we will first discuss how new insights into VR storytelling may lead towards the development of new cinematic constructs and film language. We will then investigate how existing theory on the concept of (spatial) presence can be used to support further research into the relation between the user and the medium in VR. In the next part of the paper we will discuss *Project Orpheus* [25], our own case study into trans-medial storytelling, exploring how the impact of a traditional television show may be reinforced by a VR experience. The movie was subsequently used to conduct a small qualitative study into the use of 3D sound to guide the viewers attention in VR, which is described in the last paragraph. In the current text, we focus on issues that evolve around storytelling and user experiences and we will not go into technological details that have to do with the use of a 360° camera or the specific characteristics of VR post-production, such as stitching and editing.

DEVELOPING A NEW FILM LANGUAGE

Filmmakers who start to explore the possibilities of cinematic VR, find themselves challenged in a way that is almost as overwhelming as it is fascinating. Harrison Weber, journalist of Venturebeat, described the impact of VR on filmmakers like this: *'It's a lot like film, only it puts the audience inside your story. With it, you can create entire worlds for your audience but none of the original rules of cinema apply. How do you create your art when all of your tools have changed?'* [24].

In a private interview, TV-producer Kaja Wolffers of Nl-film formulated his initial confusion like this: *'As a director, I can point out the importance of a character's words or reaction by zooming in on a face. But here I can't do that anymore...'* Indeed, control over the frame is the first thing that filmmakers have to let go when telling their story in a surround setting. In cinema, the four techniques that have traditionally formed the 'tools' that filmmakers

rely on to tell their stories are cinematography, mise-en-scene, sound and editing [2]. With the introduction of cinematic VR however, each of these tools are in need of reconsideration, and the medium may actually require the development of new cinematic constructs and film language [8]. Filmmakers not only need to let go of control over the frame, they also can no longer direct what it is that their audience is looking at, at any specific moment during a viewing of their film. Because the image is projected in 360°, the viewer has the freedom to look around in the scene, and focus her attention on the people, objects and details that she chooses, instead of the ones that are pointed out to her by the creator of the film. This inability to control the audience's attention poses a problem when a filmmaker intends to present a narrative that relies on a specific sequence of events to unfold the plot in the most effective way. But while the director can not use camera movement or frame to guide the viewers attention, there still are a number of other tools available that can be used for this purpose. Actors themselves, for instance, can give all kinds of signals to the viewer, by looking, pointing or walking in a certain direction. Also use of light and shade can be manipulated to direct the user's glance. Sound is also a powerful tool to direct the viewers attention, as we will discuss later in this text. Academic studies that intend to gain knowledge about the various techniques to guide the user's attention within a VR experience and the consequences that these techniques may have on the engagement of the user with the film, have only recently started to be published [15].

Because the user has the possibility to look around freely, even a linear VR experience can be considered as an interactive experience. The interaction between the viewer and the image theoretically causes every user to have her own version of the experience, as it will never be *exactly* the same for every individual. This type of user position is not fully passive - or *lean-back* - as is the case with a traditional movie, nor is it fully active - or *lean-forward* – like playing a videogame is. Vosmeer and Schouten have therefore proposed to use the term *lean-in* for this kind of engagement with a medium [22].

PRESENCE AND IMMERSION

An important source of knowledge about storytelling in VR is the website of the Oculus Story Studio itself. On their blog, the members of the VR team write about their latest projects, and in all openness, about the challenges they encountered while creating them and the lessons they learned from it [21]. Many insights are focused on the links between presence, narrative and interactivity and how they sometimes seem to exclude or overrule each other in VR. On the blog, lead environment artist Matt Burdette states: *'The gospel around here at Story Studio is to deliver a compelling, immersive, evocative VR experience by telling a great story. But there's another mantra we believe in: "Presence is VR Magic"* [3].

Indeed, one of the most important concepts that come up in both academic and industrial debates around use and creation of VR is *presence* and, in relation to that, *immersion* [13, 19]. The term presence is usually defined as the 'sense of being there' [17] and described as a 'feeling of actually being on location in a story rather then experiencing it from the outside' [8]. Immersion is the other term that often comes up in debates about presence and VR. Roth differentiates immersion from presence by defining immersion as an objective criterion which depends on hardware and software [18]. Presence is subsequently defined as the psychological more subjective sense of being in the environment, and mainly influenced by the content of the mediated world. Immersion could be seen as a quality of the medium, in this case a VR movie, while presence is a characteristic of the user experience. Hence, higher immersion may lead to or result in deeper presence.

Riva et al analyzed the possible use of VR as an affective medium and conclude that there may be a circular interaction between presence and emotions: while the sense of presence is higher in environments that have an emotional impact on their users, their emotional state is also influenced by the level of presence [17]. North and North have pointed the importance of evaluating the user experience within design and development of VR systems, and state that there is therefore an increased need to conduct empirical studies in which the factors that create a higher sense of presence are investigated [16]. In their study on the difference between immersive VR and traditional VR they conclude that the immersive 360° experiences lead to a higher sense of presence.

However, while the presence is currently almost being proposed as the single defining aspect of immersive VR, theoretical investigations into the presence (or spatial presence, or telepresence) started many years ago, as Wirth and all already stated in 2007 [26], when they identified *"...the rapid career of the concept of presence"* and connected presence to existing concepts within media psychology such as attention, involvement, perceived reality and transportation and indicate that also more traditional media such as books or television shows have the property to transport their readers or viewers to a different world. Busselle and Bilandzic discuss the distinction between presence that stems from sensory stimulation, such as the visual and audio cues in a 360° immersive environment, and transportation that has more to do with the narrative itself and may refer to, for instance, feeling present in a novel [4]. Lombard and Ditton have described presence as a 'perceptual illusion of nonmediation' [12], indicating that in an ideal experience of presence, the user is no longer aware of the fact that there is technology involved (for instance the pages of a book, the screen of a television or a head mounted display). With sensory induced presence, this illusion of nonmediation may be caused by technology that is working flawlessly, without bugs or lags or other cues that might distract the user's attention. Kratky also stresses the need for investigation into VR user interfaces that strive towards invisibility, in order to confront the user with technology as little as possible [11].

Sanchez-Vives has pointed out how the measurement of presence has thus become an important challenge in VR research [20]. By measuring the level of presence that a user experiences, the relative 'effectiveness' of different elements of film language and cinematic constructs may be evaluated. In other words: if a filmmaker wants to find out if a certain audio technique or lighting design helps to heighten immersion, she can make use of questionnaires that have been developed within the field media psychology to measure the level of presence that is experienced by her viewers.

In this way, Vosmeer, Roth and Schouten [23] have used the questionnaire that Roth [18] developed to evaluate the impact of auditory feedback during an interactive narrative VR experience. They found that users who received a short audio signal on interactive points in the movie, reported a lower level of presence than users in the control condition, in which interactive points could be touched without audio signal. This finding can be linked to the beforementioned illusion of nonmediation, meaning that an audio signal can be interpreted as an unwelcome reminder of the fact that one is surrounded by technology.

CASE STUDY: *PROJECT ORPHEUS*
Although the VR video *Project Orpheus* can be watched as a stand alone production, it was set up as a 'VR-companion piece' to accompany the new Dutch television drama series of the same title, that was broadcasted in the Netherlands in the spring of 2016. The project is a collaboration project with students and researchers of the Amsterdam University of Applied Sciences and the national television broadcasting company AVROTROS, the television production company NL Film and the VR production company WeMakeVR [25]. The challenge that the students were confronted with was: *'Can you create a VR experience that reinforces the impact of a traditional TV-show?'* The TV-show *Project Orpheus* was used as the starting point for this trans-medial storytelling experiment. In this show a group of young doctors and hospital interns experiment with near-death experiments, which leads to all kinds of dramatic events. While the VR production was set up as a student assignment, it also served as a research instrument for the academic partner, as a demo tool for the VR company and as a publicity generator for the television partners. In this paragraph we will discuss some issues that were confronted while producing the VR video, and describe a short exploratory study into the user experience that was conducted using this movie.

User perspective

In a VR experience, the producer has to make certain decisions on how the user will eventually be connected to the narrative. It can for instance be decided to exclude the viewer completely from the story and give her a 'fly on the wall'-perspective. However, during earlier experiments in the narrative design process it was found that this could lead to a feeling of awkwardness, as users in test groups described it. To overcome this, in *Project Orpheus* the user is directly addressed in the first scene, when she wakes up in a hospital bed. In this scene, a senior medic enters the hospital room, looks straight into the camera and starts telling 'you' – the patient in the bed – about a terrible tragedy that happened in the hospital some years ago, when a little boy died. The ghost of the little boy apparently still comes back to haunt patients who are under anesthesia and the doctor begs 'you' to help him. 'You' are asked to go under anesthesia as well, and use your willpower to force the boy to leave the hospital. While in the 'near death'-scenes that follow there is no direct contact between the user and the characters anymore, the sense of presence and of being part of the story that been established in the first scene, is enough to guide the user through the next three VR scenes.

Reinforcing the Impact of a traditional TV-show

As the VR scene was shot in the original sets of the TV-series, the 'VR companion-piece' did indeed give viewers the sense of being in the same hospital that they had seen on television. For publicity purposes, this already was a novel and attractive fact to communicate to the outside world. On the level of narrative, however, the experience is also an interesting experiment towards trans-medial storytelling. The viewer who is watching the series on television witnesses characters that undergo a near-death experience, from the perspective of an outsider. In the VR experience, however, the perspective becomes first-person, and she now participates herself in the same adventure that she has seen the characters on the screen be engaged in. The supernatural near death-theme in *Project Orpheus* is therefore transferred much more intensely when the user feels that she herself is undergoing it, instead of having to imagine what characters on the screen may feel. This sense of presence makes the VR experience a powerful way to engage the viewer in the overall narrative of a trans-medial storytelling project, and can therefore reinforce the impact of the TV-show on multiple levels.

Guiding the Viewers Attention

As mentioned earlier, in cinema, the four techniques that have traditionally formed the 'tools' that filmmakers rely on to tell their stories are: cinematography, mise-en-scene, sound and editing [2]. With the introduction of cinematic VR however, each of these tools are in need of reconsideration. In the first scene of *Project Orpheus*, the viewer has been primed by the doctor to focus her gaze on the ghost of the little boy who wanders around in the hospital. During the research design process of the VR movie, it was found that in order to guide the viewer's attention, sound seemed to be of utmost importance. When the little boys appears, his giggling or the sound of his footsteps should ideally inspire the user to direct her gaze in his direction. For a 360° environment, it is possible to create a 3D sound design that enables sound to come from all directions, instead of just left or right. The next issue that came up in the testing phase, was about whether the sound should exactly match the image, or whether it should be used as a notification for the user to turn her head in a right direction. In other words: if the little boy comes up from behind, should his giggling and footsteps be heard in advance, so the user has time to look behind her – or should the sound exactly match his visual appearance. In the last case, there is a risk that the user first needs to 'search' for him, and thus might miss the entrance of the boy altogether.

Experiment with 3D sound design

The application of 3D sound design can be seen as one of the traditional filmmakers tools that needs to be re-evaluated for use in VR. Using the VR movie *Project Orpheus*, we conducted an qualitative exploratory study on how 3D sound design may work best to guide the viewers attention. In order to do this, we had two different sound designs developed for the movie: in the standard version the sound exactly matched the image, while in the experimental version, the sound was used to 'announce' the image, giving the viewer time to look around and locate the point of interest that the director intended. We showed the movies to 16 respondents, who watched either the standard or the experimental version, and interviewed them afterwards about their experience.

Without exceptions, the respondents all enjoyed the movie. Especially first-time users were quite overwhelmed when they experienced the immersive qualities of cinematic VR. As none of the respondents had watched the television series, we were not able to further investigate the impact that the VR experience may have had on the appreciation of the show. However, *Project Orpheus* can also be viewed as a stand alone movie, and all respondents reported to have had a strong sense 'of being there' in the hospital narrative, most of them indicating it would be a 4 on a scale from 1 to 5. When asked specifically about the qualities of the sound, respondents in the experimental condition more often reported to have been distracted by the sound. They mentioned, for instance, that they heard the giggling but did not see the boy yet. As distraction by sound means that the attention is drawn towards the system, instead of letting the user experience non-mediation, we might interpret this as a sign that the experimental version, in which sound is used as an announcement for the visuals, leads to lesser presence than the standard version.

However, we also noticed that other variables may have had more effect on the user experience than the sound design itself. Differences between experienced users and people who had not been confronted with a VR movie before seemed extensive: experienced users often immediately started to investigate the VR world by looking around in all directions to find out where they were, while first time users were often quite overwhelmed and remained fairly motionless. The experienced users also reported different details, and were more critical about the narrative itself. Therefore, in the current setting it has almost been impossible to make a clear distinction between users of the standard version or the experimental version of the movie.

CONCLUDING THOUGHTS

Virtual reality is currently going through a phase of worldwide excitement, and both industry and academic researchers curiously explore the ways stories can be told within this new kind of *lean in* media experience. It promises to be an interesting means to engage television audiences with the content of a traditional television show, by offering the possibility to re-enact scenes from the show from the perspective of a character in the show.

For VR, traditional filmmaking tools need to be reconsidered. To determine how storytelling- and filmmaking strategies function in VR, the concept of presence is currently being re-evaluated for its possibilities to be used as a measurement of their relative effectiveness. In our current exploratory study, we investigated how 3D sound design may guide the viewers attention. It seemed that for 3D sound to be as unobtrusive as possible, it needs to match the image, instead of being used as an announcement of action. However, in order to be able to make clear distinctions between different groups of respondents, differences between users, especially their level of previous experiences with VR, needs to be taken in consideration. For our further research into the ways to guide the viewers attention in VR, we aim to transport our current findings towards a quantitative study in which this issue will be included.

ACKNOWLEDGMENTS

This research project is funded by the Amsterdam Creative Industries Network and by SiA RAAK – Nationaal Regieorgaan Praktijkgericht Onderzoek.

REFERENCES

1. Kristina Berntsen, Ricardo Colomo Palacios and Eduardo Herranz. 2016. Virtual reality and its uses: a systematic literature review. In *Proceedings of the Fourth International Conference on Technological Ecosystems for Enhancing Multiculturality* (ACM), 435-439.
2. David Bordwell, Kristin Thompson, and Jeremy Ashton. *Film art: An introduction*. Vol. 7. New York: McGraw-Hill, 1997.
3. Matt Burdette. 2016. The Swayze effect. https://storystudio.oculus.com/en-us/blog/the-swayze-effect/ Retrieved 12 April 2017.
4. Rick Busselle and Helena Bilandzic. 2009. Measuring Narrative Engagement, *Media Psychology*, 12,4: 321-347.
5. Jaehee Cho, Tsung-Han Lee, Joel Ogden, Amy Stewart, Tsung-Yu Tsai, Junwen Chen, and Ralph Vituccio. 2016. Imago: presence and emotion in virtual reality. In *ACM SIGGRAPH 2016 VR Village* (ACM), 6.
6. Julia Diemer, Georg W. Alpers, Henrik M. Peperkorn, Youssef Shiban, and Andreas Mühlberger. 2015. The impact of perception and presence on emotional reactions: a review of research in virtual reality. *Frontiers in psychology* 6: 26.
7. Stuart Dredge. 2014. Facebook closes its $2bn Oculus Rift acquisition. What next? https://www.theguardian.com/technology/2014/jul/22/facebook-oculus-rift-acquisition-virtual-reality Retrieved 12 April 2017.
8. Rorik Henrikson, Bruno Araujo, Fanny Chevalier, Karan Singh, and Ravin Balakrishnan. 2016. Multi-Device Storyboards for Cinematic Narratives in VR. In *Proceedings of the 29th Annual Symposium on User Interface Software and Technology* (ACM): 787-796.
9. Gray Hodgkinson. 2016. Lock up your stories - here comes Virtual Reality. *TECHART: Journal of Arts and Imaging Science* 3,4: 10-14.
10. Martijn Kors, Gabriele Ferri, Erik van der Spek, Cas Ketel, and Ben Schouten. 2016. A Breathtaking Journey: On the Design of an Empathy-Arousing Mixed-Reality Game. In *Proceedings of the 2016 Annual Symposium on Computer-Human Interaction in Play* (ACM), 91-104.
11. Andreas Kratky. 2016. Metaphor and Storytelling in Interface Design for Virtual Reality. In *International Conference on Universal Access in Human-Computer Interaction*: 287-300.
12. Matthew Lombard and Theresa Ditton. 1997. At the heart of it all: The concept of presence. *Journal of Computer - Mediated Communication* 3, 2: 0-0.
13. Moynihan, T. The Stunning Allumette Is the First VR Film Masterpiece. 2016. http://www.wired.com/2016/04/alumette-groundbreaking-vr-film-tribeca/ Retrieved 12 April 2017.
14. New York Times. 2015. http://www.nytimes.com/marketing/nytvr/ Retrieved 12 April 2017.
15. Lasse Nielsen, Matias Møller, Sune Hartmeyer, Troels Ljung, Niels Nilsson, Rolf Nordahl and Stefania Serafin. 2016. Missing the point: an exploration of how to guide users' attention during cinematic virtual reality. In *Proceedings of the 22nd ACM Conference on Virtual Reality Software and Technology (ACM)*, 229-232.
16. Max North and Sarah North. 2016. A comparative study of sense of presence of traditional virtual reality and immersive environments. *Australasian Journal of Information Systems*, 20.

17. Giuseppe Riva, Fabrizia Mantovani, Claret Samantha Capideville, Alessandra Preziosa, Francesca Morganti, Daniela Villani, Andrea Gaggioli, Cristina Botella, and Mariano Alcañiz. 2007. Affective interactions using virtual reality: the link between presence and emotions. *CyberPsychology & Behavior* 10, 1: 45-56.

18. Christian Roth. 2016. Experiencing Interactive Storytelling. PhD thesis. http://dare.ubvu.vu.nl/handle/1871/53840 Retrieved 12 April 2017.

19. Marie Laure Ryan. 2015. Narrative as virtual reality 2: Revisiting Immersion and Interactivity in Literature and Electronic Media. JHU Press.

20. Maria Sanchez-Vives and Mel Slater. 2005. From presence to consciousness through virtual reality. *Nature Reviews Neuroscience* 6,4: 332-339.

21. Unfeld, S. 5 lessons learned while making Lost. https://storystudio.oculus.com/en-us/blog/5-lessons-learned-while-making-lost/ Retrieved 12 April 2017.

22. Mirjam Vosmeer and Ben Schouten. 2014. Interactive cinema: Engagement and interaction. In *International Conference on Interactive Digital Storytelling*, 140-147.

23. Mirjam Vosmeer, Christian Roth and Ben Schouten. 2015. Interaction in surround video: the effect of auditory feedback on enjoyment. In *International Conference on Interactive Digital Storytelling*, pp. 202-210.

24. Harrison Weber. 2016. How filmmakers are inventing the language of VR. https://venturebeat.com/2016/05/04/how-filmmakers-are-inventing-the-language-of-vr/ Retrieved 12 April 2017.

25. WeMakeVR. 2016. *Project Orpheus. (*available in the Appstore for both Android and iOS, embedded in the free app *WeShareVR)*

26. Werner Wirth, Tilo Hartmann, Saskia Böcking, Peter Vorderer, Christoph Klimmt, Holger Schramm, Timo Saari, Jari Laarni, Niklas Ravaja, Feliz Ribeiro Gouveia, Frank Biocca, Ana Sacau, Lutz Jäncke, Thomas Baumgartner & Petra Jäncke. 2007. A process model of the formation of spatial presence experiences, *Media Psychology*, 9, 3: 493-525.

Enhancing Interaction with Dual-Screen Television Through Display Commonalities

Timothy Neate[1], Michael Evans[2], Matt Jones[1]

[1]FIT Lab, Department of Computer Science, Swansea University, Swansea, UK
[2]BBC Research and Development, Salford, Greater Manchester, UK
[1]firstname.lastname@swansea.ac.uk, [2]firstname.lastname@rd.bbc.co.uk

Figure 1: A user utilising display commonalities. In a) we can see the feed from the TV duplicated in the corner of the tablet as the user browses related information on the web; then in b) the same concept is implemented for a companion application; in c) the TV material is mirrored behind a companion application; and, in d), the user is casting her companion application into the corner of the TV.

ABSTRACT

Second screening – engaging with a mobile device while watching TV – is ubiquitous. Previous research demonstrates that this is hampered by cognitive and physical disjuncts between the simultaneous content streams. To engage effectively with more than one screen, users must manage their attention, for example, by frequently adjusting their gaze or posture. This can lead to cognitive effort, which leads to disengagement, content sacrifice, and ultimately, affects user experience (UX) negatively. In this paper, we look to improve the design of the dual-screen scenario through *display commonalities*; the mirroring of one content stream (e.g., TV material or second screen content) within the other. We evaluate this design space with professional broadcast practitioners, and then conduct an empirical investigation to determine the impact of the most successful methods towards understanding their impact, and designing towards positive UX with multi-device scenarios.

ACM Classification Keywords

H.5.m. Information Interfaces and Presentation: Misc.

Author Keywords

Second screening; screen mirroring; attention; TV; companion content; display commonalities; multi-device

Permission to make digital or hard copies of all or part of this work for personal or classroom use is granted without fee provided that copies are not made or distributed for profit or commercial advantage and that copies bear this notice and the full citation on the first page. Copyrights for components of this work owned by others than ACM must be honored. Abstracting with credit is permitted. To copy otherwise, or republish, to post on servers or to redistribute to lists, requires prior specific permission and/or a fee. Request permissions from permissions@acm.org.
TVX 2017, June 14–16, 2017, Hilversum, The Netherlands.
Copyright is held by the owner/author(s). Publication rights licensed to ACM.
ACM ISBN 978-1-4503-4529-3/17/06 ...$15.00.
http://dx.doi.org/10.1145/3077548.3077549

INTRODUCTION

This decade has seen mobile devices spread into and disrupt almost every commonplace routine. Second screening – the act of engaging with one's mobile device while watching TV – is a salient example of this. Whether users are engaging with social media, searching an actor they recognise, or playing-along with a gameshow, the opportunities for designing cross-device media are evident and numerous. As many of us as 87% are second screening [27], with an even higher proportion of younger audiences having this kind of experience [18], suggesting a strong upwards trend; media entertainment veering strongly towards non-linear, time shifted, and ultimately, multi-device experiences.

Our living rooms are becoming increasingly connected and many of us now have internet-enabled TVs and regularly connect devices to them. Broadcasters, developers and interaction designers now wish to design for this use case by providing multi-device experiences. These are often termed as *companion experiences*. Such content supports a TV programme by providing additional material on a secondary device. This material can vary from interesting related facts and social media, to a full interactive play-along game.

Whether driven by companion applications or by users freely second screening, researchers working in the domain of second screens have surfaced some cognitive and physical constraints of the scenario, which generally reduce the quality of the experience. Second screening typically involves a user gazing down towards their mobile device and, therefore, away from the TV. This means users must monitor the TV for events by listening and catching information in the peripheral of their vision. Then, to engage with the TV and the second screen visually, the user must adjust their gaze, and often their physical posture. The use case implies significant cognitive and physical switching cost, which is not ideal for such leisure scenarios. Moreover, such effects are exacerbated for those who are engaging with complex material, using subtitles, or have some degree of auditory or visual disability.

In this paper, we investigate the potential of duplicating elements of a user experience over multiple devices, so that a user may monitor the visual events of an unattended display on the screen they are focusing on. We term this concept *display commonalities*, illustrated in Figure 1. We investigate this concept by first conducting a focus group with professional content designers at a major broadcaster. By creating prototype dual-screen applications and their respective design space with the practitioners, we establish the most promising designs to focus on. We then use our findings to conduct an empirical investigation of display commonalities with 40 participants in the two most common second screen use cases, with an aim to evaluate their effect and consider how they may be utilised as a design lever for supporting inter-device experiences.

BACKGROUND
The focus of this paper is the duplication of elements across dual-screen UIs to improve UX. Much of the work in the second screen scenario explores how we may measure [7, 22], and intervene in [33, 34] users' attention. However, this work does not consider the full capabilities of the connected living room for the second screen use case. The research around screen mirroring, though fruitful for shared experiences in the living room, generally focuses on how we may design to enhance shared viewing experiences (c.f., the work of McGill et al. [29]). We, in this paper, seek to combine the research around screen mirroring to extend and embellish the UX of multi-device media.

Screen Mirroring
Statistics from a 2013 study with 2600 users suggests that screen mirroring awareness was at around 40% [20]. As of 2016, little recent data exists on screen mirroring penetration, however, given the increasing proliferation of casting services such as Google's Chromecast [19] and Apple's AirPlay [5], it is likely to be an increasing trajectory. The interactions afforded by casting services allow us to utilise the superior interaction capabilities of our touchscreen handheld devices, in tandem with the superior visual capabilities of a large display, such as a TV.

Empirical investigations have looked at how to best cast a device's whole screen to a TV. For example, Fleury et al. [14] investigated user preferences for screen mirroring with a mobile and a TV. Screen mirroring has been further explored with an aim to promote mutual sharing of content between users from their personal mobile devices. For instance, McGill et al. [29] look at how, in a shared viewing experience, we may use the affordances of screen mirroring to foster enhanced collaboration between users of a TV towards equal participation in mirroring.

Second Screening and Cross-Device Experiences
Over the past few years, for users in relatively affluent economies, it has become hard to imagine the living-room media landscape without interactions on a second screen personal device. A nuanced and vast set of second screen behaviours has been noted by the HCI community [10, 23, 38]. These focus around unrelated interactions, such as social media and, more pertinently, related interactions such as searching for information related to a programme, or engaging with points in a debate on social media. It is these related interactions that have fuelled major broadcasters and developers to aspire to create engaging, meaningful cross-device experiences.

Many companion applications address user inclination to discover more about things they have seen in a programme, and much empirical work has explored the provision of programme-specific second screen companion content: typically complementary information [11, 12, 32], related social media [21, 26], and play-along games [8]. Many broadcasters and developers have created companion apps for public distribution (e.g., [1, 30, 31]). These apps aim to support pre-existing behaviours and allow users to better tie together the television programme and the second screen material, creating a more unified cross-device experience.

The HCI community has considered how to improve companion UX using supporting, tangential information: Geerts et al. [17] use a companion application live-synced to a programme to examine the perspectives of users and producers, yielding qualitative and analytics-based insights; Fallahkhair et al. [13] described the potential for supporting language learning through combining a foreign television programme with a companion application; and, much work has looked at how we can provide second screen applications to simplify complex plot lines and concepts [11, 32, 40]. Another avenue of exploration has looked at support for social second screeners through dedicated apps. For example, early work by Regan and Todd [37] on instant messaging in a media centre, has more recently been extended by systems which allow people to share and communicate while watching TV; to become further engaged with their programmes, both when co-located [3, 29] and distributed [6].

In terms of large-scale adoption, many online streaming services now offer interactions on a second screen to support their viewing, for example Amazon Prime Video allows for the casting of video to another display (typically a TV) while engaging with second screen content: the *X-Ray* [2] service provides encyclopaedic, time-synchronised, content and information about people featured in a film when a user interacts.

Dual-Screen Attention: Hinderances and Enhancements
Although, in general, companion experiences are positively received by audiences, there are some clear constraints around the amount of audio-visual information we can attend to. For instance, we are poorly cognitively equipped to deal with simultaneous reading and listening [39]. Deployments and empirical investigations of dual-screen scenarios have suggested that additional cognitive load is introduced when compared to traditional TV use: Basapur et al. [6] note in their deployment of a companion system that users considered this 'active' TV, and not necessarily something one would unwind to. Such findings were also observed by Geerts et al. [17], who noted that viewers had to manage a good balance between engage-

ment and distraction with the second screen application, and return to some details in the application later (i.e., when the TV material was no longer relevant). Moreover, such scenarios are driven by the effect of visual separation (both angular and depth of field) between the TV and the mobile device, which introduces a switching cost [36] and have shown to inhibit presentation of content across screens [42].

In terms of overcoming such issues, viewers regularly pause or rewind to catch up with material they miss during a programme [35]. However, these behaviours mean users are required to to re-watch scenes, or may miss key points in live programming – likely hampering UX. Therefore, towards understanding dual-screen visual attention more completely, work by Holmes et al. [22] and Brown et al. [7] has sought to better comprehend the nuances of this use case through eye-tracking users when engaging with TV and a companion application.

In extension to this work, proactive solutions have been investigated. Geerts et al. [17], for example, suggest that by informing the user when a piece of content will become available, using a timer, that they may then adjust attention in a timely manner. Further, Neate et al. [34] have looked at how to effectively shift a user's attention between screens in a cross-device experience, and how one may vary visual complexity on a handheld device to compensate for the perceived complexity on the TV material [33]. Finally, Valuch et al. [43], when considering the effect of cinematic cuts on a single screen, noted that viewers were able to better re-orient their attention more quickly if visual content is repeated from a pre-cut scene, suggesting that a similar approach may aid reorientation of visual attention in a cross-device experience.

DISPLAY COMMONALITIES DESIGN SPACE

When considering the design space for integrating video feeds into a second screen we sought inspiration from the early interactive TV literature, which often focused on the design of EPGs (Electronic Programme Guides). Although historically remote controlled EPGs often consisted of a video embedded into the top right-hand corner of the TV (screen-in-screen), so that a user may attend to a programme and channel surf, handheld EPGs (c.f, [9, 41]) have not incorporated this. More recently, however, browser-based video experiences have used similar design ideas (e.g., the Floating Youtube Chrome extension [15]). As the user scrolls down the page using this extension (to read an article, for example) the video embeds into the corner and follows as they scroll. Further, to allow for multitasking, recent iPad devices also implement a screen-in-screen feature to allow users to attend to video [4]. Such designs, however, only allow for the direct mirroring of the mobile device's screen, and do not afford users the opportunity to integrate individual elements of the TV display into a mobile user interface.

In considering alternative approaches for embedding a video stream into the periphery of a handheld display, there is a clear tradeoff between video detail and screen space: as the video feed becomes bigger more of the content that is native to the device is occluded. Knoche et al. [25] investigated users' optimum viewing ergonomics for video on mobile devices and found that given the relative smaller distance between the user and the device (compared to the user and the TV), many mobile devices afford an acceptable viewing angle. However, shrinking this video to show other content on the mobile device is likely to impact the ideal video angle; an effect which is likely to get worse for smaller devices. The optimum design, then, would allow sufficient screen real estate for the content mirrored from the 'other' device, without obfuscating the material on the display the user wishes to attend.

In addition to the loss of video detail in such screen-in-screen designs, such approaches generally cause obstruction to viewing content in the corner of the screen. To alleviate this issue, we considered the option of non-opaque displays. Kamba et al. [24] considered, in their early work on mobiles, how the transparency control widgets in a display can act as a method to extend smaller screens and to allow for all interface elements to be visible. Such methods, in our case, would allow for the whole screen to be occupied by the companion content while still allowing a user maximised resolution of the video. However, this use of transparent overlay is bound to introduce additional issues in terms of visual ergonomics.

FOCUS GROUP WITH CONTENT DESIGNERS

From the methods discussed in the literature, we mapped out the design space depicted in Figure 2. To progress our investigation, we were inspired by work which uses experts to whittle down a large set of designs before exposing them to users (c.f. Marsden et al. [28]). In particular, we considered work such as that by Geerts et al. [17], where the opinions of experts are garnered towards designing better second screen applications. To further consider methods which would be viewed feasible in terms of an editorial perspective we engaged with content designers and creators at a major broadcasting corporation through a focus group. The benefits of doing so are practical and ecological; it allowed the expert consideration of the fully-populated design space with a manageable set of options for audience user research determined by considered, reproducible practice. We recruited four professional designers at the broadcaster, along with a creative director. Designer participants are referred to as D1 through D5. The participants' professional practice included a focus on designing the 'live experience', to accompanying produced content, for example, real-time sports statistics and social media integration. Their core skill-sets and backgrounds were broad and ranged from graphic design to programming.

Procedure

In order to identify which were the most viable design approaches warranting further exploration we first showed the expert professional participants our designs mocked up in a graphic design package (as in Figure 2), without explaining what they may be used for to reduce the priming of genre effects. We then showed them the same designs, except as nine working prototype companion applications, each with example pieces of companion content for the BBC programme "Wild China", while casting the video to a television.

Participants freely discussed the prototypes using critical skills from their professional practice then, at the end of interacting with each UI, we asked them to reflect on their experience,

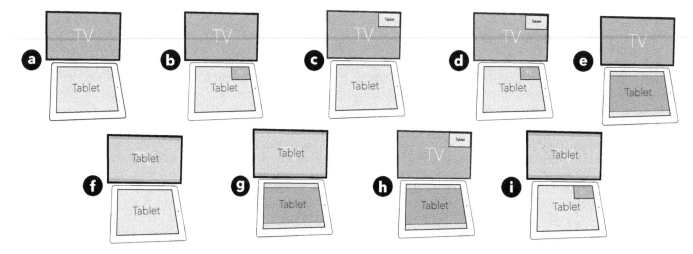

Figure 2: Initial design space: we considered the permutations of previously mentioned techniques to stimulate discussion in our focus group. a) depicts the 'default' no commonalities case, b) the TV material being mirrored from the TV to the corner of the tablet, c) the tablet being mirrored to the TV, and d) a combination of b) and c). In e) we depict mirroring the TV behind the content on the tablet, with the opacity of the content lowered to allow for the user to see through it, and method f) then reverses this concept and projects from the tablet to the TV. Technique g) is a combination of e) and f), and h) considers a hybrid of projecting from the tablet to the corner of the TV while simultaneously placing the TV content behind the tablet screen. Finally, i) shows the inverse of h) – placing the tablet content over the programme on the TV, and the TV programme in the corner of the mobile device.

noting the positives and/or negatives, along with any potential envisioned usage. Finally, after interacting with each interface arrangement, we asked them to state their informed expert preference in terms how they may utilise each UI in their content creation. All comments were recorded for later transcription and exploration through thematic analysis.

Results

In general, practitioners strongly preferred UIs that mirrored the TV on the tablet. Three preferred UI b) and two preferred UI e). A recurring theme in our discussions was that any overlay on the TV puts the designer at risk of encroaching on the TV programme, occluding important elements. The designers referred to the TV as 'sacred space': "*I just feel like that space there [the TV]. That's the primary – that's sacred. And I don't feel like you should really encroach on that*" (D1). Generally, they favoured methods that either did not cast to the TV or methods that did so discreetly (for example, h) and c)). Persistent material was viewed negatively. Participants believed that it encroached on TV's territory and that it should only be placed at very specific points as a call to action – "*kind of at trigger points letting you know that there is something on your companion screen, so that you can be involved with it.*"(D2).

Designers responded positively to on-tablet mirroring of video content, both in the corner of the handheld screen (b)), and presented behind the handheld device's native content – e). Screen-in-screen on tablet, b), was the most preferred because it was seen to work for basically all types of envisioned usage (e.g., companion content and browsing of the web). Some preferred it to the overlaid content, e), because it allowed them, as designers and viewers, to compartmentalise the mirrored TV and the supporting content.

The positive comments around mirroring from the TV to the mobile device, however, were also mixed with concerns about

users focusing wholly on their mobile device, negating the reason to have the TV in the background (despite its superior viewing quality) – "*I kind of feel like you don't have to look at the TV. But I like how you can look at the view and then back at the TV so you don't have to deal with 'both'*" (D2).

The opacity overlay was a divisive UI, with some (2/5) preferring it to the screen-in-screen. The positives for this UI mostly edged around the fact that it was aesthetically pleasing (that it worked like a wallpaper), that it afforded a larger screen, and that it allowed the users to absorb both streams of information simultaneously: "*I do actually prefer it when it's the whole video behind the screen, rather than when it's in the corner. Like I said before – you're watching the TV or reading the text. Whereas with this it feels like you're absorbing both bits of information*" (D3). Criticisms focused around the fact that opacity-overlay UIs may not work for non-designed experiences such as free browsing, as the opacity of the overlay may occlude some parts of the video display. Overlay on tablet, for example e), was generally seen to afford 'designed experiences' more – "*...information overlaid on top of video; it looks somehow compelling and seamless. But you know, if it was anything other than these pleasant meditative screens it would be a lot more competing*" (D2).

Dual-mirroring (mirrored elements on both UI) was generally seen as excessive and was seen to introduce redundancies. The designers tended to prefer more universal UI. Essentially, they preferred UIs which could be applied to the most scenarios, over powerful ones which could be used in few. UIs which were thought to afford only one type of viewing, for example the overlay on the TV, which they only saw useful for brief sharing, were generally not praised. All cases where content was mirrored onto the TV with an opaque overlay were generally noted to be good for only one use case – sharing content with others. The favoured method of mirroring to the TV was to keep the mirrored content discreet by placing it in the corner of the display c). Finally, weighing up the benefits of each, they reached a consensus that the most viable methods for future exploration were: b), the video feed from the television in the corner of the handheld device; c), the mirroring of the mobile device to the corner of the TV; and e), the TV video feed behind the material on the mobile device.

Reflections

The professional focus group allowed us to refine our design space, informed by the insight of the expert content designers who would be tasked with delivering audience value my media products using these concepts. With the experts we made the following conclusions:

– Mirroring back from the TV (e.g., b), d), e), g), h) and i)) to the device was considered viable as a commonality method;

– Screen-in-screen mirroring on the tablet and TV (b) and c) respectively) could be applied to the most scenarios they envisioned;

– The TV is sacred: the use of mirroring fully over TV content (e.g., f), g), and i)) is generally advised against for most scenarios;

– Dual-mirroring (e.g., d), g), h) and i)) was generally viewed as cluttered and redundant.

EMPIRICAL INVESTIGATION OF COMMONALITIES

The initial exhaustive design space had now been constrained to three commonality conditions selected by the professional assessment undertaken by the experts. These were then used in a large-scale empirical user study. We investigated the subjective and objective effects of display commonalities from the perspective of end users (i.e., viewers). These three, and a no-commonalities baseline, are as follows:

– C1 – the baseline condition with no commonalities, depicted as a) in Figure 2. This is the typical experience of a second screener as it stands;

– C2 – mirroring from the TV into the right hand corner of the tablet computer, represented by b) in Figure 2;

– C3 – mirroring from the TV behind the content on the tablet computer screen, as depicted in e) with the opacity of the overlaid content's alpha set to 0.7;

– C4 – mirroring from the tablet to the top right hand corner of the TV, as depicted in c).

Participants and Study Environment

We recruited 40 second screeners (P1 – P40) from a university population, both students and staff. Participation was rewarded with £5. The average age of our participants was 32.5 years old (SD = 8.6), of which 26 of identified as female and 14 male. On average, our participants watched 2.34 (SD = 1.65) hours of TV per day, and either strongly agreed (31) or agreed (9) that they regularly engage with touch screen devices, and all were second screeners to some degree. Five had noted using a companion application to support a TV programme before. All studies were conducted in HCI research lab configured as a living room (pictured in Figure 1). We used an LG 49UH620V 49 inch TV, connected to a laptop. From this, video was cast from an iPad 2 over a personal Wi-Fi hotspot enabling negligible latency between the video streams.

Study Procedure

Each study participant first read and completed a consent form, then filled out a demographics form to allow us to better understand our sample. The participants were then given their individual brief, dependent on the experimental group they were in (COMPANION or FREE-BROWSE, discussed in the next subsections). Following this, they watched a diverse set of four clips (to mitigate genre effects, which are shown to have a major effect on the viewing experience [16, 35]) from popular programmes (see Table 1), each followed by a questionnaire to evaluate their experience. Condition-wise ordering effects were mitigated against with a Latin Square design (5 rotations of 4, over each 20 participant set).

Then after watching all four clips, the participants filled out a post-study questionnaire to allow them to reflect on their whole experience, and an investigator then conducted a short semi-structured interview to capture qualitative insight. The interview questions focused on understanding if the participants noticed any of the conditions affect their attention management during the study by explicitly asking them to state a preference and to explain their perception of each method.

Clip No.	TV Programme	Summary
1	Wild China	Documentary about China
2	Australian Open Final	Tennis game
3	VW Scandal	Emissions scandal documentary
4	Eggheads	Quiz programme

Table 1: Clips used in the display commonalities complexity experiment. Each programme was edited to run for approximately 5 minutes.

The experiment followed one of two formats: the COMPANION condition, in which the TV viewing experience was accompanied by a dedicated companion app (P1 – P20), and the FREE-BROWSE condition, where the participants were free to browse the web (P21 – P40). The participants for this were assigned chronologically; after 20 participants, we began running the study with the FREE-BROWSE condition. We used both scenarios so that our findings are generic to the two common second screen cases, with varying user autonomy. To ensure the validity of our between-participants results, we conducted statistical analysis of the participants' demographics using paired t-tests and found no significant differences between the populations.

Companion and Free-Browse Conditions

To explore the effect of commonalities on a *designed* experience we built four companion applications; one for each programme, which were representative of typical applications. Each app contained four main screens of programme-relevant material, which became available at key points in the experience, at which point the participant was notified of the new content with a notification sound and a visual cue. Figure 3 illustrates the companion application layout for one of the programmes the participants watched in the experiment. The four screens are indicative of the applications we used in the experiment. In addition, to explore the effects of the commonalities on the participants when actively engaged in knowledge query we created a simplistic web browser, with 'back', 'forward', 'home', and 'refresh'

Figure 3: The Wild China Companion Application (depicted here with no commonality methods), in order of appearance to the user: a) shows a simple non-interactive plain text screen b) shows the interactive text screen of the application, here participants could swipe up and explore more text; c), the animation scree. In this case the participants explored an interactive time-lapse of desertification; d) shows the quiz; here, as influenced by [33], participants were given true/false questions related to programme and the tablet material to motivate engagement with the materials on both screens. They were free to repeat the quiz as many times as possible, while also visiting other screens to fill in gaps in their knowledge. For each clip, the applications followed this same format but with programme-related information.

buttons, with the relevant commonality methods included. We motivated the participants to engage with the TV material and the browser as they would in their regular browsing habits.

Measures and Motivations

Subjective metrics were gathered by asking participants several questions after each clip through the form of a questionnaire. We asked these questions with a motivation to understand the benefits of each commonality method in terms of how the participants take in information on the screens at the same time, how they perceive the cost of switching between them, the visual appeal of each technique, how aware of the 'other' device the participants were, and how each technique occluded the materials across the two screens (exact questions shown in Table 2). We also used a post-study questionnaire to allow the participants to compare and contrast the techniques, and reflect on the experience as a whole. In this, we asked them how they felt about each individual technique as a whole (exact questions shown in Table 3). Our hypotheses around the qualitative data were that the commonalities would allow the users to more positively manage their attention, and therefore we would expect to see this reflected in our Likert scores.

In terms of objective metrics, we measured the participants' interactions with the mobile device to determine how the conditions affected their experience. We logged time-stamped events on the device and stored them for later analysis. For the COMPANION condition, interactions were logged within the app as a proxy for participant involvement with the second screen material (as in [33]). We logged when the participants moved to a new screen on the application, when they completed a quiz, and when they interacted with an animated widget. For the FREE-BROWSE condition we logged the browser button actions, such as 'back' and 'home', along with each individual webpage they visited. In both the COMPANION and FREE-BROWSE conditions we expected to see greater interactions with mirroring methods that allowed participants to better manage their attention. We then used the interview data to frame the quantitive data and explain any anomalies.

Results: Post-clip Questionnaires

We considered a range of objective and subjective metrics to evaluate the participants' experience of the commonality methods. For the Likert scale questionnaires, we conducted

Friedman tests to determine if there was a general overall effect, running post hoc Wilcoxon tests between the conditions to determine any inter-condition effects. We set $\alpha = 0.05$ for significance testing throughout our analysis. The results for the post-clip questionnaires are shown in Table 2. These are divided into those participants who got the FREE-BROWSE condition, and those who got the COMPANION condition.

Taking in Information on Screens Simultaneously
For the COMPANION condition there was a significant effect for the participants' ability to take in the content over two screens (statement a)), with pairwise differences; the participants found it significantly easier for the C2 condition ($Z = 3.24$, $p < 0.001$) and the C4 condition ($Z = 1.95$, $p = 0.003$), compared to the C1 condition. These results were similar to those participants who had the FREE-BROWSE condition – there was a significant overall effect, and C2 was the most preferred method. From conducting pairwise post hoc tests we were able to determine that C2 was significantly preferred to C1($Z = 3.00$, $p < 0.001$) and C3 ($Z = 1.789$, $p = 0.037$). In addition, the participants felt that they were able to manage their attention across the two screens significantly better for C2 than C3 ($Z = 2.079$, $p = 0.019$).

Perceived Switching Cost
For the COMPANION scenario, there was a significant overall effect for switching cost across conditions (statement b)). Compared to the baseline (C1), all conditions were significantly better at reducing switching cost: C2 ($Z = 2.70$, $p = 0.004$); C3 ($Z = 1.94$, $p = 0.027$); C4 ($Z = 1.65$, $p = 0.026$). In general, C2 was ranked consistently the highest and ranked significantly higher than the screen-in-screen on the TV case: C4 ($Z = 1.949$, $p = 0.026$). This effect was also observed in the FREE-BROWSE condition, with a much larger effect than the companion case (COMPANION $\chi^2 = 11.86$; FREE-BROWSE $\chi^2 = 27.16$). For the case where content was mirrored from the tablet to the corner of the TV, in the FREE-BROWSE case, there was a significant difference between both the screen-in-screen on tablet C2 ($Z = 3.22$, $p = 0.005$) and the condition in which we mirrored the TV content behind the tablet's browser (C3) ($Z = 3.131$, $p < 0.001$).

Visual Appeal
For the COMPANION condition there was no significant difference in terms of visual appeal for the conditions (statement

	Statement	Mean Rank				χ^2	p
		C1	C2	C3	C4		
COMPANION	a) *I found that I could take in the content over the two screens at the same time effectively*	2.00	3.10	2.58	2.23	9.45	0.024
	b) *I had to shift my viewing between the screens a lot to take in the TV and tablet content*	3.08	1.93	2.35	2.65	11.86	0.003
	c) *I found this commonality presentation method visually appealing*	2.63	2.95	2.33	2.10	7.10	0.069
	d) *I found the commonality method used got in the way of my content viewing on the tablet*	2.85	2.35	2.40	2.40	2.76	0.490
	e) *I found that the commonality method got in the way of viewing the TV material*	2.35	2.08	2.70	2.88	5.48	0.140
	f) *I felt I had good awareness of what was happening on the TV while looking at the tablet*	2.33	2.58	2.88	2.23	4.01	0.260
	g) *I felt I had good awareness of what was happening on the tablet while looking at the TV*	2.50	2.43	2.88	2.80	2.66	0.447
FREE-BROWSE	a) *I found that I could take in the content over the two screens at the same time effectively*	2.15	3.43	2.63	1.80	23.90	0.000
	b) *I had to shift my viewing between the screens a lot to take in the TV and tablet content*	3.20	1.73	2.03	3.05	27.17	0.000
	c) *I found this commonality presentation method visually appealing*	2.63	3.28	2.48	1.63	18.43	0.000
	d) *I found the commonality method used got in the way of my content viewing·on the tablet*	2.43	2.53	3.03	2.00	9.26	0.026
	e) *I found that the commonality method got in the way of viewing the TV material*	2.55	1.65	2.48	3.33	23.44	0.000
	f) *I felt I had good awareness of what was happening on the TV while looking at the tablet*	2.15	3.28	2.70	1.88	19.36	0.000
	g) *I felt I had good awareness of what was happening on the tablet while looking at the TV*	2.60	2.75	2.25	2.40	2.52	0.410

Table 2: This table denotes the extent to which the participants agreed with the noted statement from: Strongly Agree (5); to Strongly Disagree (1). Larger numbers are indicated with darker colours for the mean ranks and the χ^2 value, and statistically significant ($p < 0.05$) are denoted in red – with increasing darkness at higher significance levels. It is clear from observation of the number of statistically significant results that the FREE-BROWSE condition results in a larger effect for many conditions.

c)). However, for the FREE-BROWSE condition, there was an overall significant effect for the conditions. In general, C2 was preferred significantly more than C1 ($Z = 1.724$, $p = 0.034$) and C4 ($Z = 2.411$, $p = 0.008$).

Occlusion of Tablet Content
There was no significant effect in the COMPANION condition for the commonality methods occluding the tablet content (statement d)). However, for the FREE-BROWSE condition it was evident that C3 – the condition where the video was placed behind the tablet content caused more interference with the web browser C4 ($Z = 2.153$, $p = 0.016$).

Occlusion of TV Material
For the COMPANION study there were no significant effects for perceived occlusion of the TV material (statement e)). However, it was evident that for the FREE-BROWSE study, the participants found that the placement of the tablet on the TV affected their perceived occlusion of the TV.

Tablet Awareness
In terms of the participants' awareness of the tablet content there was no significant effect observed for the COMPANION condition (statement f)). However for the FREE-BROWSE case there was a significant effect. Significant pairwise differences were observed between the baseline (C1), which was perceived as worse than C2 ($Z = 3.363$, $p < 0.001$) and C3 ($Z = 1.65$, $p = 0.049$). In addition it is possible to see that C3 was rated significantly worse than C2 ($Z = 1.854$, $p = 0.032$) and C4 ($Z = 2.052$, $p = 0.020$).

TV Awareness
As with tablet awareness there was no major effects for the amount to which the users were aware of the TV (statement g)). And, in contrast to the participant's reported tablet awareness, we did not see any significant effects for the FREE-BROWSE case.

Results: Post-study Questionnaires
We conducted analysis of the post-study questionnaires presented to the participants, the results of which are shown in Table 3. With regards to perceived mental effort (statement a)), as described in Table 3, a significant overall effect for the COMPANION content condition was observed. Upon conducting post hoc analysis of the data, it was evident that the video content in the corner of the tablet (C2) resulted in the participants experiencing less mental effort than the baseline case (C1) ($Z = 3.096$, $p = 0.001$). In addition, there was a similar, but not as pronounced effect, for when casting the tablet content on the TV C4 ($Z = 2.397$, $p = 0.009$), and when placing the video content behind the tablet material (C3) ($Z = 1.911$, $p = 0.028$).

There was a similar, but more pronounced difference for the FREE-BROWSE case, where all conditions were ranked significantly lower for perceived mental effort than the baseline: C2 ($Z = 3.223$, $p < 0.001$); C3 ($Z = 2.303$, $p = 0.010$); C4 ($Z = 2.236$, $p = 0.013$). In addition the TV mirrored in the top of the tablet, C2, was also ranked significantly better than when the video was mirrored behind the web browser, C3, ($Z = 2.797$, $p = 0.025$) and when compared to when mirroring the tablet content to the TV (C4): $Z = 2.753$, $p = 0.003$. Finally, with regards to the clip preference it was clear that the participants' least favourite clip was Clip 2 (statement b)). Interestingly, there was a significant effect for how much the participants enjoyed each clip for the FREE-BROWSE, but not for the COMPANION clips.

Results: Device Log Data
As shown in the bar chart in Figure 4, C2 generally elicited more interaction than any other condition. There was a significant overall effect between the four conditions: ($F(3, 17) = 3.314$, $p = 0.045$). Post hoc tests indicated that the case in which the participants had the TV screen mirrored into the corner of their device, C2, elicited significantly more interaction than the baseline case, C1 ($Z = 3.104$, $p = 0.002$) and when mirroring behind the tablet content (C3) ($Z = 2.296$, $p = 0.022$). In addition, as shown in

		Mean Rank					
	Statement	1	2	3	4	χ^2	p
COMPANION	**a)** I found that the UI for condition *N* required mental effort to view both screens	3.15	1.93	2.53	2.40	11.18	0.011
	b) I liked clip *N*	2.48	2.23	2.60	2.70	2.06	0.56
FREE-BROWSE	**a)** I found that the UI for condition *N* required mental effort to view both screens	3.23	1.63	2.50	2.65	19.34	0.000
	b) I liked clip *N*	3.10	1.75	2.50	2.65	14.17	0.003

Table 3: Post-study questionnaire: the extent to which participants agreed with a given statement. *N* refers to the particular number of the clip, or condition. It is clear that, when reflecting on their experiences, the participants saw major differences between the conditions in terms of their attention.

Figure 4, we conducted an analysis of the number of times that the participants interacted with the animation and found this was consistent across all conditions, with no significant effect.

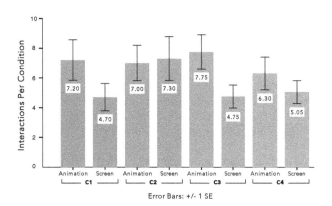

Figure 4: Mean interactions per condition, per participant: this graph describes the average number of each type of interaction per condition. Note that users were much more likely to move *screen* when in the TV was mirrored into the corner of the tablet screen – C2.

Now, turning to the FREE-BROWSE condition – it was clear that different commonality methods appeared to have an effect on the participants' browsing of the internet (F(3, 17) = 3.871, p = 0.028). As shown in Figure 5, it is clear that when the participants had the TV in the corner of the tablet screen (C2). From conducting post hoc analysis we were able to determine that the users were significantly more active browsers when searching the internet with the TV mirrored in the corner of the tablet (C2) compared to the baseline (p = 0.039) and when compared to the video underlay condition (C3) (p = 0.022).

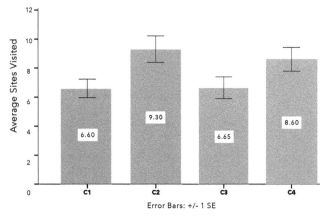

Figure 5: Mean number of sites visited per session, per participant.

Results: Post-Study Interviews

In general, the participants enjoyed the methods in which the tablet mirrored the content from the TV to the tablet. For example, to the initial question, which asked if the participants found that any of the methods were useful for taking in the content across the two screens C2, was noted as the preferred method over half of the time, with 23/40 stating that this method helped them take in the content over two screens: 10/20 for the COMPANION content study and 13/20 for the FREE-BROWSE. The case in which the TV content was mirrored under the mobile device content, C3, came second in terms of preferences: 12/40 participants favouring this option. Mirroring to the TV was not regarded as popular, as indicated by the fact that only four of our of 40 participants preferred this condition. Only one participant out of 40 said that the commonalities did not help them.

Regarding the participants' reasoning for their preferences, many of those who enjoyed the content mirrored from the TV to the tablet appeared to do so because it allowed them to get a gist of what was happening on the TV, meaning that they could better choose when to look up to view the TV content, for example, participant 34 who stated "*I could see this thing [the mirrored TV content] in the corner of the screen and if there was something I thought was really interesting and I wanted to see in full view, I could just look up at the TV. I felt like I was in control*" and participant 39 who said "*My preference is having the small screen in the corner of the device – you sort of then look at the TV if you see that something interesting is going to happen on it in more detail*".

When comparing C2 and C3 (the techniques which mirrored the TV on the tablet) the participants tended to prefer C2 because of the *way it occluded the tablet content*. For example, C2 fully occluded a small part of it, instead of partially occluding all content, as C3 does. This trade-off between size and opacity was something that the participants discussed extensively, for instance, P26 preferred C3 as it allowed for better resolution for the video content: "*I think it was easier to both watch the show and google at the same time, because of the overlay you weren't losing any size of screen.*" (P35). Many participants who preferred C2 noted that, even though the mirrored video was small, because they were using it as a cue when to look up at the full-size picture on the TV, this wasn't a major concern, as indicated by P22: "*It was handy – didn't feel it got in the way of anything. And sometimes, as it was a little small, for the more visual aspects I would look up to see what was going on*".

Participants also noted differences in the way that they experienced their eyes shifting around the tablet screen between the mobile device intra-screen conditions – C2 and C3. Some users' comments tended to indicate that they preferred C3 because it allowed them to monitor the events better on the TV as they did not need to consciously switch their gaze to the tablet computer's corner in their peripheral, but simply change their focus slightly and look 'through' the overlaid content: *"...the one that was [mirrored] behind gave me the opportunity to read what was on the screen without having to move my eyes to see what was happening"* (P8). However, on the other hand, they found that the intermixing of the video and the material on the tablet often became confusing, especially for those doing the FREE-BROWSE condition: *"I couldn't see when I wanted to look at the internet properly – it put me off what was going on behind it"* (P38). One participant even found the underlaid video content disorienting to the point where it made them feel slightly nauseous – *"yeah there was a big swooping shot and I was like *blergh*"* (P21). One participant noted a limitation of C2 may be the fact that as well as fully occluding an area, it may totally block off interface elements with some applications if not thought out properly – *I thought that it was quite useful, but if you need to interact with anything in the top corner, like to close an app or something, you can't."* (P30).

Participants generally did not respond as positively when the content from the tablet was mirrored onto the TV (C4). Generally, this was because they believed it to be occluding the larger screen, for instance, P1 noted *"it got in the way when I was watching the TV"*. Also, participants often noted that, as it was on the TV, it did not afford reading text – *"I didn't like that so much because the writing was smaller and I found it easier to read when it was right in front of me"* (P2). Another concern from the participants was typing. As they were using a non-tactile (tablet) keyboard, this meant that they had to regularly look down at the tablet to type regardless, for example, P29, who had issues typing in queries on the second screen and looking at the TV, just resorted to switching back to the tablet regardless: *"I couldn't type on the tablet and look up. I couldn't move back and forth between the screens"*.

The 'default' condition without any commonalities, which all second screeners currently experience in their day to day viewing – was the least preferred according to our data. Our interviews suggest that this is due to perceived switching cost and the mental load of the simultaneous information streams – for example P14's comment – *"...and the most difficult was the last one"* (C1) *because I had to check the TV and the tablet"*. In fact, only one participant, P18, noted disliking the commonality methods as they were not familiar with their regular second screen routine: *"In the beginning, it's a little overwhelming because you're not used to watching this way. But actually, you're used to doing the 4th method"* (C1).

Discussion

It was clear from the post-clip questionnaire that the commonality methods appeared to help the participants take in the information across the two screens, to varying degrees. Mirroring from the TV into the corner of the tablet (C2) appeared to be the most effective method for the COMPANION and the FREE-BROWSE case. And, generally, the methods in which the TV was mirrored to the tablet were considered the most effective. The interview data suggests that C3 did not perform as well as C2 because of the way that it visually clashed with the video content. Evidently, this was more predominant in the FREE-BROWSE case, where the visual content was dictated by the user freely browsing the web. As one would expect, however, there were some strong inter-participant and inter-content variances due to differences in personal preferences.

The commonality methods also appeared to reduce the perceived cost of the participants moving their focus from one display to another in both the COMPANION and the FREE-BROWSE condition. The qualitative interview data suggests that the participants were switching their focus intra-device, and then making an active decision to switch their focus when they wanted; empowering them to be more in control of their own attention. Here, the screen-in-screen method on the tablet (C2) resulted in significantly lower switching cost than when replicated on the TV (C4). This finding is likely because the TV updates faster than the tablet, and therefore the method enabled the participants to monitor the events on the TV, and to look up when their attention was caught by the visuals of the TV in the corner, or when something in the audio could not be clearly inferred from the small screen in the corner of the tablet.

When checking to determine how aware the participants were of the tablet material, we expected that the method in which we mirrored the tablet content to the TV would improve this significantly compared to the baseline (no commonalities), which it did. However, what we did not expect was that, when browsing the web, the participants appeared more aware of the tablet content for the two methods which mirrored content from the TV to the tablet. This, as indicated by the interview data, is likely because they did not have to look up at the TV as much to fill in the gaps in their (visual) perception, essentially meaning they were, as a result of this, more focused on their web browsing experience. These tablet awareness effects, however, were only seen in the FREE-BROWSE, and not the COMPANION condition. A potential explanation, here, is that it is simply the amount of information on the web browser, and the cognitive effort associated with knowledge query which exacerbated this effect. Work by Neate et al. [33] shows that the textual and graphical complexity of second screen content has a large effect on the mental effort required to engage with second screens.

Evidently, the log data shows that the participants navigated around the application much more when in the condition in which we mirrored the TV in the corner of the mobile device. In light of the subjective quantitative and qualitative data, this is likely because they experienced the least mental demand in this scenario and therefore were able to engage more with the application. The animation, however, did not show this pattern. The log data suggests that this is because most participants went through the transitions in the animation, and just stopped at the final one for each, resulting in quite uniform inter-condition data.

This propensity to search for more information when the TV was mirrored onto the tablet was also reflected in the amount of web browsing the participants did. This is likely the same effect being exhibited – as the participants can easily monitor the TV in the app, they were able to engage with it more. This effect, interestingly, was not seen when the browser was placed over the full mirrored TV screen on the tablet. The interview data indicates that this may be to do with the perceived issues some of the participants faced in this condition due to the two streams of content clashing.

IMPLICATIONS, FEASIBILITY AND THE FUTURE

Our investigations with both expert practitioners and second screeners strongly suggest that methods in which material is mirrored from the TV to a mobile device can be of significant benefit to users in mitigating the attention constraints of multi-device media. This was particularly evident when mirroring from the TV to a tablet in a screen-in-screen method. In addition, it is clear that other methods, such as placing a video stream behind content on a mobile device, are also useful techniques, but are perhaps most beneficial to scenarios in which the content on the mobile device can be designed around this (e.g., companion content scenarios). We, therefore, suggest that, in general, to improve the experience of such applications, designers should consider using techniques that use such duplication of common elements, in order to reduce the effort required in viewing companion applications or similar material.

Though we envision a future in which both persistent and non-persistent duplicate mirroring can be easily integrated into cross-device media scenarios, further research is still required. Our studies, for example, have not explored the effect of persistence: all of our commonality methods were constant, and the participants were not able to dismiss the duplicated video from their attended device. Future prototypes will transcend this experimental constraint, and allow users to control which mirroring method they employ in their browsing. Future work could then observe the appropriation of mirroring methods by users in their everyday viewing. This may uncover further concerns, for example, the issues of privacy when sharing one's screen to the television.

Longitudinal deployments, however, would open up new problems, questions and areas for design. The further investigation of such methods on a variety of devices, for example, would be of considerable interest as a next step. By exploring diverse form factors, and screen sizes of everyday mobile devices we can explore the transferability of commonality methods across device types. With smaller devices, such as smartphones and phablets, there are likely to be bottlenecks in the effectiveness of the techniques, leading to new design requirements. For example, the screen-in-screen condition in our experiments (C2), is likely to require adaption to mitigate against occlusion of the materials under the video content. In such cases, methods such as C3, C4 (and indeed methods not discussed in this paper) may begin to become more beneficial to users.

Thinking beyond the second screening scenario, the ideas and findings in this paper have implications for other use cases: for example, we could extend current mobile device EPGs by integrating the feed from the TV into the corner of the screen, allowing a user to choose a new programme while still retaining awareness of the content running on the television screen. Designs, such as those proposed in this paper, may assist designers in overcoming the issues with eyes-off interactions with non-tactile surfaces (e.g., tablets) when engaging with EPGs.

Methodologically, making use of the expertise of professional UX practitioners in this domain mitigated against subjectivity in selecting particular stimuli for the large-scale user study. Using a repeatable expert process of analysis against the full design space to derive the most valuable individual designs was a successful approach, allowing us to be confident that our user study assessed the right subset of designs. It must be noted, however, that our design space in this paper was not exhaustive and only aimed at targeting the two most frequent use cases and encourage further work refining this design space. We, therefore, encourage further mapping of the design space in future research. Finally, in terms of the infrastructure to enable such experiences, it is assumed that our users have a Smart TV, devices connected to it, and a seamless and uninterrupted internet connection. Though an increasing trend, the standards around the device-agnostic connected living room are not wholly realised for broadcast content. With recent developments in the protocols of cross-device interaction, e.g., work on frame-accurate multi-device content [44], and the increasing demand to provide users with engaging multi-device experiences, there is great potential for interaction designers and researchers to enhance the understanding and impact of this design space.

CONCLUSION

This paper has explored *display commonalities* – the concept of duplicating elements of a user experience over multiple screens, in order to lower the cognitive effort required to use the dual-screen material. Through discussions with professional content designers, we refined our initial design space and conducted an empirical investigation of the proposed techniques under the two prominent scenarios in this use case (web browsing and companion content). By analysing the objective and subjective data we have been able to determine the efficacy of the proposed techniques. In general, we found that, by duplicating the video of the television on a handheld device, we can significantly reduce the required level of cognitive effort require to engage with dual-screens. The findings and design concepts proposed in this paper which were explored, from a designer and a user perspective, can better equip content creators and developers to overcome the disjuncts in visual attention that exist in multiple screen scenarios and, therefore, improve the UX of cross-device media.

ACKNOWLEDGEMENTS

We would like thank our anonymous participants at the BBC in Salford and at Swansea University, as well as our anonymous reviewers for helping shape this paper. Timothy Neate is funded by an EPSRC DTA scholarship (EP/L504865/1) and the BBC UXRP.

REFERENCES

1. Channel 4. 2016. Million Pound Drop App. Online Article: `https://goo.gl/xySC66` - Accessed 28/07/16. (2016).

2. Amazon. 2017. Amazon Xray. (2017). Online Article : `https://goo.gl/kYUIEe` - Accessed: 15/01/17.

3. Edward Anstead, Steve Benford, and Robert J. Houghton. 2014. Many-screen Viewing: Evaluating an Olympics Companion Application. In *Proceedings of the 2014 ACM International Conference on Interactive Experiences for TV and Online Video (TVX '14)*. ACM, New York, NY, USA, 103–110. DOI: `http://dx.doi.org/10.1145/2602299.2602304`

4. Apple. 2016. About Multitasking on your iPhone, iPad, and iPod touch. (2016). Online Article : `https://goo.gl/QbcCnB` - Accessed: 15/01/17.

5. Apple. 2017. Apple Airplay. (2017). Online Article : `https://goo.gl/4cO3MR` - Accessed: 15/01/17.

6. Santosh Basapur, Gunnar Harboe, Hiren Mandalia, Ashley Novak, Van Vuong, and Crysta Metcalf. 2011. Field Trial of a Dual Device User Experience for iTV. In *Proceedings of the 9th International Interactive Conference on Interactive Television (EuroITV '11)*. ACM, New York, NY, USA, 127–136. DOI: `http://dx.doi.org/10.1145/2000119.2000145`

7. Andy Brown, Michael Evans, Caroline Jay, Maxine Glancy, Rhianne Jones, and Simon Harper. 2014. HCI over Multiple Screens. In *CHI '14 Extended Abstracts on Human Factors in Computing Systems (CHI EA '14)*. ACM, New York, NY, USA, 665–674. DOI: `http://dx.doi.org/10.1145/2559206.2578869`

8. British Broadcasting Corporation. 2015. BBC Gory Games App. (2015). Online Article: `https://goo.gl/6bxNoG` Accessed: 04/01/16.

9. Leon Cruickshank, Emmanuel Tsekleves, Roger Whitham, Annette Hill, and Kaoruko Kondo. 2007. Making Interactive TV Easier to Use: Interface Design for a Second Screen Approach. *The Design Journal* 20 (2007).

10. Evelien D'heer, Cédric Courtois, and Steve Paulussen. 2012. Everyday Life in (Front of) the Screen: The Consumption of Multiple Screen Technologies in the Living Room Context. In *Proceedings of the 10th European Conference on Interactive Tv and Video (EuroiTV '12)*. ACM, New York, NY, USA, 195–198. DOI: `http://dx.doi.org/10.1145/2325616.2325654`

11. John Dowell, Sylvain Malacria, Hana Kim, and Edward Anstead. 2015. Companion apps for information-rich television programmes: representation and interaction. *Personal and Ubiquitous Computing* (2015), 14. DOI: `http://dx.doi.org/10.1007/s00779-015-0867-7`

12. Dillon Eversman, Timothy Major, Mithila Tople, Lauren Schaffer, and Janet Murray. 2015. United Universe: A Second Screen Transmedia Experience. In *Proceedings of the ACM International Conference on Interactive Experiences for TV and Online Video (TVX '15)*. ACM, New York, NY, USA, 173–178. DOI: `http://dx.doi.org/10.1145/2745197.2755520`

13. Sanaz Fallahkhair, Lyn Pemberton, and Judith Masthoff. 2004. A dual device scenario for informal language learning: interactive television meets the mobile phone. (2004).

14. Alexandre Fleury, Jakob Schou Pedersen, and Lars Bo Larsen. 2013. Evaluating user preferences for video transfer methods from a mobile device to a TV screen. *Pervasive and Mobile Computing* 9, 2 (2013), 228–241. DOI: `http://dx.doi.org/10.1016/j.pmcj.2012.05.003`

15. Floating for Youtube. 2016. Floating Youtube App on Google Play Store. (2016). Online Article : `https://goo.gl/3k9xtc` - Accessed: 15/01/17.

16. David Geerts, Pablo Cesar, and Dick Bulterman. 2008. The Implications of Program Genres for the Design of Social Television Systems. In *Proceedings of the 1st International Conference on Designing Interactive User Experiences for TV and Video (UXTV '08)*. ACM, New York, NY, USA, 71–80. DOI: `http://dx.doi.org/10.1145/1453805.1453822`

17. David Geerts, Rinze Leenheer, Dirk De Grooff, Joost Negenman, and Susanne Heijstraten. 2014. In Front of and Behind the Second Screen: Viewer and Producer Perspectives on a Companion App. In *Proceedings of the 2014 ACM International Conference on Interactive Experiences for TV and Online Video (TVX '14)*. ACM, New York, NY, USA, 95–102. DOI: `http://dx.doi.org/10.1145/2602299.2602312`

18. Google. 2012. The New Multi-screen World:Understanding Cross-platform Consumer Behaviour. Google. `http://goo.gl/xdbOe1`

19. Google. 2017. Google Chromecast. (2017). Online Article : `https://goo.gl/xgbwOb` - Accessed: 15/01/17.

20. NPD Group. 2013. Screen Mirroring Awareness Reaches 40 Percent of Smartphone and Tablet Owners. (2013). Online Article: `http://goo.gl/2obWuQ` - Accessed: 04/01/16.

21. Jan Hess, Benedikt Ley, Corinna Ogonowski, Lin Wan, and Volker Wulf. 2011. Jumping Between Devices and Services: Towards an Integrated Concept for Social Tv. In *Procceddings of the 9th International Interactive Conference on Interactive Television (EuroITV '11)*. ACM, New York, NY, USA, 11–20. DOI: `http://dx.doi.org/10.1145/2000119.2000122`

22. Michael E. Holmes, Sheree Josephson, and Ryan E. Carney. 2012. Visual Attention to Television Programs with a Second-screen Application. In *Proceedings of the Symposium on Eye Tracking Research and Applications (ETRA '12)*. ACM, New York, NY, USA, 397–400. DOI: `http://dx.doi.org/10.1145/2168556.2168646`

23. Christian Holz, Frank Bentley, Karen Church, and Mitesh Patel. 2015. "I'M Just on My Phone and They'Re Watching TV": Quantifying Mobile Device Use While Watching Television. In *Proceedings of the ACM International Conference on Interactive Experiences for TV and Online Video (TVX '15)*. ACM, New York, NY, USA, 93–102. DOI: http://dx.doi.org/10.1145/2745197.2745210

24. Tomonari Kamba, Shawn A. Elson, Terry Harpold, Tim Stamper, and Piyawadee Sukaviriya. 1996. Using Small Screen Space More Efficiently. In *Proceedings of the SIGCHI Conference on Human Factors in Computing Systems (CHI '96)*. ACM, New York, NY, USA, 383–390. DOI: http://dx.doi.org/10.1145/238386.238582

25. Hendrik O. Knoche and M Angela Sasse. 2008. The Sweet Spot: How People Trade off Size and Definition on Mobile Devices. In *Proceedings of the 16th ACM International Conference on Multimedia (MM '08)*. ACM, New York, NY, USA, 21–30. DOI: http://dx.doi.org/10.1145/1459359.1459363

26. Mark Lochrie and Paul Coulton. 2011. Mobile Phones As Second Screen for TV, Enabling Inter-audience Interaction. In *Proceedings of the 8th International Conference on Advances in Computer Entertainment Technology (ACE '11)*. ACM, New York, NY, USA, Article 73, 2 pages. DOI: http://dx.doi.org/10.1145/2071423.2071513

27. Gavin Mann, Francesco Venturini, Robin Murdoch, Bikash Mishra, Gemma Moorby, and Bouchra Carlier. 2015. *Digital Video and the Connected Consumer*. Technical Report. Accenture.

28. Gary Marsden, Andrew Maunder, and Munier Parker. 2008. People are people, but technology is not technology. *Philosophical Transactions of the Royal Society of London A: Mathematical, Physical and Engineering Sciences* 366, 1881 (2008), 3795–3804. DOI: http://dx.doi.org/10.1098/rsta.2008.0119

29. Mark McGill, John Williamson, and Stephen A. Brewster. 2014. Mirror, Mirror, on the Wall: Collaborative Screen-mirroring for Small Groups. In *Proceedings of the 2014 ACM International Conference on Interactive Experiences for TV and Online Video (TVX '14)*. ACM, New York, NY, USA, 87–94. DOI: http://dx.doi.org/10.1145/2602299.2602319

30. Liz Miller. 2012a. Can Breaking Bad's Story Sync get viewers to give up their DVRs? (2012). Online Article : https://goo.gl/B0jyCI - Accessed: 28/07/16.

31. Liz Miller. 2012b. Why Avengers super fans should assemble for Marvel's second-screen experience. (2012). Online Article: https://goo.gl/3q8WAh - Accessed: 28/07/16.

32. Janet Murray, Sergio Goldenberg, Kartik Agarwal, Tarun Chakravorty, Jonathan Cutrell, Abraham Doris-Down, and Harish Kothandaraman. 2012. Story-map: IPad Companion for Long Form TV Narratives. In *Proceedings of the 10th European Conference on Interactive Tv and Video (EuroiTV '12)*. ACM, New York, NY, USA, 223–226. DOI: http://dx.doi.org/10.1145/2325616.2325659

33. Timothy Neate, Michael Evans, and Matt Jones. 2016. Designing Visual Complexity for Dual-screen Media. In *Proceedings of the 2016 CHI Conference on Human Factors in Computing Systems (CHI '16)*. ACM, New York, NY, USA, 475–486. DOI: http://dx.doi.org/10.1145/2858036.2858112

34. Timothy Neate, Matt Jones, and Michael Evans. 2015. Mediating Attention for Second Screen Companion Content. In *Proceedings of the 33rd Annual ACM Conference on Human Factors in Computing Systems (CHI '15)*. ACM, New York, NY, USA, 3103–3106. DOI: http://dx.doi.org/10.1145/2702123.2702278

35. Timothy Neate, Matt Jones, and Michael Evans. 2016. Interdevice Media: Choreographing Content to Maximize Viewer Engagement. *Computer* 49, 12 (2016), 42–49. DOI: http://dx.doi.org/doi.ieeecomputersociety.org/10.1109/MC.2016.375

36. Umar Rashid, Miguel A. Nacenta, and Aaron Quigley. 2012. The Cost of Display Switching: A Comparison of Mobile, Large Display and Hybrid UI Configurations. In *Proceedings of the International Working Conference on Advanced Visual Interfaces (AVI '12)*. ACM, New York, NY, USA, 99–106. DOI: http://dx.doi.org/10.1145/2254556.2254577

37. Tim Regan and Ian Todd. 2004. Media Center Buddies: Instant Messaging around a Media Center. In *Proceedings of NordiCHI*.

38. John Rooksby, Mattias Rost, Alistair Morrison, Marek Bell, Mathew Chalmers, and Timothy Smith. 2014. Practices of Parallel Media: Using Mobile Devices When Watching Television. In *CSCW – Designing with Users for Domestic Environments: Methods, Challenges and Lessons Learned*. ACM.

39. Jacqueline Sachs. 1974. Memory in reading and listening to discourse. *Memory and Cognition* 2, 1 (1974), 95–100. DOI: http://dx.doi.org/10.3758/BF03197498

40. Pedro Silva, Yasmin Amer, William Tsikerdanos, Jesse Shedd, Isabel Restrepo, and Janet Murray. 2015. A Game of Thrones Companion: Orienting Viewers to Complex Storyworlds via Synchronized Visualizations. In *Proceedings of the ACM International Conference on Interactive Experiences for TV and Online Video (TVX '15)*. ACM, New York, NY, USA, 167–172. DOI: http://dx.doi.org/10.1145/2745197.2755519

41. Barry Smyth and Paul Cotter. 2001. Personalized electronic program guides for digital TV. *Ai Magazine* 22, 2 (2001), 89.

42. Desney Tan and Mary Czerwinski. 2003. Effects of Visual Separation and Physical Discontinuities when Distributing Information across Multiple Displays.

Human-Computer Interaction–INTERACT '03 (November 2003), 252–255. https://goo.gl/XZtpm6

43. Christian Valuch, Ulrich Ansorge, Shelley Buchinger, Aniello Raffaele Patrone, and Otmar Scherzer. 2014. The Effect of Cinematic Cuts on Human Attention. In *Proceedings of the 2014 ACM International Conference on Interactive Experiences for TV and Online Video (TVX '14)*. ACM, New York, NY, USA, 119–122. DOI: http://dx.doi.org/10.1145/2602299.2602307

44. Vinoba Vinayagamoorthy, Rajiv Ramdhany, and Matt Hammond. 2016. Enabling Frame-Accurate Synchronised Companion Screen Experiences. In *Proceedings of the ACM International Conference on Interactive Experiences for TV and Online Video (TVX '16)*. ACM, New York, NY, USA, 83–92. DOI: http://dx.doi.org/10.1145/2932206.2932214

On Time or Not on Time: A User Study on Delays in a Synchronised Companion-Screen Experience

Christoph Ziegler[1], Christian Keimel[1], Rajiv Ramdhany[2] and Vinoba Vinayagamoorthy[2]

[1]IRT, Munich, Germany, ziegler@irt.de
[2]BBC R&D, London, United Kingdom, vinoba.vinayagamoorthy@bbc.co.uk

ABSTRACT

One major challenge in creation of compelling companion screen experiences, are the time delays between the presentation of content on the TV compared to the presentation of content on the companion screen. Through the use of a synchronised, interactive textbook application, we conducted a user study to evaluate the potential influence of different delays, between the TV and the companion screen, on how users experience watching a Shakespearean play on the TV. Our results indicate that although users do not notice delays of up to 1000 ms, for the kind of experience tested, they feel significantly more distracted by the tablet content for increasingly higher delays. We discuss the implications of our findings with regards to the time delay tolerances users might have when using a synchronised text accompaniment to these kinds of TV programmes.

ACM Classification Keywords

H.5.2. Information Interfaces and Presentation (e.g. HCI): User Interfaces – User-centered design

Author Keywords

Companion screen; connected experiences; interaction techniques; second screen; television; synchronisation; impact of delays.

INTRODUCTION

The ubiquity of smart devices, such as mobile phones and tablets, and their widespread use in almost every aspect of human life including, TV viewing in the home, is well documented in market research surveys such as [14, 24].

Previous studies have stressed the untapped potential of additional services that accompany the TV programme on tablets or smart phones. This includes engaging viewers further with the programme and thus enriching the overall TV experience [25]. Although the concept of presenting accompanying content on companion devices is not entirely new, a key component for creating compelling *companion applications* is the technical

ability to enable tight synchronisation of content presentation on TV and companion devices as demonstrated by [27, 28].

Different solutions for achieving companion screen synchronisation exist. They differ in underlying technical principles, end-users' hardware requirements, delivery mechanisms, and achievable synchronisation accuracy. These are important considerations for broadcasters or content providers in terms of the design decisions and commitments implied by the enabling technology. Whilst perfect zero-delay synchronisation of companion content with the TV remains the ideal case, it may not be cost effective to achieve, or even technically possible by commodity devices. Low-delay sync may not even be necessary for particular types of user experiences; a sample-accurate media synchronisation solution may be superfluous if delays of the order of a few seconds in magnitude are not noticeable by users.

We argue that it is essential to determine how the synchronisation inaccuracy (delay) impacts the user experience[1]. This knowledge will enable broadcasters and content providers to evaluate and optimise the trade-off between user experience and synchronisation accuracy based on their distribution platforms and/or media-synchronisation technologies. A better understanding of the perception of delays and their impact on the user experience of synchronised companion applications would also help in the design of degradation of services offered in companion screen applications based on the technologies being used in homes.

In this study, we examine the impact of two main factors. The first is the delay of presentation of content between the TV and the companion device. The second is three different types of interaction offered to the user in the companion application. This study is based on a potential use case involving the synchronised presentation of the transcript of a Shakespeare play (*Richard II* [4]) in time with a video recording of the play on the TV. This combines the use of subtitles in TV programmes with *surtitles* often used in theatres to increase the accessibility and comprehensibility of performances. The script on the companion screen is also augmented with synchronised highlighting of the text based on the elocution of lines by characters in the scene. The companion application developed for this study further allows for three different types of interaction modes: *passive*, *exploration* and *call-to-action*, allowing us to assess the impact of different types of interactions on the users' experience.

---

[1]A person's perceptions and responses that result from the use or anticipated use of a product, system or service[15].

Permission to make digital or hard copies of all or part of this work for personal or classroom use is granted without fee provided that copies are not made or distributed for profit or commercial advantage and that copies bear this notice and the full citation on the first page. Copyrights for components of this work owned by others than ACM must be honored. Abstracting with credit is permitted. To copy otherwise, or republish, to post on servers or to redistribute to lists, requires prior specific permission and/or a fee. Request permissions from permissions@acm.org.

TVX '17, June 14-16, 2017, Hilversum, Netherlands
© 2017 ACM. ISBN 978-1-4503-4529-3/17/06...$15.00
DOI: http://dx.doi.org/10.1145/3077548.3077557

In the following sections we present related work in human factors with respect to media synchronisation, we discuss their applicability to companion screen scenarios and examine potential shortcomings. We then provide an overview of the companion screen application developed for this study. Then, we layout a description of the experimental design and state the hypotheses to be addressed by the study presented. Finally, we discuss the results of the experiments and conclude with a short summary of our key findings.

RELATED WORK

Understanding when media streams are perceived to be synchronised is helpful in determining the requirements for the temporal accuracy of different streams within single devices and between multiple devices.

Steinmetz et al. [26] studied the perception of delays between audio and video streams to find the permissible delay at which streams were perceived to be in "*lip sync*". Their studies provided a threshold for absolute delays in addition to an indication that users may adapt to constant delay between audio and video. Murray et al. [21] investigated perception of synchronisation between olfactory data and video. They observed that perception thresholds are significantly different if participants were presented olfactory data and video with audio as opposed to olfactory data and video only. This implies that there are different cues for perception of skews in synchronisation.

Looking at a scenario similar to the type of applications relevant to this paper, there are studies that explored the impact of timing on the perceived quality of TV subtitles [1, 5, 17]. Similar to findings from the study on synchronisation between audio and video, a threshold effect was observed in the studies on subtitle timing. Of course, for subtitles, the users' attention is not split between two devices as it inevitably will be for experiences delivered concurrently between multiple screens as discussed in this study.

Other studies examined media streams played back at different devices at different physical locations, a scenario that is also referred to as inter-destination media synchronisation (IDMS). Montagud et al. [19] reviewed use cases for IDMS. Technical solutions for IDMS have been proposed for example by [2, 16, 20]. Geerts et al. [10] investigated delays between video presentation and simultaneously using text or voice chat, identifying thresholds depending on the frequency of the chat messages and modality. The test subjects, however, were not exposed to two synchronised media streams, but had processed implicit clues from their chat partners in order to detect delays. Mu et al. [20] observed a content dependency of the delay between audio and video streams on different devices on the Quality of Experience, suggesting that high temporal complexity content may mask delays better than low temporal complexity content. The content on the different devices, however, was the same, unlike the typical companion screen scenario.

STUDY OBJECTIVES AND HYPOTHESES

Vinayagamoorthy et al. [28] theorised that synchronisation accuracy requirements depend on the type of companion-screen experience: responsive guide app (~1 s) versus a companion application which delivers spatial audio effects (10 μs to 10 ms). There is evidence from previous research which supports this assumption. For example, in a study on the impact of delays on the Quality of Experience during synchronised audio presentation different companion devices, Mu et al. [20] found content genre is a determining factor on the thresholds values for delay perception (noticeable-delay and annoying-delay) by viewers. We argue that content genre is a generalisation of content characteristics (including interaction-complexity) in terms of the content factors that influence the way viewers perceive and experience delays in a companion-screen scenario. Research needs to systematically explore the impact of different dimensions of content characteristics.

We selected *interaction* as one of the dimensions of content-complexity to include in our study. The effect of interaction on delay-perception during a synchronised companion screen experience is of significant interest since interaction is a key element of the user experience in many companion applications (e.g. quiz or poll applications). There is no reported insight in the literature about how different types of interaction affect delay perception in synchronised companion screen experiences.

Further, the focus of previous user studies on media synchronisation has been on the impact of delays on the Quality of Experience (QoE)[2]. We consider the determination of QoE deterioration function based on delay-tolerance thresholds to have been amply covered by previous studies, for example [20, 21, 26]. These studies indicate that delay-tolerance thresholds (level at which delays start getting annoying) are always higher than the perception[3] thresholds (the delay value at which users start noticing delays).

Instead, this study focuses on aspects of the user experience such as visual attention split as indicated through gaze behaviour. It is plausible to theorise that more subtle aspects of the user experience might be affected before users start actively noticing delays. *Attention split* is a salient UX factor as it interferes with the editorial message content creators want to convey in their programme. The goal in the creation of many companion applications is that they should not distract users from the key content delivered on the TV screen, but rather add to the TV experience. If there is a threshold at which delays start driving the user's attention, this threshold can be used as a decision criterion for selecting a specific companion-screen synchronisation system.

Hypotheses

In order to address the question of the influence of delays on the user experience in the proposed application scenario, we formulated the following five hypotheses to be examined in our study:

H1 *At a higher interaction levels, participants have a higher threshold for perception of delays.*

---

[2]the degree of delight or annoyance of a person experiencing an application, service, or system [18]
[3]the conscious processing of sensory information [18]

H2 At higher delay levels participants spend more time looking at the companion.

H3 At higher delay levels participants' gaze switches more frequently between TV and companion.

H4 At higher delay levels participants interact less frequently with the companion application.

H5 At higher delay levels participants feel more distracted by the companion content.

Hypothesis H1 builds on the assumption that interaction requires the users' attention and that users are less sensitive to delays, if their attention is shifted from the synchronisation cues to other aspects of the application.

Hypotheses H2 and H3 build on the assumption that users anticipate a certain timed behaviour from the companion experience. They rely on the companion screen showing a certain piece of content at a certain point in time, without having to look at it. If this expectation is not met due to delays, users might start reading along on the companion or might start looking back and forth between screens to contextualise the presentations on both devices, which results in a higher dwell on tablet or in a higher gaze change frequency.

Straining themselves to make sense of the relation between tablet and TV content, users might feel distracted by the additional screen, which explains hypothesis H5. Furthermore, the overload might hinder them from interacting with the companion application, which justifies hypothesis H4.

THE COMPANION SCREEN EXPERIENCE

The candidate user experience selected for the study involves a TV emulator playing a Richard II Shakespeare play [4] and a synchronised companion screen application on a mobile device that engages users through different levels of interaction.

Companion Screen Application

The companion application was an interactive and synchronised transcript of a Shakespeare play. The concept was inspired by theatre *surtitles* which aim at improving the comprehensibility of opera libretti and plays presented in foreign or ancient languages. The user interface design adopts the layout of a textbook. This presentation layout allowed the viewer to read text lines presented by the scene characters, as well as reading ahead. The shape of a tablet fits the aspect ratio of a book and we feel it inherently supports the textbook metaphor. The companion application was designed to operate in three modes to enable the three interaction levels which we planned to study: *passive*, *exploration* and *call-to-action*. Figure 1 shows screen shots of the graphical user interface (GUI) in all three modes.

Levels of Interaction

In *passive* mode, the GUI showed the synchronised text but did not respond to user input. Participants were only able to consume the companion content and had no control over the presentation. In this mode, the GUI comprised of the following elements: a menu bar and a container displaying the synchronised transcript. The menu bar showed icons containing pictures of the characters who had active roles (lines) in the current scene. The icon corresponding to the current speaker was highlighted. Highlighting was achieved by enlarging the icon and changing its border colour. The line that was being spoken on the TV was highlighted in the textbook within the paragraph that contained the line. The current paragraph was highlighted by a vertical black bar on the left hand side of the paragraph. The current line was emphasised by changing its background colour.

The *exploration* mode provided a casual form of interaction with the companion content. The character icons in the menu bar were linked and activated. When an icon was clicked, a menu appeared from the top of the screen to offer information on the relevant character. The character information comprised of the characters name, their picture, their role in the play, relationships to other characters in the play, the actors name and other productions of the Royal Shakespeare Company the actor starred in. The information menu was presented as an overlay (middle image in Figure 1). To ensure that the highlighted line was still visible, the text container got repositioned with the highlighted line in the vertical centre of the remaining visible part of the text container.

In the *call-to-action* mode, the participant was presented with a play-along experience in the form of quiz questions on the tablet. The quiz questions were not directly relevant to the exact scene shown on the TV. Instead, they were related to the general subject of the play (Richard II [4]) and Shakespeare in general. Users needed to select one of four responses to the question within 20 seconds. The time left to select an answer was indicated by a progress bar on top of the quiz menu. Like the character information menu, the quiz menu appeared from the top of the screen. An accompanying flash notification (the call-to-action) appeared on the bottom right corner of the TV to inform the user about the new question on the companion screen.

Synchronisation

Synchronisation between the companion and the TV content was achieved by means of the DVB-CSS suite of protocols [7, 8], which are also part of the HbbTV 2.0 specification [6]. First implementations of the protocol have been shown to allow frame accurate synchronisation between devices [28]. Unfortunately, at the time of this line of experimentation, no TV sets implementing the DVB-CSS protocols were publicly available. Thus a TV emulator based on an open source Python implementation [12] of the DVB-CSS protocols was used. The front-end of the emulator consisted of a JavaScript-based Web application which instantiated the Shakespeare video in a full screen video player.

The companion application consisted, similar to the one presented by Vinayagamoorthy et al. [28], of a DVB-CSS client on an iOS device. It connected the companion screen to the protocol endpoints of the TV emulator to receive updates of the TV's video presentation time. The user interface of the companion application was implemented as a web application running in an embedded browser (web view). The compan-

Figure 1. Screen-shots of the companion application in modes of interaction: passive (left), exploration (middle) and call-to-action (right)

ion's estimates of the TV's presentation time are reported from the DVB-CSS client to the web application.

The time which elapses from the DVB-CSS client sending a timing update and the web view rendering a corresponding presentation to companion screen is unknown. To determine this duration, the DVB-Sync-Timing Framework [13] was used. The result was then used as a timing-calibration offset in the web application.

The textbook application on the companion device and the video on the TV are defined to be in sync, if the highlight on a text line in the textbook application is set at the same point in time as the character on the TV starts speaking the corresponding line. Content timings, the points on the video presentation timeline at which a certain text line on the companion shall be highlighted was authored to allow the best possible control over the synchronisation cues.

To do this, we extracted the audio stream from the TV content and imported it into a digital audio workstation (DAW), which supports visualisation of the audio waveform. To measure the timing of a text line, the play position marker was placed at the beginning of the waveform corresponding to this line. The position of the marker is read from DAW's play position display. Timings are recorded in JSON format for later interpretation by the companion application. The authoring process is illustrated in Figure 2.

EXPERIMENT METHODOLOGY
In this section, we describe the experimental set-up used to evaluate hypotheses defined above.

Experiment Variables
During the experiment values of two independent variables are varied. These were *a)* the delay between the content on the

TV and the companion device and *b)* the type of interaction. Table 1 summarises the choice of variables.

The choice of delay levels is based on results of a pilot experiment with engineers working in the broadcast sector who were skilled at noticing delays in synchrony. In the pilot, we tested delays in the order of magnitude of perceived lip sync (± 50 ms and ± 100 ms) [26], of the average speech rate (± 200 ms, ± 500 ms) [29] as well as values in the order of magnitude of accepted delays for TV subtitles ± 1000 ms and 2000 ms [5, 17]. Positive delays indicate that the tablet content is behind the TV content, negative values that tablet content is ahead. As only a few of the participants noticed the delays in lip-synchronism range, the delay values ± 50 ms and ± 100 ms were excluded from the set of factor levels to study in the main experiment. In order to reduce the size of the experiment, the largest negative and the largest positive delays were removed. The subset of participants who noticed the positive delay in the pilots were the same for 1000 ms and 2000 ms. In addition, previous research on media synchronisation showed a symmetrical effect for large negative and positive delays [26]. The final set of time delay levels used in the main experiment was composed of the reference control condition 0 ms and the five delay values ± 250 ms, ± 500 ms and 1000 ms.

Three levels of interaction were defined: *passive*, *exploration* and *call-to-action*. The interaction level 'passive' was defined to be the lowest interaction level, as participants have no way to interact other than to follow the rolling text. Level 'call-to-action' was defined to be the highest level of interaction, as the application engaged the participant to interact, while at level 'exploration', participants were free to interact with the companion content.

Two objective measures were applied to record participants responses. To gain data which might give us an insight into the participants gaze behaviour (attention split), we annotated

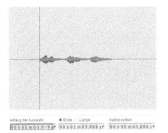

```
[//…
{
    "category": "dialogue",
    "who": "KING RICHARD II",
    "text": "Old John of Gaunt,
        time-honour'd Lancaster",
    "time": {
        "m": 2,
        "s": 3.009
    }
}
//…
]
```

Figure 2. Authoring of text timings: amplitude of the audio recording in the DAW, corresponding chunk of the JSON representation of the text timings and presentation of the highlighted text line in the companion application.

participants gaze while watching the experiences through the use of video recordings taken during the experiment. Obviously, gaze recordings do not mirror what participants actually think but they provided us with an indication of people's visual attention. In prior work, Neat et al. [23] used gaze recordings as an objective measure in an experiment as a means for mediating viewers attention between a companion screen and a TV. In their analysis, they correlated gaze changes with different triggers to assess the effectiveness of these triggers to drive the users attention between screens. We chose to derive two values from our gaze recordings: the *dwell* on tablet p_{tablet} and the gaze change frequency f_{focus}. p_{tablet} is the share of time the user looks at the companion whilst being exposed to an experiment condition. f_{focus} tells us how often users' gaze switches between the TV and companion screen.

To gain information on how participants interact with the companion application, we logged all interaction (button presses, swipe gestures) into a database. From the interaction logs we compute the interaction frequency $f_{interact}$, which tells us about how participants interact while being exposed to an experiment condition.

As a subjective measure, participants ratings on questions from a questionnaire were recorded. A 7-point Likert type scale, as recommended by [9], was chosen to capture ratings. Questions cover perception of delays (Q1 to Q3) and attention split (Q4 and Q5) between companion and TV:

Q1 I felt the TV and the Tablet were well timed to each other.

Q2 I felt like I was waiting for the TV to "catch up" to the Tablet.

Q3 I felt like I was waiting for the Tablet to "catch up" to the TV.

Q4 I felt I was missing part of the programme on the TV because of the Tablet.

Q5 I felt I was missing content on the Tablet because of the TV.

Previous QoE-centric studies on media sync asked participants if they noticed a delay and whether this delay was annoying, for example [20, 21, 26]. This approach might prime users to watch out for delays and suggest that delays affect QoE. The design of Q1 to Q3 aimed at avoiding these effects. Q4 and Q5 where derived from a questionnaire by Neate et al. [22], which they used in a study on attention split between TVs and companion screens.

Setup

The study was planned as a repeated-measures within-participant design. All subjects were exposed to all conditions including reference conditions. As there were six factor levels for the delay and three levels of interaction, there were 18 conditions each participant experienced.

To eliminate the influence of order-effects, conditions were counterbalanced across subjects. This was achieved by dividing participants into three groups of six participants. Each participant was presented three blocks of six clips. Each block was assigned to one interaction level. Within one block, each participant saw all delay levels. Participants within a group were presented the same sequence of interaction levels. Within one block of a group, delay levels were counterbalanced by means of 6×6 latin squares [3]. To prevent an effect of the order in which participants were exposed to the same interaction levels, the interaction level is varied across the three groups of participants in a 3×3 latin square.

Combinations of delay levels and experiences were applied to 18 different clips of a recording of the Shakespeare play Richard II performed at the Royal Shakespeare Company. Clips were chosen with equal amount of dialogue and scene complexity to eliminate the influence of the clip order or type on the measurement. However, the order of clips was randomised to avoid a specific semantic relation between subsequent clips.

Before the experiment started participants were shown a demo clip (at zero delay and at interaction level passive) so they got acclimatised to the new experience. Before being exposed to each block of six clips, participants were briefed on the type of interaction. After each clip, participants were asked to answer questions Q1 to Q5. After 12 clips participants were asked to take a 15 minutes break to prevent viewing fatigue. Clips had an average length of 90 seconds. In general, participants spent about one minute to fill the questionnaire in between conditions. Including welcome, briefings, collecting questionnaire responses, break and debrief one experiment session took about 120 minutes.

Name	Domain	Unit	Hypothesis
Independent variables			
Delay (d)	$\{-500, -250, 0, 250, 500, 1000\}$	ms	all
Level of interaction (e)	$\{P, I, Q\}$	-	all
Dependent Variables			
Questionnaire rating (r)	$\mathbb{N} \wedge 1 \le r \le 7$	-	H1, H5
Dwell on tablet (p_{tablet})	$\mathbb{R} \wedge -1 \le p_{tablet} \le 1$	min/min	H2
Gaze change frequency (f_{focus})	$\mathbb{R} \wedge 0 \le f_{focus} < \infty$	$1/min$	H3
Interaction frequency ($f_{interact}$)	$\mathbb{R} \wedge 0 \le f_{interact} < \infty$	$1/min$	H4

Table 1. Independent and dependent variables and related hypotheses (interaction levels: passive P, explorative I, call-to-action Q).

Experiments were conducted in a user experience lab arranged to look as close to a natural TV viewing environment. It contained a TV on a sideboard along with peripheral devices like a set-top box and gaming consoles. It was surrounded by sofas and a coffee table. The room was equipped with cameras and microphones to observe the participants during the experiment. Recordings were used after the experiment for gaze observations as shown in Figure 3.

Participants
The 18 participants recruited for the experiment were chosen to represent the population of potential users of the companion screen application. This included requirements with regard to affinity for Shakespearean plays or theatre in general, TV viewing behaviour, tablet or smart phone usage. Recruitment was done by a specialised agency. Participants received an incentive of about the equivalence of €70.00. We also collected demographics data and media usage behaviour from participants.

Participants were between 18 and 55 years of age (M=38, SD=13) and gender balanced. The youngest participant was 18 years of age and the oldest was 55. Participants watched on average 2.26 hours of TV per day (SD=1.95 hours, Max=9 hours, Min=0.5 hours). Participants were asked to indicate their perceived level of computer literacy. 14 participants (77.78%) self-reported a rating of ≥ 5 on a 7-point Likert type scale and 3 participants (5.56%) estimated their computer literacy ≤ 3. Asked on whether they liked watching Shakespeare plays, 10 participants (55.56%) gave a rating ≥ 5 and 2 participants (11.11%) a rating of ≤ 3. 17 participants (94.44%) gave a rating of ≥ 5 when asked if they often used a touch-screen device such as tablet or smart phone. No participant gave a rating of ≤ 3. All participants stated that they used a secondary device (smart phone, tablet, laptop) to search for information related to the TV programme.

In summary, all participants appeared to be familiar with the technology used in the experiment. The majority of participants assessed themselves as frequent users of touch-screen devices and feel familiar using a computer. All participants had experience of using a secondary device whilst watching television and most of the participants stated an interest in Shakespeare plays.

RESULTS
Delay Perception Threshold (H1)
Participants responses to questions Q1, Q2 and Q3 were analysed to test hypothesis H1. Single-factor analysis was conducted across the responses captured for each of the delay

values at the controlled interaction level. This allowed for finding the delay-perception tolerance at each interaction level. Shapiro-Wilk tests showed that samples could not be assumed to come from normally distributed populations. Therefore, the non-parametric Friedman test was applied to test the influence of the delay on the participants ratings. Table 2 depicts the corresponding test results. A significant effect of the delay level on the participants rating was not found for any of the questions on synchronisation accuracy. This result is also outlined by Figure 4, which shows similar medians and quartile ranges of ratings on Q1 across the different delay values at all levels of interaction. The delay-tolerance level was not determined within this study. Thus there is not enough information for a final judgement on H1.

e	Dependent variable	χ_r^2	n	p	H_0
	r_3	4.28		0.51	accepted
P	r_4	5.23	18	0.39	accepted
	r_5	5.9		0.32	accepted
	r_3	1.9		0.83	accepted
I	r_4	3.96	17	0.56	accepted
	r_5	3.08		0.69	accepted
	r_3	9.81		0.09	accepted
Q	r_4	6.8	17	0.24	accepted
	r_5	7.12		0.22	accepted

Table 2. Tests on hypothesis H1: Results of the Friedman test show no significant influence of the delay on the subjects' ratings r on questions on synchronisation accuracy Q1, Q2 and Q3 for different levels of interaction e (P passive, I explorative, Q call-to-action) ($df = 5$).

Dwell (H2) and Gaze-Change Frequency (H3)
For an assessment of H2, the influence of the delay on the participants' mean dwell on the tablet was analysed. Shapiro-Wilk tests showed that samples could be assumed to come from normally distributed populations. Hence, a parametric test, the repeated-measures single-factor analysis of variance (rANOVA), was applied to analyse the effect of the delay. Results are presented in Table 3. A significant effect caused by the delay was not found across the interaction levels. Hence, results do not confirm H2. p-values were calculated under the assumption of sphericity. The results of the Mauchly test for sphericity are also provided in Table 3. For each interaction level, mean ratings were at similar levels across delay levels ($min(\mu_{p_{tablet}}(P)) = 0.39$ vs. $max(\mu_{p_{tablet}}(P)) = 0.48$, $min(\mu_{p_{tablet}}(I)) = 0.52$ vs. $max(\mu_{p_{tablet}}(I)) = 0.57$, $min(\mu_{p_{tablet}}(Q)) = 0.56$ vs. $max(\mu_{p_{tablet}}(Q)) = 0.59$), which is inline with the results of the hypothesis test.

To test H3, the influence of the delay on the participants' relative gaze-change frequency was analysed. A Shapiro-Wilk test showed that samples could be assumed to come from a

Figure 3. Lab: left picture is taken from behind the participants seat. Right picture is taken from a camera mounted next to the television and shows the participants seat. The latter picture is used for the gaze observation.

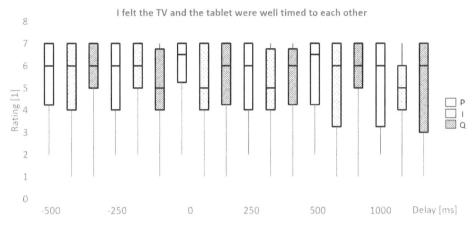

Figure 4. Box plots off participants' ratings on Q1 for different levels of interaction.

normally distributed population. Thus, rANOVA was applied. p-values were calculated under the assumption of sphericity. A significant impact of the delay was found for interaction level *exploration*. As H3 hypothesises claims a higher f_{focus} at higher delay levels, a one-tailed t test was used for pairwise comparison of samples applying Bonferroni correction of p-values. The results are presented in Table 4. Row "Expected" in Table 4 marks those pairs of samples, where H_0 (with alternative hypothesis $H_1 : \mu_{d_1} < \mu_{d_2}$) is expected to be rejected in order to support H3. Results show that f_{focus} was significantly larger at a delay level of -500 ms ($\mu(-500) = 19.82\,\text{min}^{-1}$, $S(-500) = 5.59\,\text{min}^{-1}$) as opposed to -250 ms ($\mu(-250) = 16.08\,\text{min}^{-1}$, $S(-250) = 5.93\,\text{min}^{-1}$).

However, no such effect was found between sample pairs at the reference condition 0 ms and the largest negative or positive delay values -500 ms and 1000 ms respectively, or any other of the sample pairs that were expected to show an effect. Also the mean value of f_{focus} at 250 ms ($\mu(-250) = 21.40\,\text{min}^{-1}$, $S(-250) = 9.82\,\text{min}^{-1}$) was found to be significantly larger than at -250 ms, though both delay levels have the same absolute values. An effect of the delay on f_{focus} was observed. Grounded on Cohen's f the effect size is small to medium ($f = 0.167$). However, the direction of the effect of the delay on f_{focus} claimed by H3 was not confirmed by the experiment results. An additional post-hoc test was conducted to find out, if there was complementary direction of the effect ($H_1 : \mu_{d_1} < \mu_{d_2}$). The results are provided in Table 5. An effect was only found between the reference level

($\mu(0) = 20.02\,\text{min}^{-1}$, $S(0) = 7.32\,\text{min}^{-1}$) and -250 ms. A complementary direction of the effect of the delay on f_{focus} is, therefore, not confirmed.

Influence of the delay on interaction frequency (H4)

To evaluate hypothesis H4, the influence of the delay on the interaction frequency was tested at interaction levels *exploration* and *call-to-action*. Shapiro-Wilk tests showed that the majority of the samples could not be assumed to come from normally distributed populations. Thus, the Friedman test was applied. Results are presented in Table 6. No significant effect of the delay on the interaction frequency was found. For interaction level Q, median values vary within a narrow range of $min(\theta_{f_{interact}}) = 0,70\,\text{min}^{-1}$ and $max(\theta_{f_{interact}}) = 0,81\,\text{min}^{-1}$. This observation is in line with the result of the Friedman test. For interaction level I medians vary within a larger range of $min(\theta_{f_{interact}}) = 0,80\,\text{min}^{-1}$ and $max(\theta_{f_{interact}}) = 2.20\,\text{min}^{-1}$. The larger range of medians is also reflected in the lower p value derived from the Friedman test. However, this deviation can not be regarded as significant. The results of the experiment do not deliver evidence to support H4.

Feeling of being distracted (H5)

Validity of hypothesis H5 is assessed by analysis of the influence of the delay on participants ratings on questions Q4 and Q5 at different levels of interaction. A Shapiro-Wilk test showed that samples could not be assumed to come from normally distributed populations. Hence, the Friedman test was applied. Results of the Friedman test are shown in Table 7.

111

e	Dependent variable	Notes on sphericity	F	p	H_0	η^2
P	p_{tablet}	SpA (MW=0.23, $p=0.12$)	0.65	0.66	accepted	0.045
	f_{focus}	SpA (MW=0.20, $p=0.07$)	0.73	0.61	accepted	0.043
I	p_{tablet}	SpA (MW=0.37, $p=0.46$)	0.44	0.81	accepted	0.027
	f_{focus}	SpA (MW=0.43, $p=0.63$)	0.25	0.94	accepted	0.016
Q	p_{tablet}	SpA (MW=0.19, $p=0.06$)	0.39	0.86	accepted	0.024
	f_{focus}	SpA (MW=0.33, $p=0.35$)	3.13	0.01	rejected	0.164

Table 3. Tests on hypotheses H2 and H3: Results of the rANOVA on influence of the delay on p_{tablet} and f_{focus} for interaction levels ($df_{treatment} = 5$, $df_{residuals} = 80$, "SpA": sphericity assumed), "MW": Mauchly-W.

d_1 [ms]	0					-250				-500			250		500
d_2 [ms]	-500	-250	250	500	1000	-500	250	500	1000	250	500	1000	500	1000	1000
Expected	*	*	*	*	*	*		*	*			*	*	*	*
p	1	1	1	1	1	0.04	0.04	0.45	1	1	1	1	1	1	1
H_0	A	A	A	A	A	R	R	A	A	A	A	A	A	A	A

Table 4. Post-hoc analysis for hypothesis H3: pairwise one-tailed ($H_1 : \mu_{d_1} < \mu_{d_2}$) T tests with Bonferroni-corrected p-values on samples of f_{focus} measured at different delay levels at interaction level call-to-action. Columns, where rejection of H_0 is expected in order support H3 are marked with "*". Columns where H_0 is accepted or rejected are marked with "A" and "R" respectively.

The Friedman test shows a significant effect of the delay on the ratings on question Q4.

A post-hoc analysis, to determine which sample pairs caused the significant effect, was conducted by means of a pairwise one-tailed ($H_1 : \pi_{d_1}^+ < 0.5$) binomial-sign test for dependent samples. Results are presented in Table 8. They show that a significantly higher amount of participants gave a higher rating on question Q4 at delay level 1000 ms as opposed to the reference condition 0 ms ($\sum D^+ = 10$, $\sum D^- = 2$) and the delay levels -500 ms ($\sum D^+ = 10$, $\sum D^- = 2$), 250 ms ($\sum D^+ = 7$, $\sum D^- = 1$) and 500 ms ($\sum D^+ = 9$, $\sum D^- = 2$). Moreover, a significant amount of participants gave a higher rating on Q4 at 250 ms as opposed to -500 ms ($\sum D^+ = 7$, $\sum D^- = 2$). Figure 5 illustrates these findings. Red circles mark median values of those samples where an effect was found. Arrows connect the pairs of samples for which an effect was found. The arrow points into the direction of the sample with significant amount of lower ratings. An additional one-tailed test in opposite direction ($H_1 : \pi_{d_1}^+ > 0.5$) did not find significant differences between samples.

DISCUSSION

We did not see a significant difference, in participants ratings of questions Q1 to Q3, across the different time delays (-500 ms to 1000 ms) for any of the chosen interaction levels. This implies that, for the type of experience discussed in this paper, our data set does not uncover a time delay at which participants are able to perceive inaccurate synchronisation for any of the three different interaction types designed for the companion application used. Therefore, our data does not deliver the information basis for a final judgement on hypothesis H1.

However, the results implies that, for the type of companion experience described in this paper, synchronisation delays between -500 ms and 1000 ms are unlikely to be noticed. This in turn suggests that prevalent technologies like Audio Watermarking or Audio Fingerprinting, which are reported to achieve synchronisation accuracy within a fraction of a second [11, 27], and DVB-CSS [7, 8, 28] are viable technological solutions for implementing companion experiences similar to the ones tested in this paper.

This also requires that errors introduced during production of content timings and errors introduced by the synchronisation system, do not accumulate to a value that exceeds the investigated delay range. Manual crafting of timings for the Shakespearean play transcript, used in the study, was comparatively time consuming. A production process that is at least partially automated will be a more practicable and efficient process. Future work could investigate efficient ways to generate the timing information, in particular the applicability of professional subtitling tools or natural language processing tools. For the specific application used in our work, a major challenge in this regard is certainly the processing of the Shakespearean language.

Hypotheses on the impact of the delay on dwell time H2, gaze change frequency H3 and interaction frequency H4 were not confirmed by the experiment. However, we observed a significant effect, across the time delay, when users were able to actively browse content on the companion screen (interaction level - exploration). This shows that delays can effect aspects of the user experience before users start noticing them.

This finding has implications on the method used to evaluate a companion application before going "live". Authors follow a certain intention, when orchestrating content across screens, for example to mediate users attention between companion and TV screens, as shown by Neate et al. [23]. Tests that only look at perceptibility of delays, may not suffice to evaluate whether a specific synchronisation system is able to support the authors' intent.

CONCLUSION

We investigated the perception of delays, between content presentation on companion screen devices and TVs, as well as the impact of delays on some aspects of the user experience. Our results indicate that, for companion screen applications which aim to present users with a synchronised rolling transcript as an accompaniment to a programme with relatively difficult subject matters (such as the Shakespearean play used in this study), synchronisation technologies are able to keep delays below the threshold at which users may perceive mistimed content across devices. With one exception, we saw no effect of the chosen delay levels in the range of $[500ms, 1000ms]$ on

d_1 [ms]	0					-250				-500			250		500
d_2 [ms]	-500	-250	250	500	1000	-500	250	500	1000	250	500	1000	500	1000	1000
p	1	0.01	1	1	0.43	1	1	1	1	1	1	0.82	1	0.34	1
H_0	A	R	A	A	A	A	A	A	A	A	A	A	A	A	A

Table 5. Post-hoc analysis for hypothesis H3: Test on complementary direction of the effect of the delay on f_{focus} as claimed by H3: pairwise one-tailed ($H_1 : \mu_{d_1} > \mu_{d_2}$) T tests with Bonferroni-corrected p-values on samples of f_{focus} measured at different delay levels at interaction level call-to-action. Columns where H_0 is accepted or rejected are marked with "A" and "R" respectively.

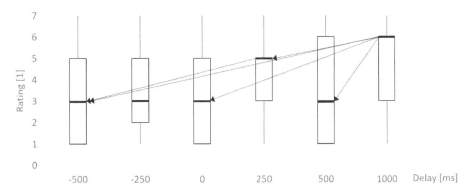

Figure 5. Box plots of ratings on Q4 for different levels of delay at interaction level exploration. Arrows connect pairs of samples for which an effect was found in the pairwise sign test as shown in Table 8. The arrows point into the direction of the samples with significant amount of lower ratings.

e	Dependent variable	χ_r^2	n	p	H_0
I	$f_{interact}$	8.86	16	0.12	accepted
Q	$f_{interact}$	5.29	14	0.39	accepted

Table 6. Test on hypothesis H4: results of the Friedman test on the influence of the delay ($df = 5$) on the interaction frequency for different levels of interaction e.

e	Dependent variable	χ_r^2	p	H_0
P	r_5	4.90	0.43	accepted
	r_6	8.16	0.15	accepted
I	r_5	11.56	0.04	rejected
	r_6	6.42	0.27	accepted
Q	r_5	9.64	0.09	accepted
	r_6	5.79	0.33	accepted

Table 7. Test on hypothesis H5: results of the Friedman test ($df = 5$, $n = 17$) on the influence of the delay on subjects' ratings r on questions Q4 and Q5 for different levels of interaction e.

participants responses. During the conditions in which participants were able to actively browse additional content on the companion-screen, users' felt more distracted by the tablet at a delay of 1000 ms as opposed to lower delay values. The participants lack of noticing any delays within the given range may be an indication that evaluation methods focussing on users perception of delays may not suffice to assess the overall requirements on timing accuracy to support specific goals in user experience design.

ACKNOWLEDGMENTS
We would like to thank the participants who took part in our experiment, our colleagues who participated in pilot trials and the reviewers for helping us improve this paper. The research leading to these results has received funding from the European Union's H2020-ICT-2015 programme under grant agreement n° 687655 (2-IMMERSE).

REFERENCES

1. Mike Armstrong. 2013. *The Development of a Methodology to Evaluate the Perceived Quality of Live TV Subtitles*. White Paper WHP 259. British Broadcasting Cooperation.

2. Ingar M. Arntzen, Njål T. Borch, and Christopher P. Needham. 2013. The media state vector: a unifying concept for multi-device media navigation. In *MoVid '13 Proceedings of the 5th Workshop on Mobile Video*. 61–66.

3. R. A. Bailey. 2008. *Design of Comparative Experiments*. Cambridge University Press, Chapter Row-column designs, 105–116.

4. British Broadcasting Cooperation. 2016. Richard II. `http://www.bbc.co.uk/programmes/p03rr1v1`. (2016). Online; accessed: 2016-08-27.

5. D. Burnham, J. Robert-Ribes, , and R. Ellison. 1998. Why captions have to be on time. In *Audio-visual speech processing*. 153–156.

6. European Telecommunications Standards Institute (ETSI) 2015a. *ETSI TS 102 796 V1.3.1 / HbbTV 2.0 – Hybrid Broadcast Broadband TV* . European Telecommunications Standards Institute (ETSI).

7. European Telecommunications Standards Institute (ETSI) 2015b. *ETSI TS 103 286-1 – Companion Screens and Streams; Part 1: Concepts, roles and overall architecture* (DVB BlueBook A167-1 ed.). European Telecommunications Standards Institute (ETSI).

8. European Telecommunications Standards Institute (ETSI) 2015c. *ETSI TS 103 286-2 – Companion Screens and Streams; Part 2: Content Identification and Media Synchronization* (DVB BlueBook A167-2 ed.). European Telecommunications Standards Institute (ETSI).

d_1 [ms]	0					-250				-500			250		500
d_2 [ms]	-500	-250	250	500	1000	-500	250	500	1000	250	500	1000	500	1000	1000
Expected	*	*	*	*	*	*		*	*			*	*	*	*
p	0.37	0.37	0.1	1	0.02	1	0.37	1	0.1	0.02	1	0.02	1	0.002	0.02
H_0	A	A	A	A	R	A	A	A	A	R	A	R	A	R	R

Table 8. Post-hoc analysis for hypothesis H5: results of pairwise one-tailed binomial-sign test ($H_1 : \pi_{d_1}^+ < 0.5$) on responses to Q4 at interaction level explorative. P values are Bonferroni corrected. Columns, where rejection of H_0 is expected in order support H5 are marked with "*". Columns where H_0 is accepted or rejected are marked with "A" and "R" respectively.

9. Kraig Finstad. 2010. Response Interpolation and Scale Sensitivity: Evidence Against 5-Point Scales. *Journal of Usability Studies* 5, 3 (2010), 104–110.

10. David Geerts, Ishan Vaishnavi, Rufael Mekuria, Oskar van Deventer, and Pablo Cesar. 2011. Are we in Sync? Synchronization Requirements for Watching Online Video Together. In *CHI '11 Conference on Human Factors in Computing Systems*. 311–314.

11. Leandro Gomes, Pedro Cano, Emilia Gomez, Madeleine Bonnet, and Eloi Batlle. 2003. Audio Watermarking and Fingerprinting: For Which Applications? *Journal of New Music Research* 32, 1 (2003), 65–82.

12. Matt Hammond. 2016. Python DVB Companion Screen Synchronisation protocol library. https://github.com/BBC/pydvbcss. (2016). Online; accessed: 2016-08-08.

13. Matt Hammond and Jerry Kramskoy. 2016. DVB companion synchronisation timing accuracy measurement. https://github.com/bbc/dvbcss-synctiming. (2016). Online; accessed: 2016-08-24.

14. Nielsen Holdings. 2011. In the U.S., tablets are TV buddies while eReaders make great bedfellows. http://www.nielsen.com/us/en/insights/news/2011/in-the-u-s-tablets-are-tv-buddies-while-ereaders-make-great-bedfellows.html. (2011). Online; accessed: 2016-09-02.

15. International Organization for Standardization (ISO) 2010. *ISO 9241-210:2010: Ergonomics of human-system interaction – Part 210: Human-centred design for interactive systems*. International Organization for Standardization (ISO).

16. Internet Engineering Task Force (IETF) 2014. *RFC 7272 – Inter-Destination Media Synchronization (IDMS) Using the RTP Control Protocol (RTCP)* (Request for Comments 7272 ed.). Internet Engineering Task Force (IETF).

17. Ichiro Maruyama, Yoshiharu Abe, Eiji Sawamura, Tetsuo Mitsuhashi, Terumasa Ehara, and Katsuhiko Shirai. 1999. Cognitive experiments on timing lag for superimposing closed captions. In *Sixth European Conference on Speech Communication and Technology*. 575–578.

18. Sebastian Moeller and Alexander Raake. 2014. *Quality of Experience – Advanced Concepts, Applications and Methods*. Springer, Chapter Quality and Quality of Experience, 11–33.

19. Mario Montagud, Fernando Boronat, Hans Stokking, and Ray van Brandenburg. 2012. Inter-destination multimedia synchronization: schemes, use cases and standardization. *Multimedia Systems* 18, 6 (2012), 459–482.

20. Mu Mu, Steven Simpson, Hans Stokking, and Nicholas Race. 2016. QoE-aware Inter-stream Synchronization in Open N-Screens Cloud. In *13th Annual IEEE Consumer Communications & Networking Conference (IEEE CCNC)*. 907–915.

21. Niall Murray, Yuansong Qiao, Brian Lee, A. K. Karunakar, and Gabriel-Miro Muntean. 2013. Subjective evaluation of olfactory and visual media synchronization. In *4th ACM Multimedia Systems Conference (MMSys '13)*. 162–171.

22. Timothy Neate, Michael Evans, and Matt Jones. 2016. Designing Visual Complexity for Dual-screen Media. In *Proceedings of the 2016 CHI Conference on Human Factors in Computing Systems (CHI '16)*. ACM, 475–486.

23. Timothy Neate, Matt Jones, and Michael Evans. 2015. Mediating Attention for Second Screen Companion Content. In *CHI '15 Proceedings of the 33rd Annual ACM Conference on Human Factors in Computing Systems*. 3103–3106.

24. Ofcom. 2016. Communications Market Report 2016. https://www.ofcom.org.uk/__data/assets/pdf_file/0024/26826/cmr_uk_2016.pdf. (2016). Online; accessed: 2017-03-28.

25. Red Bee Media Ltd. 2012. Broadcast industry not capitalising on rise of the second screen. http://www.redbeemedia.com/sites/all/files/downloads/secondscreenresearch.pdf. (2012). Online; accessed: 2013-07-15.

26. Ralf Steinmetz. 1996. Human perception of jitter and media synchronization. *IEEE Journal on Selected Areas in Communications* 14, 1 (1 1996), 61–72.

27. Vinoba Vinayagamoorthy, Matt Hammond, Penelope Allen, and Michael Evans. 2012. Researching the User Experience for Connected TV – A Case Study. In *CHI EA Extended Abstracts on Human Factors in Computing Systems*. 589–604.

28. Vinoba Vinayagamoorthy, Rajiv Ramdhany, and Matt Hammond. 2016. Enabling Frame-Accurate Synchronised Companion Screen Experiences. In *TVX '16 Proceedings of the ACM International Conference on Interactive Experiences for TV and Online Video*. 83–92.

29. J. Yuan, M. Liberman, and C. Cieri. 2006. Towards an integrated understanding of speaking rate in conversation. In *Interspeech 2006*. 541–544.

Don't Leave – Combining Sensing Technology and Second Screens to Enhance the User Experience with TV Content

Daniela Huber, Daniel Buschek, Florian Alt

LMU Munich
Ubiquitous Interactive Systems Group
Amalienstrasse 17, 80333 Munich, Germany
Contact Author: florian.alt@ifi.lmu.de

ABSTRACT

In this paper we explore how the use of sensing technologies can enhance people's experience during perceiving TV content. The work is motivated by an increasing number of sensors (such as Kinect) that find their way into living rooms. Such sensors allow the behavior of viewers to be analyzed, hence providing the opportunity to instantly react to this behavior. The particular idea we explore in our work is how a second screen app triggered by the viewer's behavior can be designed to make them re-engage with the TV content. At the outset of our work we conducted a survey (N=411) to assess viewers' activities while watching TV. Based on the findings we implemented a Kinect-based system to detect these activities and connected it with a playful second screen app. We then conducted a field evaluation (N=20) where we compared (a) four hints to direct users' attention to the second screen app and (b) four types of second screen content requiring different levels of engagement. We conclude with implications for both practitioners and researchers concerned with interactive TV.

Author Keywords

Interactive TV; User Behavior; Kinect; advertisements;

ACM Classification Keywords

H.5.2. User Interfaces: Screen Design; H.5.1. Multimedia Information Systems: Video

INTRODUCTION

TV has come a long way from being a family event for many years to a medium that many people today consume alone [14]. During the last 20 years, the number of people watching alone has doubled. Yet, smart TVs are growing in popularity (over 50% market penetration as of today [8]), indicating that the living room's couch is still the prime spot to watch TV. As of 2015, 73% of the generation X and 55% of millennials are watching TV on a TV [11].

Permission to make digital or hard copies of all or part of this work for personal or classroom use is granted without fee provided that copies are not made or distributed for profit or commercial advantage and that copies bear this notice and the full citation on the first page. Copyrights for components of this work owned by others than the author(s) must be honored. Abstracting with credit is permitted. To copy otherwise, or republish, to post on servers or to redistribute to lists, requires prior specific permission and/or a fee. Request permissions from Permissions@acm.org.

TVX '17, June 14–16, 2017, Hilversum, Netherlands.
Copyright is held by the owner/author(s). Publication rights licensed to ACM.
ACM ISBN 978-1-4503-4529-3/17/06 ...$15.00.
http://dx.doi.org/10.1145/3077548.3077561

Figure 1. We address the challenge of re-engaging users as they direct their attention away from TV content, for example to interact with their mobile device or to get something to eat/drink during commercial breaks. We implemented a system that allows such activities to be recognized from Kinect data and to react to them by means of a second screen application. We compare the effectiveness of different visual hints and examine how their degree of engagement impacts on user behavior.

At the same time, our TV viewing behavior changed considerably. On one hand, TV watching is in many cases not constrained anymore to one TV in the living room – rather, people often have TVs also in their bedroom, the kitchen, or even their bathroom – and, on the other hand, the viewer's attention easily shifts away from the screen, not only as people get something to eat or drink during commercial breaks, but mainly as they attend to their mobile devices, for example, reading and replying to instant messages (WhatsApp, etc.).

There is an undisputed need to find ways as to how such changes in behavior can be accounted for. In particular, sensing technologies that are increasingly finding their way into living rooms (for example, Microsoft Kinect or cameras integrated with TVs) create novel opportunities by allowing the current behavior of the viewer to be sensed, analyzed and reacted to. For example, systems could try to direct viewers' attention back to the TV or, as content gets more personalized, to instantly adapt the content to user behavior, such as providing a brief summary of content viewers potentially missed as soon as they direct their attention back to the screen.

In this work, we present a system that allows the behavior of users in front of a TV to be analyzed by means of a Microsoft Kinect. We then show how this information can be exploited in a particular use case, that is a second screen app trying to make the user re-engage with the actual TV content.

In recent years, second screen applications have become a popular means to prevent users from engaging in other activities [2]. According to the MyScreens study [7], 74% of all TV viewers were using a second screen as of 2015. They direct their visual attention to apps about 30% of the time in general [6] and about 90% of the time during commercial breaks. With 47%, the smart phone is the most used second screen, followed by the laptop (38%) and the tablet (20%) [7].

However, previous work showed that second screen apps may draw more of the viewer's attention away from the screen than desired [3, 5, 9, 10]. The reason for this is that much prior work focused on how second screen apps could be better integrated with the TV content rather than putting the user into focus. For example, Schroeter et al. [12] showed how certain content (ads, shows) can be detected in real-time to immediately show fitting content on the second screen. Basapur proposed to synchronize content updates on second screens based on the viewer's social circle [1]. And Weber et al. investigated how to embed notifications with smart TVs [15]. As sensing technologies enables a real-time assessment of user behavior, we can add a new quality to second screens. In contrast to previous work, we detect when viewers direct their attention away from the screen and only then try to re-engage them.

CONTRIBUTION STATEMENT

The contribution of this work is threefold. First, we conducted a *survey* (N=411) to obtain an understanding of viewers' activities while watching TV. Second, we then implemented a Kinect-based *system* that is able to detect these activities in real time. Third, we *showcase* how a second screen app can benefit from this knowledge. We report on the implementation of the app and present results from a field study (N=20) in which we deployed our system in users' homes. We compared (a) the ability of different visual triggers to re-engage viewers, as well as (b) various types of content that require different levels of engagement.

Our findings are relevant for researchers and practitioners working on interactive TV systems that take viewers' behavior into account in general, as well as for designers of second screen apps which aim to re-engage viewers in particular.

OBJECTIVE AND METHODOLOGY

The main objective of our work is to understand how viewers' behavior while perceiving TV content can be determined and how this knowledge be used for different purposes, including but not limited to enhancing the viewing experience as well as increasing exposure of content by making viewers re-engage as they turn away attention. As a result, both viewers as well as content providers can benefit from this approach. With our work we hope to support research primarily concerned with the considerable change in TV viewing behavior over the past decades and how to account for it.

Our research consists of multiple steps. At the outset, we conducted a survey with the main goal of understanding how people watch TV today and, in particular, in which activities they engage while doing so. From this we obtained a broad set of activities, which we aimed to detect in the second step. Therefore, we implemented a system, capable of determining

the viewers' activities by means of a Microsoft Kinect. The third and final step of our research was to demonstrate how the ability to determine a viewer's behavior can be exploited. While our use case here is a second screen app that tries to re-engage users as they shift their attention away from the screen by means of interactive content, we would like to stress, that there are many more use cases that can benefit from this approach, some of which are discussed in the future work section at the end of this paper.

ONLINE SURVEY: UNDERSTANDING VIEWER BEHAVIOR

At the outset of our work we conducted an online survey to assess user behavior while watching TV and using second screens. The survey contained 36 questions grouped into four categories (demographics, second screen usage, behavior while watching TV, behavior during commercial breaks).

Recruiting

We recruited participants through University mailing lists and in social media groups. Three 30 Euro Amazon vouchers were raffled among all participants. During two weeks, 557 persons participated in the survey – 411 surveys were completed until the end and considered for further analyses.

Results

Participants (42% female) had a mean age of 27 years (range: 13-68). Most were students (67.9%) and employees (13.2%).

The majority of participants (75.7%) aged 14 to 49 stated to *watch TV alone* occasionally to very often. Participants also watch TV with their partner (56.7%), with their family (46.1%) and with their friends (31.3%).

Among participants aged 14 to 29, 79.1% of male and 85.0% of female participants use a *second screen* while watching TV. With 84.8% the smartphone is the most popular device among both genders, followed by laptop (74.3%) and tablet (32.6%). A Mann-Whitney U test shows that participants using a second screen spend significantly more time watching TV than participants who do not (+37 minutes on weekdays, +67 minutes on weekends), $U = 7683.00$, $p = 0.001$, $r = -0.16$.

Usage of second screen apps is highest during a commercial break (74%). Regarding which apps were used, the younger generation (aged 14 to 29, N=267) prefers communication with friends while consumers over 30 years (N=64) favor surfing the internet and searching for general information.

Almost every second participant (47.2%) stated to play on the smartphone – mainly for pastime (95.4%), because it is fun to play (91.2%), and because they like competing with friends (33.0%). Top-ranked apps are quiz and knowledge games played by 70% of all participants, followed by brain games (60%), strategic games (49%), and skill games (46%).

During a commercial, most participants stated to use their second device (86.3%), followed by switching to another TV channel but switching back (85.4%) or doing other things not related to the TV or second screen (82.8%). Participants not using a second screen mainly do things unrelated to the TV program (73.2%), followed by switching to another TV channel but switching back (62.49%) and switching to another TV channel and not switching back (42.9%).

Figure 2. Hints in the study: we used three textual hints (bandage, slider, split screen) and a spoken tutorial. Each hint provided a brief description of the second screen app as well as a QR code and a URL for accessing the content.

Feedback from participants showed that non TV related activities during a commercial break include doing the household (41.8%), going to the bathroom (46.2%) getting something to drink or do some cooking (53.6%). Very few learned, read, called somebody, or listened to music (<5%).

People using a second screen keep in touch with friends through social media (63.4%), read or write emails (27.1%) play games (17.9%) or browse the internet for general information (14.4%). Only few people call somebody, work or learn, do online-shopping or listen to music.

Summary

Through the survey we identified a list of activities that ought to be recognized as interactive TV systems should react to viewer behavior. This includes (1) leaning forward to grab a phone, (2) looking away from the TV (e.g., to the phone), and (3) standing up to get something to eat/drink. As will be described in the following sections we used these activities as requirements for our behavior analysis tool.

In addition, we learned that the use of smartphones as second screen is particularly popular and that the majority of people favor playful apps. Hence, we focus our investigation on a use case including a playful second screen app.

VIEWER BEHAVIOR ANALYSIS & SECOND SCREEN APP

To investigate how TV can benefit from real-time knowledge on user behavior in the future, we first implemented a *behavior recognition* component that allows to detect when users shift their attention away from the screen by using a Microsoft Kinect. Our simple recognizer can determine the following behaviors: looking right/left/up/down, standing up, leaning forward/backward, grabbing something with the left/right hand, and looking at a smart device. Head direction and leaning forward/backward can be inferred from a comparison of the viewer's head angles, standing up is available from the Kinect SDK, and a custom implementation was used to recognize the other behaviors. The recognition was implemented in C#.

The second component we built allows for *embedding different hints with TV content* that are triggered as one of the aforementioned types of behavior is recognized. Note, that in general each behavior could trigger a different action. Triggers differ with regard to the amount of presented information, how information is presented, and where it is presented (see Figure 2). For the purpose of our work we implemented four triggers: in the *bandage* a hint is shown at the bottom of the screen in a distinct area overlaying the TV content. The *slider* is shown in the top-right corner of the screen with shorter text. For the *split screen* the TV content is scaled down and shown in the top-left corner. Hints are shown below the video. In contrast to

the other triggers, in the *tutorial* information about the second screen app is presented by a speaker. Content is continued to be shown in the top-right corner of the screen. In the context of our work, we use the hints to make users aware of a second screen app. All hints depict a QR code as well as the URL to the second screen app. Hints are shown for 20 seconds.

The third component is a *second screen app*. This app enhances TV content [4] by showing information or questions that are synchronized and closely related with the TV program. Information can consist of different types of media, in our case text and images. Questions have different answer options and a time constraint. After having answered a question, the correct answer is displayed to the user. All questions, answering options and timestamps are received from a database. The application is realized with HTML5, CSS, JavaScript and responsive design. Figure 3 shows the different content types of the second screen app.

USER STUDY

The system described above forms the basis for a user study in which we investigated how people could be re-engaged with TV content by responding to their behavior. In particular, we were interested in 1) comparing different hints, as well as in 2) understanding design considerations for second screen apps used while watching TV. We decided to conduct a field study in participants' homes to ensure more natural behavior than under lab conditions. For example, this allowed participants to go to the toilet or to grab food – at home they are more likely to really stand up and leave the TV than in the lab.

TV and Second Screen App Content

For the study, we worked together with a national German TV station, who provided us with 60 minutes of professionally produced video content. Thus we increased the ecologic validity of our data. The program consisted of a cooking show and was interlaced with three 7-minute commercial blocks.

For the second screen app, we designed four different types of content. Hereby we followed Schulmeister's classification of interactivity levels of multimodal learning systems [13]. In particular, we distinguished non-interactive content and interactive content requiring different levels of engagement. The content took the form of background information or questions, all of which were related to the TV program (Figure 3).

Background Information in the form of short text provides additional information on the program. Such information could tell participants how many people are usually involved in shooting an episode of the cooking show (such as several authors, camera-men make-up artists, designers, editors, and cutters.)

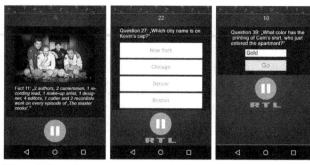

Figure 3. Second screen app content: information, yes/no question (not depicted), questions with four answer options, question with text input.

Yes/No Questions are also related to the current content. For example, users were asked whether or not they could imagine using a particular tool one of the cooks was using during the show for preparing their meals.

Multiple Choice Questions provide users multiple answer options, for example 'Which city name is on Kevin's (one of the cooks) cap? – New York, Chicago, Denver, or Boston?'.

Open Question require users to freely type text, hence requiring the highest level of engagement. An example question asked users on the color of one of the people's shirts.

Study Design
The study followed a repeated measures design with two independent variables – hints and required level of engagement. *Hints* capture the attention of the audience. We compared four hints described before: bandage, slider, tutorial, split screen. As a baseline we used a push notification sent to the participant's smart phone. *Engagement* was also compared on four levels, as described before: in addition to static program information (low engagement) we compared yes/no questions (moderate engagement), questions that included multiple, more complex answering options (high), and finally questions requiring free text (very high) (Figure 3).

As dependent variables we collected (1) number and duration of different activities; (2) number and duration of app use beyond the second screen app; (3) number, type and time of appearance of hints; (4) number of answered questions per question type; (5) when the second screen app was opened.

Setting & Procedure
Participants watched TV at home, sitting on a couch or chair in front of the TV screen with a small table being placed between seating and TV screen. The Kinect was placed right below the TV screen to capture the scene and participant. A laptop with the Kinect program was attached to the TV. Participants could place their smart phone or something to eat or drink on the table. We used the TV and second screen app content as described above.

As the researchers arrived at the participants' home they would first explain the purpose of the study. In particular we told them that a second screen app was to be tested during the study but not that the hints were triggered through their behavior. The second screen app was installed on the participant's phone.

Furthermore, we told them that images would occasionally be taken by the Kinect but that they would have the opportunity to look through these immediately after the study and decide which to delete. After being instructed to watch TV in an accustomed manner, they signed a consent form.

After the instructions, participants were left alone and watched one hour of the pre-cut TV program. Afterwards the technical setting was removed while the participant was browsing through and potentially deleting pictures taken by the Kinect.

Then, participants answered a questionnaire. The questionnaire assessed the opinion of the participant on the second screen app and its content. In particular we wanted them to rate the following statements on a 4-Point Likert scale[1]: 'I would be motivated to use the second screen app again.' 'Perceiving the background information required a lot of effort. Responding to the {yes/no questions | multiple-choice questions | open questions} required a lot of effort.' 'Using the {yes/no questions | multiple-choice questions | open questions} was fun.' Furthermore, we asked them whether they considered the TV program to be attractive. Finally, we provided statements on the displayed hints: 'The {bandage | slides | split screen | tutorial | push notification} was easy to understand.' 'The {bandage | slides | split screen | tutorial | push notification} motivated me to use the second screen app.' 'The {bandage | slides | split screen | tutorial | push notification} was disturbing.' In addition, we conducted semi-structure interviews, assessing whether participants noted that the second screen app reacted to their behavior, whether they preferred accessing the second screen app using QR code or the URL, and asking them how our system could be further improved. Finally, each participant received a 15 Euro gift voucher.

Limitations
We are aware of several limitations of our study. Many homes have more than one TV (for example, in the living room, the bedroom, the kitchen, and even the bathroom). In this work we focused exclusively on TVs located in the living room. Future work could look into how user tracking could be realized for other locations, how user behavior is different, and which opportunities arise from the ability to track viewers across multiple TVs. Furthermore, our results may have been influenced by a novelty effect. Yet, we expect this to be minimal, since it was not apparent to participants that hints were triggered through their behavior and we were not primarily interested in how often the approach triggers a response from the participants. Then, participants' behavior may have been influenced by their awareness of being recorded via Kinect. Yet, we tried to minimize any potential bias by telling participants in the beginning about the opportunity to delete images immediately after the study. Finally, we only focused on single user interaction. Future work could take the interplay between second screen apps and multiple users into account.

Results
A total of 20 participants (iPhone and Android users) recruited through University mailing lists and from social networks took part in the study. On average, participants were 24.4 years (age range 15-46, 12 female). Eleven participants were students.

---

[1] We chose a 4-Point scale to minimize the central tendency bias.

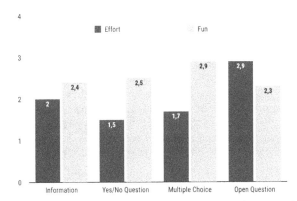

Figure 4. User rating of the second screen app content: Open questions were perceived to require more effort compared to the other types of content. Users liked multiple choice questions due to their high fun factor.

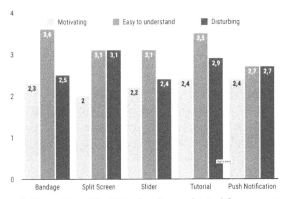

Figure 5. User rating of the hints: Bandage and tutorial were most easy to understand. Slider and bandage were perceived as least disturbing. Hints were perceived similarly with regard to motivation.

Detection Accuracy

Manual inspection revealed that in 264 of 304 cases, the behavior of participants was recognized correctly (87%). The remaining cases were a result of body postures being misinterpreted, mainly due to participants being positioned in a way such that the skeleton could not be detected properly.

Second Screen Application Usage

On average, participants with Android phones used the second screen app (N=13, M=1369.62 s, SD=272.72) longer than other applications (N=13, M=1045.38 s, SD=273.71) on the smartphone. Note, that this data cannot be logged on iPhones.

65% of the participants preferred the QR code compared to the URL. For seven participants it was very easy and for four it was rather easy to scan the QR code from the TV screen.

Perception of the Second Screen App & Content

Figure 4 shows the average rating for the second screen content. Overall, participants rated the second screen app to be fun to use (Mdn=3). Looking more closely at the results, we found the questions to be perceived more fun (Mdn=3) compared to the information (Mdn=2). With regard to the required effort, the open question was perceived as rather demanding (Mdn=3), whereas all other questions as well as the information were perceived as rather undemanding (Mdn=2). We found a significant correlation between the effort for answering a question and the fun factor for that type of question, R=-0.29, p <0.05. The higher the effort, the lower the fun factor was rated.

People who used the the second screen app more often than other apps (Mdn=3) rated the watched TV program significantly more attractive than participants who in the majority of cases used other apps (Mdn=1), U=6.00, s, r=-0.63.

Response to Hints

During the study none of the participants realised that the hints were triggered by their behavior. Neither did they consider them to be particularly disruptive. Being debriefed afterwards, two participants mentioned that they found it creepy that the system was capable of detecting their activities.

Following Geerts et al. who found discoverability to be crucial for second screen apps [5], each hint was accompanied by a short sound. 30% of participants stated that they didn't notice this sound whereas 45% fully agreed that the sound gained

their attention. Visual inspection of the images revealed, that some of them, though they stated not to have noticed the sound, raised their head from looking at the smartphone and watched the screen. This suggests that the sound is an effective way to attract attention while not being too disturbing.

We were furthermore interested in how quickly participants responded to the hints. Hence, we looked at all cases, where a hint was shown for the first time. Participants who were shown the split screen as the first hint were fastest to open the second screen app (N=4, M= 83.5 s, SE=27.45 s). Slightly slower were the participants who were first shown the bandage (N=3, M=307.67 s, SE=58.46 s) and the slider (N=4, M=311.75 s, SE=26.07 s). Time was measured from when the hint was first displayed until the second screen app was opened first.

Figure 5 depicts the average ratings for the different hints. We did not find strong differences with regard to how *motivating* the hints were. Participants found the bandage and tutorial most easy to *understand* (Mdn=4), followed by split screen and slider (Mdn=3). As expected, push notifications were ranked lowest. Concerning *disturbance*, all hints that strongly affected the TV content (split screen, tutorial) as well as push notification were rated as rather disturbing (Mdn=3) whereas bandage and slider were rated as less disturbing (Mdn=2).

Influence on User Behavior

We reviewed the video material and log files to gather insights into people's behavior during a commercial break. Whereas 18 people watched the first block of commercials, only 12 did so for the third block. Likewise, also the number of people using the second screen app decreased between the first and third block of commercials. The second break was used by participants mainly to stand up and get something to eat or drink, whereas this was not the case for blocks one and three.

We observed several occasions (17) where participants used the second screen app during watching the program and continued using it during the break. In five cases, usage even lasted throughout the entire break into the next program. During all breaks about the same number of participants used the second screen to surf the internet while the number of persons who used our app increased each break. Continued use even in a break suggests that viewers were more engaged with the TV content than if they had left the room.

Qualitative Feedback
Two persons found the second screen app to be distracting while watching TV and two persons would have liked the information hints to be displayed longer. Four participants would have liked shorter time intervals between two questions.

DISCUSSION & LESSONS LEARNED
Our findings are relevant for both researchers and practitioners aiming at exploiting knowledge on user behavior in general as well as for using second screen apps that are strongly linked with the TV program in particular.

Assessment of User Behavior
Our work demonstrates that an assessment of viewers' behavior is a promising means to enhance the way we will watch TV in the future. From a technical perspective, we found that with *off-the-shelf devices* such an assessment is possible with high accuracy (in our case, behavior was correctly identified in 89% of all cases). As such devices are available in many viewers' homes or could be easily integrated in consumer TVs, we envision such approaches to find wider application in the near future. Challenges may arise from situations, such as users walking around while watching TV (e.g., as screens are located in the kitchen) or watching while lying in bed.

From a viewers' perspective there is a clear need to investigate *acceptance* of such a technology, since recording Kinect data in viewers' homes may be considered a severe invasion of privacy. In contrast to the use of microphones (for example, Amazon Alexa[2]) or cameras (as in many of Samsung's current TV models) which easily allow users to be identified and conversations to be tracked, we use skeleton data only which is neither buffered nor stored. Yet, viewers' privacy concerns need to be understood and taken seriously as such technologies find their way into our homes. Whereas some participants found the technology 'creepy', others seemed not to bother. Yet, the question remains to which degree users understand that an analysis of data from the Kinect's depth camera could be ultimately used to not only track behavior but to also identify people (for example, among other family members).

Beyond acceptance, there is also a need to investigate how much *control* viewers would want to have as their behavior is recorded and which *incentives or benefits* they would consider appropriate. Apart from the use case explored in this work, we envision that adaptations of (personalized) content that takes into account what users are currently doing and supports them in re-engaging could further leverage the potential of this approach.

Using Second Screen Apps to Re-engage Viewers
Our findings center around four important aspects: discoverability, disturbance, motivation, and ease of use.

One major challenge seems to be how to *introduce the second screen app*. The tutorial was both motivating and easy-to-understand. Furthermore, it led to users opening the second screen application quickly and was remembered well after the study. In particular the fact that no text had to be read on the screen seemed to facilitate participants' willingness to access

[2]http://alexa.amazon.com

the app. In contrast, the bandage was perceived to be less *disturbing*, yet understandable. We conclude, that to introduce the second screen app, a tutorial is clearly advisable. Once users saw the tutorial, less disturbing hints could be used – yet a balance needs to be striven between too subtle hints that are potentially overlooked and too prominent hints. To then access the app, participants preferred the QR code compared to the URL. Yet, to not exclude people without an installed QR code scanner, it is advisable to show both options. It turned out that displaying the QR code for 30 seconds was a good choice.

We found that no hint stood out with regard to motivating the use of the app. This may well be a result of the study situation, since users knew the app was under investigation. Future work should more closely investigate means to increase viewers' *motivation* to use the app, for example through benefits such as the opportunity to download the current sound track.

Our second screen app, in particular the questions, was well received by participants due to its *fun* factor and its ability to increase the attractiveness of the TV program. At the same time, perceived *effort* is crucial: free text answers required a lot of effort and were hence perceived to be less fun compared to the other types of questions. Participants also liked the informative text. Our findings suggest that second screen applications should offer a mixture of interactive and non-interactive content. For answers in quizzes, immediate feedback should be provided. The time between two content pieces should not be too long (e.g., max. 30 seconds), since else viewers are likely to again direct their attention away.

CONCLUSION AND FUTURE WORK
In this paper we showed how future interactive TV applications could make use of knowledge on TV viewers' behavior. In particular, we demonstrated how to leverage this knowledge to re-engage viewers in front of the TV by means of a second screen app. Our findings revealed that the way hints are presented impacts on how quickly users access the second screen app, and how understandable and motivating the concept is. Furthermore, we found that whereas too engaging tasks should be avoided, people liked a mixtures of content requiring different levels of engagement.

We see a lot of opportunities for future research, including a long-term deployment and evaluation of the system as well as an extension to multi-device and multi-user scenarios. Furthermore, additional sensors could be included (for example, physiological sensors) to obtain more fine-grained information not only on the viewers' behavior but also on their state (Where do they focus their attention? Which content did they perceive? What is their current emotion?). This, finally, provides opportunities for further use cases and applications that adapt to the viewers and their context. As a result, the TV watching experience could be further enhanced. For example, systems could adjust the presentation of content in a way, such that important information (e.g., news a viewer is particularly interested in) is presented in phases of high attention. Or content could be better tailored to the viewers' behavior, such as pausing content as they temporarily engage in other activities or providing a brief summary of what happened in a plot or during a sports events as users briefly left the TV.

ACKNOWLEDGEMENT
We thank Heiko Brantsch, Anika Koch and Barbara Dander from RTL2 for their help with producing the content used in the user study. Furthermore, we would like to thank Christian Andre from RTL2 for his valuable input and feedback on this work. Work on this project was partially funded by the Bavarian State Ministry of Education, Science and the Arts in the framework of the Centre Digitisation.Bavaria (ZD.B).

REFERENCES
1. Santosh Basapur, Hiren Mandalia, Shirley Chaysinh, Young Lee, Narayanan Venkitaraman, and Crysta Metcalf. 2012. FANFEEDS: Evaluation of Socially Generated Information Feed on Second Screen As a TV Show Companion. In *Proceedings of the 10th European Conference on Interactive Tv and Video (EuroiTV '12)*. ACM, New York, NY, USA, 87–96. DOI: http://dx.doi.org/10.1145/2325616.2325636

2. E. D'heer C. Courtois. Second Screen Applications and Tablet Users : Constellation , Awareness, Experience , and Interest. In *Proceedings of the 10th European Conference on Interactive Tv and Video.*

3. J. Castillo. 2013. The Rise of the Second Screen: Zeebox, GetGlue, Viggle, and More. StreamingMedia. (2013). http://www.streamingmedia.com/Articles/Editorial/Featured-Articles/The-Rise-of-the-Second-Screen\-Zeebox-GetGlue-Viggle-and-More-89008.aspx

4. Pablo Cesar, Dick CA Bulterman, and AJ Jansen. 2008. Usages of the secondary screen in an interactive television environment: Control, enrich, share, and transfer television content. In *European Conference on Interactive Television*. Springer, 168–177.

5. David Geerts, Rinze Leenheer, Dirk De Grooff, Joost Negenman, and Susanne Heijstraten. 2014. In Front of and Behind the Second Screen: Viewer and Producer Perspectives on a Companion App. In *Proceedings of the 2014 ACM International Conference on Interactive Experiences for TV and Online Video (TVX '14)*. ACM, New York, NY, USA, 95–102. DOI: http://dx.doi.org/10.1145/2602299.2602312

6. Michael E. Holmes, Sheree Josephson, and Ryan E. Carney. 2012. Visual Attention to Television Programs with a Second-screen Application. In *Proceedings of the Symposium on Eye Tracking Research and Applications (ETRA '12)*. ACM, New York, NY, USA, 397–400. DOI: http://dx.doi.org/10.1145/2168556.2168646

7. initiative. 2015. My Screen 2014/02. initiativeMedia. (February 2015). http://www.initiative-media.de/initiative-studie-my-screens-ii-zur-parallelnutzung\-von-tv-und-zweitbildschirmen/

8. Michelle Jones. 2016. How Netflix Is Changing Our TV-Watching Behaviors. ValueWalk. (June 2016). http://www.valuewalk.com/2015/06/how-netflix-is-changing-our-tv-watching-behaviors/

9. Jan Kallenbach, Silja Narhi, and Pirkko Oittinen. 2007. Effects of Extra Information on TV Viewers' Visual Attention, Message Processing Ability, and Cognitive Workload. *Comput. Entertain.* 5, 2, Article 8 (April 2007). DOI: http://dx.doi.org/10.1145/1279540.1279548

10. Timothy Neate, Matt Jones, and Michael Evans. 2015. Mediating Attention for Second Screen Companion Content. In *Proceedings of the 33rd Annual ACM Conference on Human Factors in Computing Systems (CHI '15)*. ACM, New York, NY, USA, 3103–3106. DOI: http://dx.doi.org/10.1145/2702123.2702278

11. Lara O'Reilly. 2015. Most Young People Say They Have Stopped Watching TV. BusinessInsider. (Jan 2015). http://www.businessinsider.com/forrester-video-and-tv-consumption-report-2015-1?IR=T

12. A. Schroeter. 2015. So vernetzen Sie TV-Werbung effizient mit dem Second Screen. W&V. (April 2015). http://www.wuv.de/medien/so_vernetzen_sie_tv_werbung_effizient_mit_dem_second_screen

13. Rolf Schulmeister. 2005. Interaktivitaet in Multimedia-Anwendungen. (2005). https://www.e-teaching.org/didaktik/gestaltung/interaktiv/InteraktivitaetSchulmeister.pdf

14. Flint Stephens. 2016. Women or men, young or old: Who really watches the most TV. KTAR News. (May 2016). http://ktar.com/story/724853/women-or-men-young\-or-old-who-really-watches-the-most-tv/

15. Dominik Weber, Sven Mayer, Alexandra Voit, Rodrigo Ventura Fierro, and Niels Henze. 2016. Design Guidelines for Notifications on Smart TVs. In *Proceedings of the ACM International Conference on Interactive Experiences for TV and Online Video (TVX '16)*. ACM, New York, NY, USA, 13–24. DOI: http://dx.doi.org/10.1145/2932206.2932212

Understanding Secondary Content Practices
for Television Viewing

Frank R. Bentley
Yahoo, Inc.
Sunnyvale, CA USA
fbentley@yahoo-inc.com

ABSTRACT

Secondary content experiences related to television viewing have been a frequent topic of study in the TVX community. While many new interfaces have been created and studied in the small scale, we are not aware of any larger quantitative work to study current practices now that many secondary content experiences are publicly available. We conducted a survey with a broad sample of the American population to explore current secondary content use. We report on our findings, including that 80% of these experiences occur before or after viewing the primary content, and not as simultaneous experiences, and that social posting about television content remains quite low, even for one's favorite show. We conclude with implications for the design new secondary content systems based on our findings.

Author Keywords

Television; Second Screen; Survey; Related Content; Mobile Devices.

ACM Classification Keywords

H.5.1 Multimedia Information Systems: Video; H.5.m. Information interfaces and presentation (e.g., HCI): Miscellaneous

INTRODUCTION

The experience that a viewer has with a television program is no longer limited to the 30 or 60 minutes that they spend watching the linear content of the program. Secondary information about television programs is now widely available in the form of Tweets, Facebook posts, Tumblr GIFs, fan forums, official content from show websites, actor bios and episode summaries on sites such as IMDB and Wikipedia, and second screen apps specifically created for shows or networks.

This explosion of online content has the power to transform

Permission to make digital or hard copies of all or part of this work for personal or classroom use is granted without fee provided that copies are not made or distributed for profit or commercial advantage and that copies bear this notice and the full citation on the first page. Copyrights for components of this work owned by others than ACM must be honored. Abstracting with credit is permitted. To copy otherwise, or republish, to post on servers or to redistribute to lists, requires prior specific permission and/or a fee. Request permissions from Permissions@acm.org.

TVX '17, June 14-16, 2017, Hilversum, Netherlands
© 2017 ACM. ISBN 978-1-4503-4529-3/17/06 $15.00
DOI: http://dx.doi.org/10.1145/3077548.3077554

a television watching experience – from reading up before the program, through gathering additional information and understanding during the program, to connecting with others during and after the viewing experience.

While the TVX community has been exploring second screen interactions around television content for many years, little is known about what people are actually doing in practice when it comes to supplementary content. Multiple research systems have been built that have provided companion apps on mobile devices [13, 18], parallel feeds of related content [2, 3], social interactions [7, 8], and related sports stats [6] – among many others. These systems were often tested in the field at specific events, or in multi-week field studies. But none is currently deployed at scale in the world.

It remains unclear how these types of experiences have made it into real-world, natural use in the 14 years since TVX started (as EuroITV) and researchers began to create these types of systems. What types of secondary content experiences are people currently engaging with? What types of information are they seeking? When do they seek this information with respect to viewing the program content?

We set out to answer these questions through an online survey aimed at a wide section of the American population. In this survey, we asked participants a variety of questions relating to their secondary content use in order to better quantify the spread of these technologies into the world.

The insights from this analysis helped us to focus new secondary content experiences towards the types of content people want to engage with, on the devices where they want it, and at the appropriate time to not interfere with the program. We offer several implications for design based on our findings.

RELATED WORK

A wide variety of secondary content systems have been created over the years, both in academic settings as well as commercially viable solutions. A variety of studies have mostly explored their use qualitatively, without providing quantitative insights as to the prevalence of use in the broader audience.

Early work in this community explored social television systems [7, 8]. In these systems, users could exchange textual or voice content with each other during a television broadcast. While in field studies heavy use was observed, these types of systems never made it into the mainstream of readily available technology on set-top boxes or streaming sites.

The types of secondary content around TV programs that did emerge into public use were primarily on social network sites such as Twitter or Facebook. Multiple researchers in the TVX community [15, 16] have studied the use of these social platforms for particular shows or events. However, little academic work has sought to quantify the use of these social platforms for TV-related content more generally. Twitter's own TV page points to MacMillan [11], which shows that while there were 350,000 Tweets in a month relating to Game of Thrones (#GoT), these only maxed out at 18 Tweets per minute during one of the 60-minute episodes, showing that Tweeting during a show was hardly a mass phenomenon. Nielsen's Social Content Ratings [14] shows a similar pattern, with only tens of thousands of users Tweeting for the top TV shows during the week of January 8th, 2017, the most recent week available, for shows with audiences in the millions of viewers.

Other research has focused on timecode-synchronized feeds of related content for television shows. Parallel Feeds [3] provided a stream of content related to events in the show, such as links to related Wikipedia pages or related YouTube videos. Fan Feeds [2] took this further and allowed fans to create their own related content feed for others.

Companion apps, taking this idea of related content to a point of rich navigation, have also been created in research environments for shows such as Justified [13] and Game of Thrones [18]. Television networks have created their own apps for popular shows as well that have been more widely released. Amazon and IMDB partnered to create X-Ray [1], which provides additional content about actors in particular scenes of popular shows and movies. However, to our knowledge the use of these services has not been longitudinally studied in real contexts of use.

Hillman et al. [9] have explored fandom communities on Tumblr and how viewers create their own fan fiction as well as the use of animated GIFs on the platform to express reactions to events in a television program. However, it is not clear from this research how many viewers participate in these activities.

Overall, while many platforms exist today for secondary content interaction, it is not clear how often they are used and when they are used with respect to watching the program content. We set out to answer these questions through a survey deployed to a broad US-based audience.

METHOD
We conducted a survey in June 2016 to explore secondary content interactions. This was towards the end of the TV season, while popular shows such as Game of Thrones were in their final episodes of the season and traditional network television had just gone on its summer break. Therefore asking about interactions that participants had performed in the past month would capture the peak of the TV season as many shows aired their season finales.

The survey was deployed on Amazon Mechanical Turk to an audience of 153 diverse participants aged 19-69. 56% of participants were male and 47% had college degrees (compared to 42% nationally). Income ranged from <$15k to >$150k per year. In earlier work, we have found that these panels accurately represent technology usage behaviors within 7% of larger, professionally-commissioned market research samples and are accurate enough to discover which behaviors are common, prevalent, or rare in the broader American population [4]. Data from similar studies has been presented at TVX in the past [5].

Specific questions from the survey will be discussed below in the Findings. Broadly, we asked about particular secondary content experiences that participants had engaged in within the past month, and at any time in the past for their favorite show. We asked about recent experiences in order to reduce bias in self-reporting, as people are more likely to remember specific recent interactions. In addition to the type of experience, we asked questions around the timing of that interaction with respect to watching the show as well as the devices that they used to access both the primary and secondary content.

FINDINGS
In this section we will explore the specific questions that we asked and the data received from our participants. We will refer heavily to the tables shown on the next page, which summarize the data received. Overall, this data helps to quantify current use of secondary content experiences on a variety of platforms, and thus to understand the opportunities for new content experiences that can be created for mass-market adoption.

Secondary Content Consumption
Table 1 shows the percentage of respondents who have engaged in particular secondary content consumption interactions in the past month. The most popular category of content was "Additional Information about the Show," with 73% of participants looking for this type of information. "Information about Actors" followed closely behind, with 62% of participants looking for this type of information in the past month.

Most interesting to us are the types of interactions that participants were not engaging in. Only 15% were reading celebrity news articles about actors, and only 6% were engaging with fan fiction. Interestingly, if asked to choose between viewing social content from the show's official account (or actor's accounts) versus seeing content from fans, 67% of participants chose the official show content

What additional/related content have you looked at for a TV show you watched in the past month?	
ABOUT THE SHOW	**73%**
Trailers/Teasers for future episodes	49%
Information related to the episode (summaries, details about a scene)	40%
Behind the Scenes Videos, Actor/Director Interviews	29%
Episode Recap Videos	25%
ACTOR INFO	**62%**
Actor Bios/Profiles (e.g. IMDB, Wikipedia)	45%
Actor Filmography (Other movies/shows they have been on)	32%
Social Network Posts from Actors/Shows	27%
Celebrity Articles / Gossip about Actors	15%
SOCIAL	**50%**
What other people are saying about the show (Posts about the show, comments, Tweets, etc.)	50%
FANDOM	**43%**
GIFs/Memes about the show	41%
Fan Fiction (i.e. stories written by people using characters from the show)	6%

Table 1: Percentage of respondents who have looked for particular types of secondary content in the past month.

Which of the following information sources have you used in the past month to find additional information about a TV show, actor, or character?	
DATA SOURCES	
IMDB	68%
Google/Yahoo/Bing Search	64%
Wikipedia	62%
TOP SOCIAL SOURCES	
Reddit	47%
Facebook	41%
Twitter	32%
OTHER SOCIAL SOURCES	
Instagram	15%
Tumblr	5%
Snapchat	4%

Table 2: Percentage of respondents who turned to particular information sources for secondary content in the past month.

Think about the show you feel most passionately about. Which of these have you done?	
Read content online about the show (reviews, interviews, official social network posts, etc.)	90%
Talked to/messaged a friend about the show.	69%
Posted on social media about the show	42%
Joined an online community about the show	22%
Created content related to the show (GIF, Meme, Review, Fan Fiction)	7%

Table 3: Percentage of respondents who have engaged in secondary content behaviors for the show that they feel most passionately about.

used social sources such as Instagram, Tumblr, and Snapchat were the least frequently used.

With all of the attention in the TVX community about "second screening" – or looking at information related to a show simultaneously to watching a program, we were interested in when people were looking for this information. Consistent with findings from Holz et al. [10], we found that relatively few instances of related content consumption occurred while watching a particular show. When asked to think about the last time that they looked for related television content, only 20% of participants had looked while the show was on. 60% looked after the show, while another 20% had looked before the episode started.

Secondary Content Creation

Turning from consumption to creation, we now look at the percentage of participants who were involved in creating a wide variety of related content for television shows. As shown in Table 3, we asked participants to think about their favorite television program, and the types of interactions that they had engaged in about this show.

While 90% of participants had consumed secondary content related to that show, only 42% had posted online about that show, 22% had joined an online community about the show, and only 7% had created content about that show, such as a GIF, meme, or review. We note here that these behaviors could have occurred any time in the past (even years ago) for a participant's favorite show, thus indicating a likely upper bound on these behaviors that is still rather low, and lower than we expected.

Age Differences

We observed age effects in social network interactions including creating a GIF/meme ($t=5.15$, $p<10^{-7}$), and going to Tumblr ($t=6.59$, $p<10^{-6}$), Instagram ($t=2.95$, $p=0.005$), Snapchat ($t=3.60$, $p=0.009$), or Reddit ($t=3.67$, $p=0.0003$) for related information, where younger participants were significantly more likely to engage in these interactions. There were no differences based on age in viewing second screen content before, during, or after a show or in other aspects presented in the tables.

showing a strong preference for an official voice from the show and more insight from the actors themselves.

When it comes to where users are turning to find this information, we can look at Table 2 for more details. IMDB, web search, and Wikipedia were the most common sources with over 60% of users turning to each of these within the past month. Social sources such as Reddit, Facebook, and Twitter come in next with between one third and one half of participants turning to each of these. Lesser-

LIMITATIONS

This study only explores behaviors in the United States. Understanding secondary content experiences in other markets remains a topic for future work. We are also lacking the qualitative data to more deeply explore why particular participants engaged in the behaviors that they mentioned. We have conducted a few preliminary interviews in this area, however a full qualitative exploration is beyond the scope of this short paper. Finally, we rely on a sample from Amazon Mechanical Turk. While we have shown in other work [4] that these samples can be trusted to provide results within about 7% from larger, prohibitively expensive market research studies, we have seen some instances where for particular questions the responses are off by more than 7%. Findings should be taken to be approximations of the broader US population and to indicate what many people are doing, some are doing, or few are doing.

DISCUSSION

This data has allowed us to get a deeper picture into what people are actually doing out in the world when it comes to secondary television-related content. What we have found most interesting is that most secondary content experiences occur after a program (60%) with only 20% occurring while the program is on. This validates earlier smaller-scale studies (e.g. [10]) and shows that this behavior is the norm and not the exception in the broader population. With the large focus on second screening and real-time companion apps at TVX, perhaps there is a need for a deeper focus on systems that help prepare viewers for an episode or help them deconstruct and share afterwards.

When it comes to sharing, we were surprised by the relatively low frequency of social and creation behaviors around television content. For their most loved television program, only 42% had ever posted online about it, and only 7% had ever created any sort of content about it. If this is for the show they are most passionate about, social numbers for other programs are bound to be even lower. It is worth exploring more deeply through qualitative interviews why people are averse to sharing viewpoints and media around television programs. Fear of spoiling [15] and differing political views [19] might be some of the reasons, and developing systems that help combat these issues could offer promise in increasing social behaviors around television content.

What is promising is that the data most often sought by viewers is structured data that is readily available online. Information about the show (air dates, number of seasons, shooting locations, etc.), actors (biographies, photos, filmographies, etc.), and related media (such as trailers, episode summaries and behind the scenes clips) could easily be aggregated to create a compelling post-viewing experience.

It would still be interesting to investigate this topic further and to observe viewers as they go through a post-show content exploration experience. This would help understand exactly what they are engaging with, in what order, how they discover new related content, and how other members of the household factor into this content exploration. We leave this to future work beyond the scope of this short quantitatively-focused paper.

IMPLICATIONS FOR DESIGN

The emergence of online video portals to find and watch large numbers of popular television series has dramatically changed the opportunities to create secondary content interactions. Content portals such as Netflix, Hulu, and Yahoo View provide viewers with a single place to gain access to vast content libraries.

While these sites have already done some work to integrate secondary content experiences (e.g. Amazon X-Ray [1], or the Tumblr GIFs and Behind the Scenes clips in Yahoo View), our survey points to new opportunities.

Focus on After the Show

Television is often watched because it is an immersive experience [12] that takes people out of their living rooms and into rich new worlds. This is fairly incompatible with being removed from this world to engage with secondary content while a program is being watched.

Our participants demonstrated a clear preference for viewing related content after a show was over, or before it started, accounting for 80% of recent secondary content interactions. Systems that attempt to engage users in related content to should focus on this time frame so that viewers can focus on the program and engage with related content before or after the program with more of their attention.

Aggregate Content Based on Structured Data

Most of the media that users were consuming relating to a television show was based on structured data that is readily available. While 64% of users turned towards a web search for this data, media platforms can easily aggregate this data in one place.

Basic show metadata and actor information, such as that from IMDB and Wikipedia can be used to find additional content. News articles about the actors, recent social media posts, clips of them from YouTube and other online video sources could all be aggregated together with biographies and links to related shows directly in the post-viewing experience instead of launching viewers directly into the next episode.

Provide More Targeted Social Experiences

We have observed that viewers are often hesitant to post to social media, even about their favorite shows. Creating more targeted social media experiences, harkening back to systems that connect users 1-1 (e.g. [8]) or in small groups (e.g. [2]) can help overcome reluctance to post and share content from favorite shows to broad and heterogeneous networks.

One way that this could be done is with time-synchronized comments in small social groups. Another way could be with easy-to-create simultaneous small-group watching experiences, similar to Shamma et al.'s system for online video clips [17].

CONCLUSION

In this short paper, we have explored current practices around secondary content viewing and creation in the broader American population. We have identified that viewers most commonly look for information about a show or an actor after a show is over, not while it is playing. We have also shown that fewer than half of participants had created content relating to their most favorite show, showing that content creation (including social content such as Tweets and Facebook posts) remains a niche activity for most general TV watching. Exploring ways to increase social engagement in television programs remains an area for future work.

ACKNOWEDGEMENTS

I would like to thank the Yahoo View team. Their practical product questions inspired much of this work to better understand second screen experiences before, during, and after shows. I would also like to thank the broader User Experience Research team at Yahoo for providing a place to conduct work that is both practically useful for products and also has an academic impact.

REFERENCES

1. Amazon.com Press Release. For the First Time Ever, X-Ray for Movies and TV Shows Now Available Directly on Your TV — Answer the Classic Movie-Watching Question "Who's That Guy?" with Your Amazon Fire TV. http://phx.corporate-ir.net/phoenix.zhtml?c=176060&p=irol-newsArticle&ID=2034369&highlight= Accessed 1/23/17.

2. Santosh Basapur, Hiren Mandalia, Shirley Chaysinh, Young Lee, Narayanan Venkitaraman, and Crysta Metcalf. 2012. FANFEEDS: evaluation of socially generated information feed on second screen as a TV show companion. In *Proceedings of the 10th European conference on Interactive tv and video* (EuroiTV '12). ACM, New York, NY, USA, 87-96. DOI=http://dx.doi.org/10.1145/2325616.2325636

3. Santosh Basapur, Gunnar Harboe, Hiren Mandalia, Ashley Novak, Van Vuong, and Crysta Metcalf. 2011. Field trial of a dual device user experience for iTV. In *Proceedings of the 9th international interactive conference on Interactive television* (EuroITV '11). ACM, New York, NY, USA, 127-136. DOI=http://dx.doi.org/10.1145/2000119.2000145

4. Frank Bentley, Nediyana Daskalova, and Brooke White. 2017. Comparing the Reliability of Amazon Mechanical Turk and Survey Monkey to Traditional Market Research Surveys. In Extended Abstracts of *the SIGCHI Conference on Human Factors in Computing Systems* (CHI '17). ACM, New York, NY, USA. DOI=http://dx.doi.org/10.1145/3027063.3053335

5. Frank Bentley and Janet Murray. 2016. Understanding Video Rewatching Experiences. In *Proceedings of the ACM International Conference on Interactive Experiences for TV and Online Video* (TVX '16). ACM, New York, NY, USA, 69-75. DOI: http://dx.doi.org/10.1145/2932206.2932213

6. Frank R. Bentley and Michael Groble. 2009. TuVista: meeting the multimedia needs of mobile sports fans. In *Proceedings of the 17th ACM international conference on Multimedia* (MM '09). ACM, New York, NY, USA, 471-480. DOI: http://dx.doi.org/10.1145/1631272.1631337

7. David Geerts and Dirk De Grooff. 2009. Supporting the social uses of television: sociability heuristics for social tv. In *Proceedings of the SIGCHI Conference on Human Factors in Computing Systems* (CHI '09). ACM, New York, NY, USA, 595-604. DOI=http://dx.doi.org/10.1145/1518701.1518793

8. Gunnar Harboe, Crysta J. Metcalf, Frank Bentley, Joe Tullio, Noel Massey, and Guy Romano. 2008. Ambient Social TV: drawing people into a shared experience. In *Proceedings of the SIGCHI Conference on Human Factors in Computing Systems* (CHI '08). ACM, New York, NY, USA, 1-10. DOI=http://dx.doi.org/10.1145/1357054.1357056

9. Serena Hillman, Jason Procyk, and Carman Neustaedter. 2014. Tumblr fandoms, community & culture. In *Proceedings of the companion publication of the 17th ACM conference on Computer supported cooperative work & social computing* (CSCW Companion '14). ACM, New York, NY, USA, 285-288. DOI=http://dx.doi.org/10.1145/2556420.2557634

10. Christian Holz, Frank Bentley, Karen Church, and Mitesh Patel. 2015. "I'm just on my phone and they're watching TV": Quantifying mobile device use while watching television. In *Proceedings of the ACM International Conference on Interactive Experiences for TV and Online Video* (TVX '15). ACM, New York, NY, USA, 93-102. DOI=http://dx.doi.org/10.1145/2745197.2745210

11. Gordon MacMillan. #GoT: Conversation last month about Game of Thrones. https://reverb.guru/view/671647250248877730 Accessed 1/23/17.

12. Janet Murray. Hamlet on the Holodeck: The future of narrative in cyberspace. Simon and Schuster (1997).

13. Abhishek Nandakumar and Janet Murray. 2014. Companion apps for long arc TV series: supporting new viewers in complex storyworlds with tightly synchronized context-sensitive annotations. In *Proceedings of the 2014 ACM international*

conference on Interactive experiences for TV and online video (TVX '14). ACM, New York, NY, USA, 3-10. DOI=http://dx.doi.org/10.1145/2602299.2602317

14. Nielsen Social Content Ratings. http://www.nielsensocial.com/socialcontentratings/weekly/ Accessed 1/23/17.

15. Steven Schirra, Huan Sun, and Frank Bentley. 2014. Together alone: motivations for live-tweeting a television series. In *Proceedings of the SIGCHI Conference on Human Factors in Computing Systems* (CHI '14). ACM, New York, NY, USA, 2441-2450. DOI=http://dx.doi.org/10.1145/2556288.2557070

16. David A. Shamma, Lyndon Kennedy, and Elizabeth F. Churchill. 2009. Tweet the debates: understanding community annotation of uncollected sources. In *Proceedings of the first SIGMM workshop on Social media* (WSM '09). ACM, New York, NY, USA, 3-10. DOI=http://dx.doi.org/10.1145/1631144.1631148

17. David A. Shamma, Marcello Bastea-Forte, Niels Joubert, and Yiming Liu. Enhancing online personal connections through the synchronized sharing of online video. In *CHI'08 extended abstracts on Human factors in computing systems*, pp. 2931-2936. ACM, 2008.

18. Pedro Silva, Yasmin Amer, William Tsikerdanos, Jesse Shedd, Isabel Restrepo, and Janet Murray. 2015. A Game of Thrones Companion: Orienting Viewers to Complex Storyworlds via Synchronized Visualizations. In *Proceedings of the ACM International Conference on Interactive Experiences for TV and Online Video* (TVX '15). ACM, New York, NY, USA, 167-172. DOI=http://dx.doi.org/10.1145/2745197.2755519

19. Emily K. Vraga, Kjerstin Thorson, Neta Kligler-Vilenchik, and Emily Gee. How individual sensitivities to disagreement shape youth political expression on Facebook. *Computers in Human Behavior* 45 (2015): 281-289.

Virtual Reality and the Future of Immersive Entertainment

Arthur van Hoff

Jaunt

Palo Alto, California, USA

avh@jauntvr.com

ABSTRACT

Jaunt [1] has been creating cinematic virtual reality experiences since 2013. With cinematic VR, the user is transported to a place of wonder where storytelling has completely new dimensions. In this keynote, Arthur will discuss how Jaunt leverages this new technology and overcomes challenges in storytelling, production and distribution. Cinematic VR allows storytellers and brands to create an emotional connection with the viewer, using tools and techniques familiar to the industry.

ACM Classification Keywords

H.5.1 Multimedia Information Systems; Artificial, augmented, and virtual realities

Author Keywords

Cinematic virtual reality; storytelling; production; distribution.

BIOGRAPHY

Arthur van Hoff is Founder and CTO of Jaunt. Jaunt's technology provides an end-to-end solution for creating cinematic VR experiences. Arthur is serial entrepreneur and was most recently CTO at Flipboard. He started his career in Silicon Valley at Sun Microsystems where he was an early developer of the Java programming language. Since then he has started several successful companies including Marimba (IPO 1999), Strangeberry (acquired by TiVo), ZING (acquired by Dell), and Ellerdale (acquired by Flipboard). Arthur has expertise in machine learning, big data, mobile applications, 3D printing, and computational photography. He is originally from the Netherlands and has a master's degree in Computer Science from Strathclyde University in Glasgow.

REFERENCES

1. Jaunt, https://www.jauntvr.com

Permission to make digital or hard copies of part or all of this work for personal or classroom use is granted without fee provided that copies are not made or distributed for profit or commercial advantage and that copies bear this notice and the full citation on the first page. Copyrights for third-party components of this work must be honored. For all other uses, contact the owner/author(s). Copyright is held by the author/owner(s).

TVX 2017, June 14–16, 2017, Hilversum, The Netherlands.
ACM ISBN 978-1-4503-4529-3/17/06.
http://dx.doi.org/10.1145/3077548.3080529

Emerging TV Experiences:
How VR, Voice, and Emerging Audiences Have Changed the TV Landscape

Isha Dandavate
YouTube
901 Cherry Ave
San Bruno, CA 94066
ishad@google.com

Kerwell Liao
YouTube
901 Cherry Ave
San Bruno, CA 94066
kerwell@google.com

Lettie Malan
YouTube
901 Cherry Ave
San Bruno, CA 94066
lettiemalan@google.com

Nibha Jain
YouTube
901 Cherry Ave
San Bruno, CA 94066
nibha@google.com

ABSTRACT
At TVX 2015, we led an interactive workshop to explore how people, contexts, and multi-device experiences contribute to a changed landscape of TV watching behaviors. Since then, the television and video industry has developed new technologies and attracted an ever-growing audience. This one-day, interactive workshop at TVX 2017 will bring together academics and professionals to update the framework, and to understand the challenges and opportunities associated with technological developments in VR/360 video and voice interactions, and a new focus on audiences such as kids, teens, and emerging markets.

Author Keywords
Television; Interactive Workshop; Emerging Markets; Teens; Kids; Virtual Reality; Voice Interactions

ACM Classification Keywords
H.5. [Information Interfaces and Presentation] M. [Miscellaneous]

INTRODUCTION
Since the introduction of the TV, the user experience has evolved from a single use case involving groups surrounding a single screen, with viewing limited to programming on 2-3 channels, to ever more complex systems involving competing and complementary technologies, devices, services, programming, inputs and interactions, contexts, and expectations which are further convoluted by the ecosystem of user, programmer and advertiser intentions. Most recent developments in this space include virtual reality, voice controls, and video apps targeted at young and emerging audiences.

Though the idea of virtual reality has existed since Charles

Permission to make digital or hard copies of part or all of this work for personal or classroom use is granted without fee provided that copies are not made or distributed for profit or commercial advantage and that copies bear this notice and the full citation on the first page. Copyrights for third-party components of this work must be honored. For all other uses, contact the Owner/Author.
TVX '17, June 14-16, 2017, Hilversum, Netherlands
© 2017 Copyright is held by the owner/author(s).
ACM ISBN 978-1-4503-4529-3/17/06.
http://dx.doi.org/10.1145/3077548.3078626

Wheatstone's research into and development of the stereoscope in 1838, we are still trying to figure out what is practical in the near term, as well as its future applications. Virtual reality allows people to interact with content in a much more complex way than ever before. For the first time, consuming video content involves a physical aspect tied to the viewer's present context. And while increased immersion may be impressive, virtual reality content is much more difficult to create than normal video, and viewing it comes with its own set challenges and social stigmas.

The emergence of voice control as a reliable interaction mechanism has opened the door for a new suite of possibilities. People can use their voice in lieu of a remote to conduct searches on their TV, and may soon be able to use voice as an authentication mechanism. However, machine voice recognition that is robust enough for consumers is still in its early stages, can only be used for simple actions, and is riddled with recognition errors. Social stigma and challenges in exposing interaction possibilities without a visual component currently limit the widespread adoption of voice control.

In addition to new technologies, the target audiences of these experiences have also changed. While older demographics still subscribe to cable TV and traditional outlets, younger audiences (13-18 years old) show a preference for online streaming experiences and mobile devices. Parents of even younger audiences, below 13 years old, are seeking ways to give their kids access to kid-appropriate content. Even kids who can't yet read are accessing online video content.

As more users from developing countries come online, designers also have to consider their particular needs. For example, bandwidth constraints can impact how we design for latency. Users in emerging markets may also hold different cultural views and beliefs that affect their end-to-end video streaming experience: how they find content, assess its quality, and what they do with it after viewing.

These emerging technologies and audiences present new opportunities and challenges for researchers and practitioners. In order to gain a better understanding that supports design and exploration in VR, voice controls, and needs of emerging audiences, we will bring together experts in the field to collaboratively articulate a framework based on their shared experience.

AIM

This workshop aims to bring together the expertise of a diverse group of academics, industry practitioners, and others working in the television and video experiences space to build a shared understanding of the television landscape and how new technologies are rapidly evolving relevant use cases. We will lead structured discussions and brainstorming activities to explore how new technologies and audiences are shaping the design and use of video platforms. This interactive workshop should culminate in the synthesis of key opportunities of each emerging experience.

AGENDA
9:00-9:10 am INTRO

Workshop leads introduce themselves and present the workshop agenda.

9:10-10:30 am PRESENTATIONS AND HIGHLIGHTS

Workshop leads and selected participants will present research findings relevant to the three emerging areas. Participants will be invited to take notes on post-its, which will then be used in a collaborative synthesis process to identify emerging themes.

10:30-11:00 am BREAK

11:00-12:30 pm WORLD CAFE

Groups will participate in a world cafe to discuss opportunities and lessons learned for emerging experiences (VR, Voice Interactions, Designing for Children and Families, Designing for Teens).

12:30- 1:30 pm LUNCH BREAK

1:30- 2:30 pm GROUP BRAINSTORM

Participants will break out into groups, and in each group will answer key questions about how an emerging technology has changed the landscape of TV experiences. After the guided brainstorms, groups will work together to create a poster synthesizing key takeaways.

2:30- 3:00 pm COFFEE BREAK

3:00-4:00 pm PRESENTATIONS

Groups share their key takeaways with the workshop participants.

4:00- 4:30 pm CLOSING NOTES

PARTICIPATION

We will disseminate the call for participation throughout our company (Google) and to other academic and industry groups we have worked with (UC Berkeley, University of Michigan, Stanford D School, Anthrodesign, IxDA, XXUX).

Interested participants must submit their CV/resume, and a few paragraphs discussing their existing work in the TV/online video space and their background via email to yttvx2017@gmail.com.

We invite interested presenters, who have experience with VR, voice interactions, or young age groups, to submit a 2-4 page position paper by March 21. Those who are selected to present at the workshop will be notified by April 3.

The workshop can accommodate up to 30 participants, so if applicants exceed this number, participants will be selected based on both their date of application and CV/resume to ensure a variety of viewpoints and expertise are represented.

ORGANIZERS

Isha Dandavate is a User Experience Researcher at YouTube. She currently leads research focused on mobile devices and the video sharing behaviors of teens. In the past, she led research for the YouTube living room team. Prior to joining YouTube, she was a design researcher at SonicRim, a global design research consultancy based in San Francisco, where she conducted exploratory design research and co-design workshops. Isha holds a master's degree in information management and systems from the UC Berkeley School of Information, and an undergraduate degree from New York University.

Kerwell Liao has previously done research for YouTube on mobile and tablet, and currently leads multi-device and voice user experience research for YouTube. Prior to YouTube, he collaborated on a framework to explain device and account sharing, and investigated solutions for identity and account management across Google. Kerwell has an undergraduate degree in Information Science from Cornell University.

Lettie Malan is the User Experience Research lead for YouTube Kids. Previous projects include YouTube Music Key. Prior to joining YouTube, Lettie was an Interaction Designer at the Institute for the Study of Knowledge Management in Education (ISKME). Lettie has a Masters in Information Science from the University of Michigan and an undergraduate degree in Industrial Design.

Nibha Jain currently leads Emerging Markets research at YouTube. In the past, she's helped establish the cross device UX program at YouTube, helping teams understand and build for the key differences in video consumption patterns and needs on Phones, Tablets and TVs. Her past work includes contextual research at companies like Samsung and HFI. Nibha holds a masters and undergraduate degree in Industrial Design from Georgia Institute of Technology and National Institute of Design, India.

REFERENCES

1. Anderson, M. (January 2016). More Americans using smartphones for getting directions, streaming TV. Retrieved October 25, 2016 from http://www.pewresearch.org/fact-tank/2016/01/29/us-smartphone-use/

2. Anon. World Café Method. (2016). Retrieved October 25, 2016 from http://www.theworldcafe.com/key-concepts-resources/world-cafe-method

3. Nielsen. Age of Technology: Generational Video Viewing Preferences Vary by Device and Activity. (April 2015). Retrieved October 25, 2016 from http://www.nielsen.com/us/en/insights/news/2015/age-of-technology-generational-video-viewing-preferences-vary-by-device-and-activity.html

4. Wheatstone, C. (1838). Contributions to the Physiology of Vision.--Part the First. On Some Remarkable, and Hitherto Unobserved, Phenomena of Binocular Vision. *Philosophical Transactions of the Royal Society of London, 128*, 371-394. Retrieved from http://www.jstor.org/stable/108203

Converging User-Generated Material with Professional Video User Experiences

Michael Evans
BBC R&D
Salford, UK
michael.evans@bbc.co.uk

George Margetis
Foundation of Research and
Technology — Hellas
Heraklion, Greece
gmarget@ics.forth.gr

Stavroula Ntoa
Foundation of Research and
Technology — Hellas
Heraklion, Greece
stant@ics.forth.gr

Rajitha Weerakkody
BBC R&D
London, UK
rajitha.weerakkody@bbc.co.uk

ABSTRACT

This multidisciplinary workshop will contribute to a user experience (UX) research agenda for the effective combination of audiovisual material from professional and non-professional contributors. Responding to trends in developing technology and in user behaviour, the workshop will investigate a specific range of themes, deeper knowledge of which will support more coherent, higher quality integration of the creative efforts of non-professional contributors with those of professionals. The overall aim is to equip professional producers with the means to support and develop their contributors to be successful in providing material, and, therefore, optimise viewers' quality of experience when watching mixed-origin content.

ACM Classification Keywords

H.5.m. Information Interfaces and Presentation (e.g. HCI): Miscellaneous

Author Keywords

Quality of Experience; User generated content; COGNITUS

INTRODUCTION

The Internet is transforming the human experience of creating and using television content in a wide range of ways. Many of these developments come under the broad category of disruption to the historically demarcated roles of broadcaster and viewer. The rise of interactive TV and video-on-demand has shifted much of the professional broadcasters' traditionally unchallenged role in dictating and scheduling the audience's experience towards models with much more viewer agency. Moreover, current trends like *object-based broadcasting* [1],

Permission to make digital or hard copies of part or all of this work for personal or classroom use is granted without fee provided that copies are not made or distributed for profit or commercial advantage and that copies bear this notice and the full citation on the first page. Copyrights for third-party components of this work must be honored. For all other uses, contact the owner/author(s). Copyright is held by the author/owner(s).

TVX 2017, June 14–16, 2017, Hilversum, The Netherlands.
ACM ISBN 978-1-4503-4529-3/17/06.
http://dx.doi.org/10.1145/3077548.3078627

[2] further evolve the producer-consumer relationship towards a model where the professional broadcaster curates content for audiovisual experiences that are rendered responsively to individuals' requirements, preferences and contexts-of-use. Technology development—in particular bidirectional, data agnostic delivery networks and the proliferation of processing capability throughout those networks—have driven behaviour and changed expectations amongst producers and users. A related technology and behaviour change is the subject of this workshop proposal; people capturing and sharing increasing amounts of video using cameras (usually in smartphones), connected to ubiquitous high-bandwidth Internet. User-generated content (UGC), including user-generated video (UGV), has very significant potential to supplement the quantity and editorial diversity of professional coverage. Its potential effect on quality of experience (QoE), however, has both positive and negative implications. A research agenda to develop and apply knowledge about the relationship between UGC and professional content will help ensure high quality UX.

AIMS AND SCOPE

The purpose of this workshop is to bring together a diverse group of researchers and practitioners for focussed discussion and knowledge sharing. Collectively, we will generate a research and development agenda; the research questions that we must answer and the techniques and technologies that we must invent in order to maximise the value of integrating UGC with professionally-captured material. This includes accelerating the adoption and growth of behaviours in both communities; professional producers and potential contributors. Specifically, the organisers believe that the following themes are important:

Novel Quality of Experience (QoE) Metrics
The technical capabilities of an average cameraphone are increasing significantly, but there are still likely to be differences in depth of field, video codec, lens distortion and other features, compared to professional footage. Perhaps much more significantly, there are also differences in typical shot composition and construction in video from these distinct origins. Comparable issues exist in the capture of audio. Offsetting

or reinforcing these are editorial contrasts, such as viewpoint. How do these differences impact on a viewer's perceived quality of experience? What subjective metrics will we need in order to usefully distinguish between different levels of quality, and what methodologies will allow us to develop and make use of them? Critically, what additional QoE issues may be formed by the fusion of professional and user-generated material in a single experience, and how can we measure them?

Computational Enhancement of Perceived QoE
Having developed metrics for effective human assessment of QoE, how can these be deployed in computational form in systems to maximise quality?

Contributor Reward, Motivation and Development
For professional content to be enhanced by inclusion of UGC, potential contributors need to be motivated to share good quality material with the professional broadcaster. This motivation needs to persist even when the chance of being included in professional coverage is very low. What are likely motivational factors for contributors, and how do they develop with time and in different use cases? What forms of reward, social capital and other motivational support will sustain supply of UGC and how can professionals help contributors improve?

Methodological Research
What are the requirements and opportunities for new research methods, including for longitudinal study and large scale deployment in-the-wild?

Personal Data Ethics, Creative Control and Informed Choice
Scenarios in which contributors share video and audio, perhaps including footage of other people, bring issues of consent and privacy. These are supplemented by questions of contributors' and professionals' expectations of creative control. What mechanisms and responsibilities do professionals have in supporting contributors' informed choice over what to share?

WORKSHOP FORMAT
The organisers of this workshop are all members of the consortium working on the European Union Horizon 2020 project COGNITUS[1]. This runs from January 2016 to December 2018 and brings together experts in broadcast technology and UX, with the aim of enhancing ultra high definition (UHD) broadcasting through combination with UGC. Accepted papers come from inside and outside the COGNITUS consortium, encompassing academic and industrial researchers, and covering a variety of disciplines. Successful submissions will be published as a workshop proceedings via the COGNITUS website. At the workshop, each paper will be presented by its authors in a lightning talk and the rest of the day will comprise a short series of facilitated discussions on the workshop themes.

Authors and other workshop participants will be asked to each contribute a use case for discussion. These will describe applications or convergence of professional and UGC in ways that challenge existing practices, technologies and behaviours. The overall outcome will be set of research agendas, organised by theme. These will be published on the workshop website.

---

[1] http://cognitus-h2020.eu Converging broadcast and user generated content for interactive ultra-high definition services

ORGANISERS
Michael Evans is a Research Lead in the User Experience group at BBC R&D, in which human-computer interaction engineers and scientists investigate the impact of interaction technologies on BBC services, audiences and production. Before joining the BBC in 1999, Mike co-founded the Signal Processing Laboratory and lectured at the University of Reading. He is a Chartered Engineer and completed a PhD in psychoacoustics at British Telecom Labs in 1997. Mike's publications include papers on perceptual evaluation, signal processing, accessibility and HCI research methods. Mike has been Industry Chair and Associate Chair of TVX2014 in Newcastle and TVX2016 in Chicago. He was also Co-chair and Organiser of the TVUX workshop at CHI2013 in Paris.

George Margetis is a senior Research Engineer at the Human-Computer Interaction Laboratory of FORTH-ICS since 2005. His current work focuses on interaction design, Ambient Intelligence and Smart Spaces, Universal Access and Design for All. He has participated in a number of European and National research projects. His recent work includes the analysis and investigation of tools and interaction techniques for multimodal interaction in Ambient Intelligence environments. He holds a degree in Computer Science, M.Sc. in Computer Networks and Digital Communications and in Information Systems, and is a PhD candidate in Computer Science, at the University of Crete. His publications include papers on Universal Design, accessibility, Ambient Intelligence and big-data visualization.

Stavroula Ntoa holds a degree in Computer Science, M.Sc. in Information Systems and in Computer Networks and Digital Communications, and is a PhD candidate in Computer Science, at the University of Crete. She is a member of the Human-Computer Interaction Laboratory of FORTH-ICS since 2000. She is experienced in the design, development and evaluation of accessibility software for motor-impaired users, and of accessible web applications, as well as in UX design for responsive web applications. Her research interests fall in the field of Universal Access, Design for All, Web Accessibility, and eLearning, with her current work focussing on UX evaluation in Ambient Intelligence environments.

Rajitha Weerakkody joined BBC R&D in 2008, and has since worked on a number of projects including audio visual archiving and digital preservation, and the 8K Ultra HD (Super Hi-Vision) trial with NHK for London 2012 Games. He currently works in the video compression research team. Rajitha got his BSc (Eng.) and PhD from the University of Moratuwa, Sri Lanka, and the University of Surrey, UK, respectively. In between he worked in the wireless telecommunications industry for 5 years. His main current interests are in video compression algorithm development, video quality assessment and UHDTV fundamentals.

ACKNOWLEDGMENTS
Part of this work has been conducted within the project COGNITUS, which has received funding from the European Union's Horizon 2020 research and innovation programme under grant agreement No 687605.

REFERENCES

1. Mike Armstrong, Matthew Brooks, Anthony Churnside, Michael Evans, Frank Melchior, and Matthew Shotton. 2014. Object-Based Broadcasting: Curation, Responsiveness and User Experience. In *Proceedings of International Broadcasting Convention*. http://dx.doi.org/10.1049/ibc.2016.0034

2. Michael Evans, Tristan Ferne, Zillah Watson, Frank Melchior, Matthew Brooks, Phil Stenton, and Ian Forrester. 2016. Creating object-based experiences in the real world. In *Proceedings of International Broadcasting Convention*. http://dx.doi.org/10.1049/ibc.2016.0034

Workshop on Interactive Digital Storytelling in Broadcasting Environment

Sebastian Arndt
Norwegian University of
Science and Technology
Department of Electronic
Systems
7491 Trondheim, Norway
sebastian.arndt@ntnu.no

Veli-Pekka Räty
Norwegian University of
Science and Technology
Department of Electronic
Systems
7491 Trondheim, Norway
veli-pekka.raty@ntnu.no

Wendy Ann Mansilla
Norwegian University of
Science and Technology
Department of Electronic
Systems
7491 Trondheim, Norway
wendy.mansilla@ntnu.no

Francisco Ibáñez
Brainstorm Multimedia
Maestro Gozalbo, 23
46005 Valencia
francisco@brainstrom3d.com

Scott Davies
never.no
Blue Tower, The Landing,
Media City,
Manchester M50 2ST, UK
scott@never.no

Andrew Perkis
Norwegian University of
Science and Technology
Department of Electronic
Systems
7491 Trondheim, Norway
andrew.perkis@ntnu.no

ABSTRACT

In this workshop, we are going to explore new ways of user interaction that cater to the attention of a distracted audience. One of the challenging aspects we will focus on is the growing user requirement for real-time mobile information and stories anytime and anywhere. This has exerted significant pressure on the importance of new forms of storytelling and information delivery on every target audiences.

We will examine how to adopt new forms of digital storytelling in traditional media such as TV broadcasting. The workshop will stimulate discussions and experiences among a broad spectrum of workshop participants, such as researchers, industry, designers, and artists on how to create stories and journalism that think about information delivery in real time. The first part of this workshop consists of presentations submitted to this workshop. Here, potential effects of using digital storytelling in creation and participation of media will be discussed. Furthermore, we will also have presentations on use cases, artistic research and demonstrations of design and storytelling. To foster creativity and discussions among participants, presentations are followed by interactive group-work. Here, participants have the chance to express their ideas and scenarios on how to effectively include audiences' opinion into TV broadcasting. The workshop will be concluded by a panel discussion on the topic of new storytelling perspectives in broadcasting, and will cover aspects of the group-work and presentation of submitted work to the workshop.

Permission to make digital or hard copies of part or all of this work for personal or classroom use is granted without fee provided that copies are not made or distributed for profit or commercial advantage and that copies bear this notice and the full citation on the first page. Copyrights for third-party components of this work must be honored. For all other uses, contact the owner/author(s).

TVX '17 June 14-16, 2017, Hilversum, Netherlands
© 2017 Copyright held by the owner/author(s).
ACM ISBN 978-1-4503-4529-3/17/06.
DOI: http://dx.doi.org/10.1145/3077548.3078628

ACM Classification Keywords

Information systems: Multimedia information systems: Multimedia content creation

Author Keywords

Multimedia Information Systems, Content Production, User Experience, Media Studies, Media Art

MOTIVATION

In the past, delivery of information was one-way, broadcasters and journalists had the sole responsibility of bringing stories to their audience. Today however, such relationship between broadcasters and its audience is harder to sustain. The audience seeks to actively participate in program formation and wants its opinions heard. This is affecting the way information should be delivered from the storytelling perspective where the audience itself is contributing to the dissemination of stories using social media channels. This is especially true in the case of breaking news, where information often spreads much faster than the traditional news companies can cope with. To preserve the relevance of traditional media, such as television broadcasting and newspapers, it becomes a necessity for them to find ways to engage the audience. This includes involving the audience into the story generation and presentation, which will facilitate the enrichment of the broadcasters' program [1].

Another observable trend is the growing appetite for real-time mobile information, and stories anytime and anywhere. The reality in storytelling and information delivery is how to seize the attention of a distracted audience. One way for breaking through and taming the wandering mind of the audience is to seamlessly bring stories into their everyday lives. This challenging new requirement exerted significant pressure on the importance of new forms of storytelling and information delivery.

One of the things that this workshop will look upon is how to create stories and journalism that think about information delivery in real time. Advancements in technology and the revolution in mobile devices, give people more opportunities to draw information from several sources, and is changing the way people connect with each other. One of the challenges is to determine the impact of these technologies on the way people communicate and interact. Bringing this technological infrastructure into broadcasting should not disrupt but rather should naturally merge with our daily lives.

Another perspective that we will present in this workshop is the possibility of using multiple screens to deliver a new form of broadcasting experience in any given time and place. Research shows that using various media and creating new types of storytelling compared to the traditional first screen or a single screen view, has a positive appeal to younger audiences because it is conforming to the way they consume media [2]. However, the enrichment of broadcasting shows using these types of media is not a straight-forward process and has to be addressed. If the new concept of digital storytelling is integrated carelessly and appeals only to selected viewers, there is a risk that others may not appreciate these new services. Traditional media has to cater to all kinds of audiences, while attracting new (younger) audience at the same time not to lose their established (and often older) audience. Therefore, it is important to develop well thought concepts for each individual show. This includes designing the appearance or image of the visual content attractive and naturally flowing with the show or second screen. This is also one the goals of the VisualMedia[1] project which is supported by the Horizon 2020 programme where most of the workshop organisers are part of.

AIM AND SCOPE OF THE WORKSHOP

The goal of this workshop is to discuss new ways of information generation and delivery and adopt them both, in the traditional broadcasting sense and in the public use. Selected presentations submitted to this workshop will focus on topics that address new ways of of technically integrated digital storytelling in broadcasted shows. This includes looking into some of the new techniques in designing interactions and audiovisual content creations. Another interesting aspect that we seek to address in this workshop is to bring in alternative forms of content delivery from a more design and creative standpoint.

We will also investigate the use of new media and its concepts in TV-, web-broadcasting, and printed media. During group-work, the workshop participants will be engaged in discussions and create new use-cases on how to utilise new media such as digital storytelling. Here, different perspectives will be covered, such as information generation, retrieval, and preparation. This workshop shall facilitate professionals, academics, designers, and digital artists to put forward discussions on multidisciplinary approaches to enhance audience experience and expectations towards information delivery at anytime and anywhere.

FORMAT AND DURATION

- **Welcome and Introduction of participants** Welcome of workshop organizers with a brief introduction to the workshop topic, to assure that all the workshop participants are aware of the topic, and are able to contribute to the interactive part of the workshop. Short introduction of the workshop participants. A presentation will be given by an industry partner who is talking about how social media can already currently being implemented and used in TV broadcasting.

- **Presentations** Will contain 4 presentations of papers, that will contain of research work done, use cases or work with design, creative and storytelling focus.

- **Group-work –Creating a use-case** Participants will be divided into groups. Each group will create one use-case show using digital storytelling on a given genre. The workshop organizers will make sure that groups consist of people with diverse backgrounds. Group work will be followed by a short poster presentation from each group.

- **Panel Discussion** Discussing about future opportunities of new media in traditional media together with the audience. Potential participants: workshop-co-organizer (from industry), and two participants from the presentations.

TYPES OF SUBMISSIONS

We invite authors to submit either **research papers**, on how digital storytelling can be used in broadcasting, and how it can and is changing the traditional media landscape, or **Use-cases, Artistic research, Design studies**, describing completed or on-going projects implementing new kinds of media and/or showcasing implementations of new ways of digital storytelling.

ACKNOWLEDGEMENT

This project has received funding from the European Union's Horizon 2020 research and innovation programme under grant agreement No 687800.

REFERENCES

1. S. Arndt, A. Perkis, and V.-P. Räty. Opportunities of Social Media in TV Broadcasting. In *Proceedings of the 9th Nordic Conference on Human-Computer Interaction*, page 123. ACM, 2016.

2. A.-S. Vanhaeght and K. Donders. Moving beyond the borders of top–down broadcasting an analysis of younger users' participation in public service media. *Television & New Media*, 2015.

---

[1]www.visualmediaproject.com

In-Programme Personalisation for Broadcast: IPP4B

Jeremy Foss
Birmingham City University
Birmingham, UK
jeremy.foss@bcu.ac.uk

Ben Shirley
University of Salford
Salford, UK
b.g.shirley@salford.ac.uk

Benedita Malheiro
ISEP/IPP – Polytechnic of Porto
& INESC TEC
Porto, Portugal
mbm@isep.ipp.pt

Sara Kepplinger
Fraunhofer Institute for Digital
Media Technology
Ilmenau, Germany
kpl@idmt.fraunhofer.de

Alexandre Ulisses
MOG Technologies
Maia, Portugal
alexandre.ulisses@mog-
technologies.com

Mike Armstrong
BBC R&D
London, UK
mike.armstrong@bbc.co.uk

ABSTRACT

The IPP4B workshop assembles a group of researchers from academia and industry – BBC R&D, Ericsson and MOG Technologies – to discuss the state of the art and together envisage future directions for in-programme personalisation in broadcasting. The workshop comprises one invited keynote, two invited presentations together with a paper and discussion sessions.

Author Keywords

In-Programme Personalisation; Interactive; Broadcast; TV; Video; Audio; Object-based.

ACM Classification Keywords

H.5.1 Multimedia Information Systems

INTRODUCTION

The growing demand for personalisation provides endless research, development and innovation opportunities for academics and industry. Personalisation is usually interpreted as the generation of personalised playlist, programme guide, product placement and advertising for viewers. However the notion explored in this workshop is the personalisation of audio, video and data elements within the broadcast programme which we are calling In-Programme Personalisation. Consequently, the IPP4B workshop focusses on the automatic personalisation of the streamed content. The likely technology to support these features is object-based media where audio, video and other elements may be placed into existing media and be rendered for consumption by the end viewer.

In-Programme Personalisation is a radical innovation for broadcast media, where network content can be personalised according to the viewer profiles. However, there are many challenges to face. The aim of the workshop is to explore both the technical issues of In- Programme Personalisation for Broadcast, also the market and production of content. A community of interest needs to be realized in order that best practice, concerted development and standardisation are appropriately addressed in the industry.

KEYNOTE

The keynote entitled "Why don't we yet have in-programme personalisation?" is given by Prof. Marian Ursu from the University of York. According to Prof. Ursu, in-programme personalisation is a concept that applies to both live and pre-recorded TV productions, and, further, to the whole space that lays in-between professional and amateur video narrative production. The keynote addresses the "in-programme personalisation" paradigm with a number of exemplar professional productions made with pre-recorded footage, followed by an exemplar associated technology for automatic real-time editing. It expands the paradigm to live content, building on similarities, highlighting major differences, but, finally, drawing the two (similarities and differences) towards each other. Then, it challenges the borderline between professional and amateur productions, and look at in-programme personalisation for productions made with user-generated pre-recorded content, user-generated live content, and extensions to smart telepresence.

PRESENTATIONS

The presentations report the progress on IPP4B at BBC R&D and at Fraunhofer IDMT.

Mike Armstrong from BBC R&D presents "The workshop Progress towards creating workflows for object-based media at BBC R&D". Specifically, BBC R&D has created a number of object-based experiences - media created as a series of separate objects which can be combined on-the-fly to provide personalisation. However, the process of creating this media has involved the extensive use of spread sheets

Permission to make digital or hard copies of part or all of this work for personal or classroom use is granted without fee provided that copies are not made or distributed for profit or commercial advantage and that copies bear this notice and the full citation on the first page. Copyrights for third-party components of this work must be honored. For all other uses, contact the Owner/Author.

TVX '17, June 14-16, 2017, Hilversum, Netherlands
© 2017 Copyright is held by the owner/author(s).
ACM ISBN 978-1-4503-4529-3/17/06.
http://dx.doi.org/10.1145/3077548.3078629

and graph databases to describe the narrative and the media, all driven by manual processes and the writing of bespoke software. The most recent Cook-Along Kitchen Experience (CAKE) was created entirely as objects from conception and has enabled BBC to understand the kind of data structures and production tools needed to build to enable object-based media to be produced in a sustainable workflow. BBC has now developed a prototype data model, based on the lessons learnt from CAKE and this is forming the core of a software toolkit from which it is aiming to build usable production tools. The aim is to share these tools with a developing community of practice with partners outside the BBC as well as in-house producers.

Sara Kepplinger from Fraunhofer IDMT presents "The Quality Taxonomy for Scalable Algorithms of Free Viewpoint Video Objects". In this case, quality assessment of free viewpoint video objects includes topics like usability and human factors in production processes, usability and human factors for end viewers, Quality of Experience (QoE) for personalisation, and User Experience (UX) of personalisation. The work analyses opportunities and obstacles, focussing on users' subjective quality of experience. The challenges are to define factors that influence quality, to formulate an adequate measure of quality, and to link the quality of experience to the technical realization within an undefined and ever-changing technical realization process. There are two advantages of interlinking the quality of experience with the quality of service: First, it can benefit the technical realization process, in order to allow adaptability (e.g., based on systems used by the end users). Second, it provides an opportunity to support scalability in a user-centred way, e.g., based on a cost or resources limitation. The outlined results consist of a systematic definition of factors that influence quality, including a research framework, evaluation activities, and lessons learned.

PAPERS

Regado et al. [1] from MOG Technologies from Porto, Portugal, present their project on "New Cloud Services for Product Placement in Television". Over the last years, the video consumption under digital format has dramatically increased together with the number of people watching television through their tablets, smartphones and computers, allowing personalised target advertising. Therefore, the goal of the reported project is to create a cloud based platform that allows an insertion of personalized ads, in real time, focused to the final user. The different objects (ads) are inserted into the viewer's programme, where the choice of which ads to display is made according to the user's location.

Bruno Veloso et al. [2] present a paper on "On-Line Feature-Based User and Item Profiling", addressing the on-line profiling of users and items, including new user and new items, using both feature frequency and feature rating (FFR). Typically, recommendation algorithms are unable to make recommendations involving new users and items due to the inherent lack of information. To overcome this problem, for each newly arrived entity, a new profile, combining general and individual components, is created. Then, as the number of entity-related events increases, the general component is faded and the individual component is strengthened. In the case of a new user, the FFR stereotype is combined with the individual FFR profile, whereas, in the case of a new item, the FFR cluster profile with the individual item FFR profile.

Ibrahim et al. [3] present their work on "TV Graphics Personalization Using In-Band Events". It is based on the concepts of overlaying personalized TV graphics on the device side, controlled and triggered by DASH in-band events. TV graphics personalization helps engaging viewers in the programme and maximizes the value of information shown to them. Today's TV graphics are encoded within the video making it difficult to modify it afterwards. Also for offerings using HTTP ABR technologies, the graphics are encoded with the video. Graphics become unreadable when the ABR algorithm switches to low quality representation, e.g., due to bad network conditions. Overlaying the graphics on the player side decouples the quality of the graphics from the quality of the video. Each viewer can resolve the events to different auxiliary media according to its profile. Graphics handling is performed at the client side where each client fetches and overlays the auxiliary media to the video, allowing personalization of graphics and provides high quality overlays independent of the current video quality.

CONCLUSION

The IPP4B workshop provides an open forum for the discussion on and advancement of the state of the art. It highlights areas the industry needs to address in terms of practice, standards and recommendations.

REFERENCES

1. André Regado, Alexandre Ulisses, Miguel Poeira and Pedro Santos. 2017. New Cloud Services for Product Placement in Television. Adjunct Proceedings of the 15th European Interactive TV Conference (ACM TVX 2017), In-Programme Personalisation for Broadcast (IPP4B) Workshop.

2. Bruno Veloso, Benedita Malheiro, Juan Carlos Burguillo and Jeremy Foss. 2017. On-Line Feature-Based User and Item Profiling. Adjunct Proceedings of the 15th European Interactive TV Conference (ACM TVX 2017), In-Programme Personalisation for Broadcast (IPP4B) Workshop.

3. Mohamed Ibrahim, Ali El Essaili, Thorsten Lohmar and Aurelien Revault D'allonnes. 2017. TV Graphics Personalization Using In-Band Events. Adjunct Proceedings of the 15th European Interactive TV Conference (ACM TVX 2017), In-Programme Personalisation for Broadcast (IPP4B) Workshop.

ACM TVX Asia Forum 2017: A Brand New Game of Online Digital Marketing in Asia

Hokyoung Ryu
Arts & Technology,
Hanyang University
Seoul, Korea
hryu@hanyang.ac.kr

Jieun Kim
Arts & Technology,
Hanyang University
Seoul, Korea
jkim2@hanyang.ac.kr

Shuichi Aoki
NHK
Tokyo, Japan
aoki.s-ha@nhk.or.jp

Donghun Chung
Communication
Kwangwun University
Seoul, Korea
donghunc@gmail.com

ABSTRACT
Digital online advertising today is struggling to find the right way to reach consumers on new digital platforms. Advertisers like social-media platforms want to gather all sorts of data on each user's age, consumption patterns, interests and so on. This means ads could be aimed at them with an accuracy that is unthinkable with analogue media. However, social networks, TV advertisers who are interested in switching to the bran new field have yet to work out what is the optimal format for online and/or integrated ads. This workshop is aimed at dealing with these issues of how Asian markets would approach to this.

Author Keywords
Digital marketing; integrated ads; SNS; Asia.

ACM Classification Keywords
J.1 Administrative Data Processing (e.g., Marketing), D.2.2 Design Tools and Techniques (e.g., User interfaces); J.4. Social and Behavioral Sciences (e.g., Economics, Psychology)

BACKGROUNDS
BMW advertised on WeChat, a popular messaging app in China, with around 550m monthly users in 2015. But its ads were shown only to those whose profiles suggested they were potential buyers of expensive cars. Others were shown ads for more affordable stuff, such as smartphones. The campaign made some angry, because those not shown the BMW ad -referred themselves as *diao*, or (putting it politely) losers [Extended from The Economist 08/29/2015].

The carmaker's experience shows the creativity of digital online advertising today, but at the same time, an example of how marketing is struggling to find the right way to reach consumers on new digital platforms, where they are spending ever more of their time. Advertisers like social-media platforms want to gather all sorts of data on each user's age, consumption patterns, interests and so on. This means ads could be correctly aimed at them with an accuracy that is unthinkable with analogue media.

For example, Chevrolet, an American car brand, has sent ads to the Facebook pages and Twitter feeds of people who had expressed an interest in, or signed up to test-drive, a competitor's vehicle. Such fine-tuned targeting means that the distinction between advertising and e-commerce is becoming blurred. Facebook, Twitter, Instagram and other platforms are selling ads containing "buy now" buttons, which let users complete a sale on the spot. It is too early to tell how many consumers want such a convenience, but the social platforms foresee a future in which they get paid by advertisers to provide instant-shopping services that make the platforms more useful to their members, and get them to spend more time on them. Some TV media have to feel much pain from the loss of ad revenue to digital rivals. As TV audiences both decline and shift to services that do not have ads, such as Netflix, the competition will be more chronically felt. However, social networks, and TV advertisers interested in switching to them, have yet to work out what is the optimal format for video ads.

To wiring the most out of the ability to target consumers precisely on social media, ad agencies are making big changes to their campaigns. However, doing with personalisation on social media costs a lot so we cannot target too much. Hence, some researchers look for how to define "online personalities", which has not been successful. Even if marketers master social media without coming across as clumsy, grating or intrusive, there will surely be a limit to how much advertising will shift to the social and online platforms. Television ads are still great for reaching big audiences with simple messages. This forum discusses the potential topics:

- Digital online marketing in Asia markets
- Digital consumers in Asia (or global)
- Online personalities
- Business models in digital marketing
- Attraction and aesthetics in digital online media (artistic experience and digital marketing)

Permission to make digital or hard copies of part or all of this work for personal or classroom use is granted without fee provided that copies are not made or distributed for profit or commercial advantage and that copies bear this notice and the full citation on the first page. Copyrights for third-party components of this work must be honored. For all other uses, contact the Owner/Author.
TVX '17, June 14-16, 2017, Hilversum, Netherlands
© 2017 Copyright is held by the owner/author(s).
ACM ISBN 978-1-4503-4529-3/17/06.
http://dx.doi.org/10.1145/3077548.3078630

Author Index

www.ingramcontent.com/pod-product-compliance
Lightning Source LLC
LaVergne TN
LVHW060143070326
832902LV00018B/2918